Uwe Seidel
Berlin and Potsdam

"Berlin, Berlin wat macht et?
Mit eenem Ooge weent et,
mit eenem Ooge lacht et."

"Berlin, Berlin, what is it doing?
It cries with one eye and laughs with the other."
colloquialism

Uwe Seidel

Berlin and Potsdam

Uwe Seidel
Berlin and Potsdam
Published by

Peter Rump Publishing Co.
Hauptstr. 198
D-4800 Bielefeld 14

© *Peter Rump, 1992*

ISBN: 3-89416-334-8

Design:
Cover: M. Schömann, P. Rump
Contents: Monika Siegmund, Gunda Urban
Maps: Catherine Raisin
Photos: Uwe Seidel and others (see page 296)
Typesetting:
digitron, Bielefeld
Translated
by Dr. Robert van Krieken
Edited by: David Henley
Printed by: Fuldaer Verlagsanstalt GmbH, Fulda

PRINTED IN GERMANY

Distributors:
Travel Bug guides are available in the countries listed below. If you can't find them, ask your bookshop to order them from one of the listed distributors. For countries not listed, write to Peter Rump in Germany.

Austria: Robo, Postfach 601, 1060 Wien
Germany: Prolit, Postfach 9, 6301 Fernwald (Annerod)
India and Nepal: India Book Distributor, 107/108, Arcadia, 195, Nariman Point, Bombay 400021
Malaysia and Singapore: S. Abdul Majeed & Co.; 2210, Malayan Mansion, Jl. Masjid India; 50100 Kuala Lumpur
Netherlands: Nilsson & Lamm bv. Postbus 195, Pampuslaan 212, 1380 AD Weesp
Switzerland: AVA-buch 2000, Postfach, 3910 Affoltern
Thailand: Bangkok Book Distributor Co. LTD., 302-4 Siam Square Soi 4 Phatumwan, Bangkok 10330
USA: SCB Distributors, P.O. Box 5446, Carson, CA 90749-5446

Send 15 US$ for a copy of the **Berlin and Potsdam Handbook** to P.R.-Distribution, Heidekampstr. 18, D-4450 Lingen, Germany, and the book will be airmailed anywhere in the world.

Foreword

Berlin, a city often buffeted by the winds of change, is once again being driven to find a new identity for itself. After decades of division both halves of Berlin stand on the threshold of a common future.

'Berlin, set yourself free!' These words, spoken by the former Mayor of West Berlin at the opening of the Wall, still ring in the ears of the city's inhabitants. Some celebrated the end of their isolation within their 'real socialist' surroundings; others, the inhabitants of the 'Capital of East Germany' were overjoyed to begin exploring a West Berlin denied to them for almost 30 years. After the initial euphoria, the first problems began to emerge in the reunification of the two very different halves of the city, but that should not have been unexpected. The stench of two-stroke engines on Ku'damm will disappear, just as the flood of Western tourists in what used to be poorly-patronised East Berlin bars will ebb to a normal flow.

Berlin's face was changed by the fall of the Wall, and will change again dramatically in the immediate future. It still stands apart (although always part of world affairs), but suddenly there is talk of a metropolis and even a capital city.

This travel guide will help first time visitors to Berlin find their feet in both pulsating halves of the city. Background information, descriptions of selected districts and many practical hints make it easier to get to know both the city and its people. It cannot and does not claim to be comprehensive. In a city as exciting as Berlin everyone has to engage in their own (successful) pursuit of personal 'highlights'. Enjoy yourself!

My thanks go to the co-authors and photographers who have made contributions to this book. Special thanks go to Robert and Annette for the translation, as well as to Karin and Lutz for their unconventional assistance. Volker Buslau and his technical 'park' were a great help in the preparation of the text. Thanks too to Josef, Hartmut, Ina, Heike, Markus, Peter, my parents and all the others who supported me with advice and encouragement.

Above all I would like to direct my gratitude and love to Carola, whose support and understanding constantly gives me new strength.

Uwe Seidel

Translator's Foreword

Some words have been left untranslated - street names, names of important locations and buildings, and particular expressions like "U-Bahn" (metro or subway). This is because it is the German version that you will see on street signs, maps, in the subway and so on, so a translation is of little use to you. We have also retained the German form of setting out addresses, i.e. Potsdamer Platz 56, instead of 56 Potsdamer Platz, again because this is the form in which you will most often encounter addresses. Often they are also accompanied with a postcode (e.g. 1-15), where the second number refers to the district postcode marked on most maps.

One particular word is worth special mention: "Kneipe". We have translated it as "tavern", but we know that this is not exactly the right term, because it refers to a particular German social institution, a sociable combination of bar, cafe and restaurant unique to Germany. All the words which may cause you difficulty are listed in the "Practical Hints" section at the back of the book, page 279. Visiting another country means encountering some of its language. Discovering at least some of the local terms and expressions will make your trip all that much more enjoyable.

Contents

Contents

Introduction

Testing the water in Berlin

How do you come to terms with a city like Berlin? How can the visitor discover as much as possible in the shortest time available, without simply scratching a glossy surface? Well, by looking behind the myths, behind the cliches, it is possible to get a little closer to Berlin's true nature.

This book will help you approach the newly reunited city of Berlin, without leading you by the nose. It will make the first steps easier with some practical directions. Those of you who want to play the 'discovering the city' game should first learn some of the rules by which we play here. The fact that the rules are constantly changing is taken into account through the listing of contact addresses.

It is advisable, in both halves of the city, to begin by visiting the local Tourist Bureau and obtaining the most recent information. Here one can acquire a multitude of glossy brochures, free. The view of Berlin promoted by these publications is naturally intended to have a particular propaganda effect, so they should be approached with some care.

If you are not lucky enough to have friends or acquaintances you can stay with, you will first have to solve the accommodation problem.

With over two million visitors a year, Berlin often bursts at the seams; the supply of empty beds is abundant, but not unlimited. If you are planning your trip well in advance, you should contact the Tourist Bureau (for addresses see Appendix) and book ahead. From tent spots to Youth Hostels to five-star hotels, Berlin's accommodation ranges across all price brackets. If you would rather stay somewhere more private, there are accommodation agencies called 'Mitwohnzentralen' which will put you in contact with Berliners wanting to rent their apartments for shorter or longer periods. As it is always an advantage to get to know a city through personal contacts, this alternative also makes life easier for the beginner.

In order to explore Berlin's 883 square kilometers one has to cover long distances. Nevertheless, a car, whether your own or rented, is not recommended. Heavy traffic, constant roadwork and poor road surfaces (particularly in the Eastern half of the city) make driving a car a misery. Why should you subject yourself to the stress of city streets when there is a well-developed public transport system? All varieties are at your disposal. Whether you travel by bus, tram, train (under and above ground), boat or taxi, every point in Berlin is easy to reach. Measures taken by the Berlin Senate (under the influence of the Alternative List, or Greens) are making public transport increasingly attractive. The introduction of bus lanes in the city, for example, has led to noticeable improvements in inner-city travel. Even at night you are not entirely dependent on expensive taxis (1 km costs DM 1.68). Many bus and recently some U-Bahn lines, on weekends at least, operate all through the night. The whole of Berlin is one fare zone, i.e. tickets bought from the Berlin Transport Authority (BVG) can be used between Glienecke and Köpenick. If you buy a Day Ticket, you can discover Berlin for a pittance.

Berlin, with its many facets, has something to offer all tastes, and these are catered for through the selection of district descriptions in this book. Naturally the inner-city districts *Charlottenburg* and *Mitte*, together with the Kurfurstendamm and Unter den Linden avenues are described in detail. Here beats the heart of the twin city, and here the historical, the cultural and of course the commercial attractions lie. But, however interesting these inner city areas may be, it is 'only' the large 'Showcase avenues' which determine the streetscape here. The achievements of a market economy are put proudly on show on the Western side, while the Eastern side is adorned above all by Prussian architectural showpieces.

Beyond these prestige streets lies the real Berlin, and this is what the descriptions of the districts *Schöneberg*, *Kreuzberg*, *Prenzlauer Berg*, and *Friedrichshain* will convey. With their own unique characters, these districts offer a multitude of sights and a 'scene' which is often charac-terised affectionately as a sub- or alternative culture. Simply stepping into 'scene life' is not always easy. Hostility towards camera-slinging tourists sometimes leads to a general rejection of all visitors. But if you use your common sense, making contact will not be that difficult, Berliners are actually regarded as quite receptive and open to novelty. It is no accident that these districts in particular reflect Berlin's multicultural character. Being districts with cheap rents, they house the majority of the working population, which in Berlin is often Turkish, Yugoslavian, Vietnamese, Italian or Greek. The various cultures these ethnic groups brought with them have permeated the city over recent years and given it a colorful, cosmopolitan flair. Naturally it is not always easy for people with different cultural backgrounds to live with each other. In recent times parti-cularly, there has been a noticeable increase in racist feeling even in Kreuzberg and Prenzlauer Berg.

The phenomenon of the Wall, of which there are now only a few remains, can be recalled with the *walk from Checkpoint Charlie to the Reichstag*. Along this seam between the two city halves one can most clearly describe the changes which the fall of the Wall represents. Even when some things described no longer exist, the encounter with history will still be exciting.

Berlin's history makes a particular-ly strong impression when you visit the district of *Spandau*. Where else

A book about Berlin would not be complete without a chapter dedicated to the city of *Potsdam*. After the fall of the Wall, Potsdam is now only a stone's throw away, its castles and gardens within quick and easy reach. For an excursion into the Prussian past you should set aside at least one whole day to roam through the historic buildings and parks at your leisure.

The selection of restaurants, bars, discos and sights in the district descriptions makes no claim to be comprehensive. Berlin's offerings are too numerous and change too quickly for that. In particular the rapid changes in the East make it impossible to keep track of the current situation. Why some places at particular times are 'in' and then just as suddenly completely 'out' is hard to explain, let alone predict. The restaurants and bars mentioned are nonetheless critically examined and will also continue to be found under their current names for some time yet.

can you walk along the old city wall, admire the oldest house in Berlin, or enjoy a traditional banquet in a centuries-old building? Here you can see history at every street-corner. Spandau's forest areas also serve as the destination for long rambling walks.

If you need to be convinced of how green Berlin really is, then visit the districts of *Wilmersdorf, Zehlendorf,* and *Köpenick*. In the suburb of *Dahlem* you will find numerous museums and the Berlin Free University. All these districts are also characterised by forests and lakes. Here you can both seek and find seclusion.

As I said, the range of offerings in Berlin is huge. In the West you can enjoy yourself round the clock without interruption. Virtually every corner has a tavern; some are inviting, most, however, are dreadful, especially the taverns east of the former Wall. These leave a lot to be desired in terms of atmosphere. This is in sharp contrast to the café and bar scene (including the Eastern districts). They cannot be compared in terms of total numbers, but there are a far greater variety of cafés and

bars. Generally they are more enjoyable and stylish than the taverns, and cater for every target group. You can breakfast in many cafés round the clock. In principle it can be said that the afternoon belongs to the inner city (in both halves), while in the evening action is best found in the outer districts.

The area around *Savignyplatz* or the scene in *Schöneberg*, *Kreuzberg* or *Prenzlauer Berg* is highly recommended in terms of night life, which in the West really begins around 10 pm. The best dance floors lie beyond the City. In the Eastern half only a few taverns or discos stay open until the early morning, so things cut loose earlier, but then more vigorously.

In culinary terms you can easily go round the world in Berlin. Just about all nations are represented by their cuisine. When the restaurants in the East improve in quality, the range will expand even more. Curried sausage stalls, as the local representative of the fast-food culture, can be found all over the city, as can the kebab stalls with Turkish specialties.

If you are on the lookout for unusual shopping opportunities, you should still concentrate on the Western half of Berlin. In the districts of Kreuzberg (e.g. Oranien-, Gneisenau- or Yorkstraße), Schöneberg (around Winterfeldplatz) and Charlottenburg (around Stuttgarterplatz) you will find small shops with the latest fashions, jewelry and other bits and pieces. In any event

you should visit the fleamarket on the Straße des 17. Juni. KaDeWe (Kaufhaus des Westens - Department Store of the West) is worth seeing, but not the place for a productive shopping trip.

All newcomers should buy one of the city magazines (*tip* or *Zitty*, see Appendix) which offer extensive hints and address lists. Here you will find descriptions of the most current trends and novelties, and a listing of the innumerable cultural events in a daily program. The road through the rich theater and cinema landscape is made easy with the help of the critics' reviews. Berlin's cinema scene has a lot to offer. The days when Berlin was a film metropolis are certainly over, but as far as the number and quality of cinemas is concerned, it is still in a leading position. There are numerous independent cinemas, i.e. beyond the inner city, and with interesting programs.

The book closes with an A-Z address list containing practical information. The prices mentioned were current in 1991, they may have changed. For accommodation the first price listed refers to a single room, the second to a double room. For the Eastern city districts and the city of Potsdam, area codes are still included in the telephone numbers.

The City's History

A Brief History of Berlin since 1945

Berlin, June 1948

World War II left a ruined Berlin with a useless currency, and joint meetings of the Allied powers were unable to agree on a replacement.

The planned introduction of the Deutsch Mark in the Western zones, together with the refusal of the Soviet Union to agree to a unitary currency for the whole of Germany, left Berlin well and truly caught between the two power blocs. The Soviet-occupied zones of the divided Germany also got their own currency, against strong opposition from the Western allies. For all Berliners this was the first noticeable division between the Western and Eastern halves of the city. The links between the Western sectors of Berlin and the Western Zones of Germany were also regarded with suspicion by the Soviets. The situation finally escalated into the *"Berlin Blockade"*, with the Soviets closing the trade routes for provisions from the Western zones to Berlin. This softening-up tactic was meant ultimately to drive West Berlin to capitulate to the Soviets and establish a "socialist" Greater Berlin.

For ten months the city's provisions came in only by air. In a historically unique rescue operation the Western allies put the patient

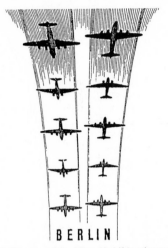

BERLIN

Berlin on a drip. The Air Lift's planes landed every one to two minutes, and brought up to 13,000 tons of provisions and materials every day. The use of the blockade as a political weapon backfired on the Soviets. The Western Allies' rescue operation, together with the stubbornness of the West Berliners, made the attempt a futile one, and world opinion condemned the Soviet Union.

The Berlin Blockade ended on 12th May 1949, and the city's ties with the about-to-be-established Federal Republic were stronger than ever. *Allied Occupiers* became *Western Protectors*, and Berlin's Western sector became an outpost of the Western world. People saw themselves as part of the Federal Republic and conducted themselves accordingly. The differences between the two social systems were expressed in open disagreements. The Western sector prospered, supported by the Marshall Plan and Federal aid. Provisions and services constantly improved, in crass contrast to the problems of the East Berliners. West Berlin was able to reconstruct, while the inhabitants of the Soviet-occupied districts were still surrounded by post-war rubble. Many West Berlin firms hired East German workers, who thus helped with the reconstruction of West Berlin. Just as the situation improved in the one part of the city, it became more desolate in the other part.

East Berlin, 17th June 1953

The dissatisfaction of East Berlin workers with a planned economy and its associated poor working conditions led in June 1953 to strikes and open protests. The standard of living bore no relationship to the productive achievements being demanded of workers. A large proportion of goods produced disappeared from East Berlin's shops, to go as war-reparations to the Soviet Union.

The quelling of a rally at a large building site in the former Stalin Allee sparked off nationwide protests. These demonstrations on 16th June gave courage to the whole GDR. Strikes and protests were held at over 270 locations on 17th June. The demonstrators demanded not just economic improvements, but also sweeping changes in society. The call for free elections could be

heard at all the rallies. In East Berlin police clashed with workers. Increasing numbers of workers laid down their tools and joined the rebellion.

The SED (Socialist Unity Party) regime was powerless against the uprising. At 1 pm on 17th of June a state of emergency was declared in East Berlin. Soviet troops intervened in the street battles, and their superior might broke the demonstrators' resistance, leaving behind an unknown number of dead and injured.

Divided Berlin, before and after 13th August 1961

Eight years after the workers' rebellion the two halves of Berlin were divided off from each other, virtually as they slept.

The preceding years had bled East Berlin dry. Hundreds of thousands of workers worked in the West, and West Berlin became the first stop in the flight to capitalism. In 1953 alone there were 300,000 registered refugees. The situation was kept on the boil by both power blocs, who used Berlin as an ideological football. The *Krushchev Ultimatum* was a further attempt by the USSR to put pressure on the Western Allies. The ultimatum expired without the Western allies leaving the city as demanded. Instead of the anticipated new blockade, the war of words escalated and the situation became increasingly unbearable. As a result, the number of refugees reached new heights.

Under a cloak of secrecy the life-lines between West and East Berlin were cut on 13th August 1961. Hemmed-in by an impossible situation, the East German (GDR) authorities saw no way out of their powerlessness other than making the division of the city inescapably clear with the building of a wall. From one day to the next families and friends were seperated from each other by barbed wire. East Berlin was now finally a part of the GDR and West Berlin an enclave. The West Berliners' fury and distress at the building of the wall was also directed at the Western Allies, who did protest formally, but ultimately shied away from a confrontation with the Soviet Union. A military counter-offensive was deliberately avoided for fear of threatening world peace. West Berlin was left with only the moral and material support of the Western world. In the first days after the Wall's construction there were a number of spectacular escape attempts over the still porous border. Houses lying on the border itself were used for "freedom jumps". Some got to the West over the Spree, through self-dug tunnels or underground service tunnels. Until the final fall of the Wall more than 5,000 people escaped, although more than 70 escape attempts ended in death.

Although it remained possible for West Berliners to visit friends and relatives in East Berlin until the end of August 1961, the atmosphere between the two German States was naturally at its lowest point. Life in West Berlin was once again completely dependent on external support. The workers who oscillated between the two halves were suddenly gone and their absence tore a hole in West Berlins' productivity. Over 30,000 West Berlin inhabitants moved to West Germany.

The total seperation of the Berliners lasted until 1963. Towards the end of that year the first visas, limited to a few days, were issued, so that West Berliners could at least

spend Christmas with their relatives. After a succession of short-lived agreements, the *Four Power Agreement* was only signed in 1971. This agreement between the victors regulated the civil transit traffic to and from West Berlin. In the first year of its operation over 3.7 million visitors arrived. Until the opening of the border, access to East Berlin or transit through the GDR was at various times hindered or eased, independently of the world political climate. Despite many links, the two halves of the city developed in very different ways. East German military service, for example, was also applied to East Berliners, in opposition to the Allied agreements. The fact that West Berlin's inhabitants did not have to enter military service

attracted many people to the city, protecting its population from ageing too rapidly.

East Berlin had to be made suitable for its role as capital and shining example. The construction of a "political, economic and cultural center" was made a national goal. Monumentally hideous government and administrative buildings appeared, but money was also invested in the restoration of historical buildings. This effort was concentrated on the city center, and old housing stock was neglected. The supply of goods was consistently better in East Berlin than in the rest of the GDR, and this naturally led to envious criticism.

The development of West Berlin, in contrast to the Eastern zone, was determined precisely by the absence of benefits normally accruing to a capital city. Attempts were constantly made to turn Berlin into as attractive a location as possible. The promotion of science and culture created an interesting and thoroughly lively atmosphere in the city. But the division was never forgotten and never overcome. It did not, however, lead West Berliners to depression or thoughts of leaving. Many new things were attempted, developed and above all experienced. It was no coincidence that the student movement and the squatting movement found their first supporters here.

Berlin, before November 1989

The *40th Anniversary of the GDR* was planned as a celebration, and turned into the beginning of the end. The flag-waving of the *Free German Youth* and workers associations in front of grey-haired men of power fell remarkably flat. The GDR had managed to avoid much of the reform movements of neighboring countries, but the embassy-occupations and strong indications of dissatisfaction did not pass East Berlin by. "History is not kind to those who come too late" was what Mikhail Gorbachev told the rulers of

the GDR in East Berlin on the 7th of October. He was to be proved right. After the demonstration of over a million GDR citizens in East Berlin on 4th November, the process could no longer be restrained. The old leadership was replaced, but the spirit remained the same. The resignation of the whole SED Politburo on the eve of the opening of the Wall ended 28 years of division.

Open Berlin, 9th November 1989

Ku'damm strollers rubbed their eyes in disbelief. A column of horn-tooting Trabants wound through West Berlin's inner city and for the first time spread the smell of freedom and two-strokes which was to characterise Berlin's air in the following months. Now the final dream was realised: the peaceful revolution had succeeded, the Wall was history.

Hair sticky with cheap champagne, eyes full of tears and sometimes only partially clothed (because of haste), the first East Berliners met the reception committees on the Western side. Satellites sent images of wild people throwing themselves into each others arms all around the world. The world once again turned its eyes to this city.

The first steps on new territory were careful ones, so deep ran the skepticism and decades of powerlessness in relation to a state apparatus which had now, so suddenly, granted them freedom of movement. Astonishment turned the

first words of the East Berliners, many younger than the Wall itself, into inarticulate stutterings. "Crazy!" and the typical GDR expression, "Unbeatable!" were mostly all that the microphones of the international media could pick up. Unbelievable scenes, in the truest sense of the word.

On a small, inconspicuous note was written the message which would change Berlin and Germany for ever. This note was quickly passed to Günter Schabowski (then fresh-faced press secretary for the SED) for him to read incredulously. Freedom of movement for all, a demand which had stood for weeks on the flags of the most impressive demonstrations, was now announced and never to be withdrawn.

No one saw this amazing development coming. Erich Honecker's senile prophecies of a *hundredth anniversary of the Berlin Wall* had been ridiculed, but for the power apparatus to fall so quickly to its knees took everyone by surprise.

The border guards were particularly amazed. In the afternoon they were still the guardians of "real socialism", by evening they had been turned into extras. One could read the confusion of these hours most clearly on the faces of these guards. And they let it show. With flowers stuck in the lapels of their olive-green uniforms or with barely concealed champagne glasses, they revealed their true feelings. The stream from East to West and back again flowed without any formalities.

New Year, 1989/90

The greeting of the new decade turned into a massive reunification party. Hundreds of thousands of Berliners gathered at Brandenburg Gate, to give unbridled expression to their amazement at the unification of the two halves of the city. Amid the fireworks and champagne the atmosphere ran out of control for the first time. Tears of wonder mixed with tears of rage and disappointment at the German-national derailment. The saddest moment was the accidental death of a youth in mysterious circumstances. A huge video screen fell into the celebrating crowd and brought the festivities to an end.

The following spring saw new growth beyond what is normal for the season. After overcoming the first anxieties, wishes and hopes also began to bloom. Just as that year's winter ended relatively early and the March sun began to warm, so the reunification process caught Berlin much earlier and swifter than expected.

West Berlin, 30th June 1990

The visitors to Ku'damm and Kreuzberg could clearly see that the great euphoria was long gone. The headlines of the tabloid press suggested a great celebratory weekend, but they did not match the West Berliners' mood.

So much is not as it was. For almost 30 years it was possible to enjoy the feeling of an exotic island.

"The Wall must go" was always the slogan yelled, especially on anniversaries like the 17th June, and particularly at the VoPo (*Volkspolizisten*, People's Police) along the inner city borders. Being able to enjoy the colorful graffiti during a "Wall walk" was part of the normal craziness which had for so long made Berlin so attractive. You were something special, culturally sophisticated, studiously youthful, autonomously rebellious, multiculturally friendly to foreigners, traditionally bourgeois, politically always prepared for a surprise, but above all "off the beaten track". You had to "travel" to Berlin, because Berliners were not just "round the corner".

Surrounded by a tabooed "Socialism" and a capital city's twin, which was never accepted as such, one was always conscious of the world's attention. No state visitors ever forgot to sign their names in the city's golden guest book. An unforgettable appearance was made by the aging Ronald Reagan, who with trembling voice and at a time best suited for an American broadcast, demanded, that the Soviet General Secretary finally tear down the Wall. The fact that his visit was accompanied by violent riots fitted well into Berlin's "we've got everything" image.

And now it's all over. The chance to experience "moments full of historical significance" became rarer with every piece torn off the Wall. Berliners knew that the days of their special status were numbered,

leaving them to finally become real cosmopolites. And that was all they had wanted all those years.....

East Berlin, 1st July 1990, 0:00

Berlin Alexanderplatz - one could be forgiven for thinking that the Eastern citizens had decided to celebrate New Year's Eve in a 6-monthly cycle. The square, surrounded by bland architecture, was normally only this full when there was tropical fruit or real coffee beans for sale. For hours the mood in the city was remarkably tense. Even those who went through the ecstasy of the peaceful revolution and the final opening of the border could not escape the discussions of this new "historical" event. Midnight comes: the exchange of "alu-chips" for hard West marks begins, completing the penultimate step towards unification of the two German states and the two halves of Berlin. Every one of the ten thousand on Alexanderplatz wanted to be the first to exchange their savings for a handful of Deutschmarks.

In accordance with the signifi-cance of the event, the *Deutsche* *Bank* opened its first branch at the bewitching hour. This symbolic act was thankfully received by the crowd.

People celebrated happily until early morning, even though the cost of beer suddenly went from 73 pfen-nig to 4 DM.

Berlin whole again, back to the future

Despite the great differences there have been between the two halves of the city in the past, they will grow together again. For the visitor the extreme contrasts which made Berlin so attractive will be translated into a metropolitan experience at least twice as exciting. It is useless and also unproductive to hanker after the past. Both parts of the city will change and adapt to the new circumstances. The youth, who have never known a Greater Berlin, will be astounded by and also have to grasp the new opportunities sud-denly offered to them. And the older generation who never accepted the division and have for a long time made fun of it, can now fully enjoy the joke.

The city was never easy to figure out, and nor will it be in the future. Whether it is the discussions about Berlin as capital, the Daimler-Benz development or the bid for the Olympics, these larger themes are not what make Berlin exciting. Much more interesting for both visitors and locals are the small, invisible changes accompanying unification, changes to be observed, experienced and shaped.

Historical Chronology

to 550	The area where Berlin now stands was first settled by various Germanic tribes, as indicated by a number of archaeological finds.
circa 660	The banks and valleys of the rivers Havel and Spree occupied by Slavic tribes, the **Wends** and the **Sorbs**.
1134	The Ascanian Count **Albert the Bear** (after the legend of Berlin's founder) takes control of the Mark (border territory) of Brandenburg.
1153	**Albert's** policy of settling the banks of the Havel with peasants from Westphalia and the Netherlands brings about an uprising by the **Wends**.
1157	The construction of fortresses and armed villages leads to the defeat of this uprising. In this period the twin town Berlin-Cölln is probably founded.
1230	Berlin and Cölln probably attain the town charters.
1237	First official mention of Cölln.
1244	First official mention of Berlin.
1251	First official recognition of Berlin as a town, under the protection of the **Ascanian House**, which guaranteed Berlin toll-freedom, the town experiences a boom period: a first city wall is built, in the surrounding areas there appear many smaller market towns, later to become Berlin's districts.
1307	Berlin and Cölln unite to form one town.
1319	The death of the last Ascanian count marks the beginning of a period of political confusion, with the Mark having to protect itself from now on against the claims of the electoral landgraves (provincial counts).
1442	**Friedrich II** takes control of the government, the Berlin-Cölln town union is dissolved, the town council defeated.

1447	Berlin and Cölln become the Elector's (prince) residence.
1460	Berlin acquires a new town emblem, the Elector's court and his officials henceforth determine the town's image, despite numerous epidemics the population doubles up to 1600 to reach 12,000.
1500	**Fugger** and **Welser** set up trading establishments in Berlin.
1517	**Luther** publishes his 95 theses in Wittenberg.
1566	Beginning of the Counter-Reformation.
1582	Gregorian Calendar reform.
1608	**Protestant Union** founded.
1615	Lutheran Berliners rebel against their Calvinist Elector **Johann Sigismund**.
1617	First Berlin weekly newspaper printed in the **Grey Cloister**.
1618	Beginning of the **Thirty Years War.**
1631	**Wallenstein** and his Swedish troops lay siege to the town, leading to a famine in the winter of 1631/32.
1635	Berlin plundered.
1640	Elector **Friedrich-Wilhelm** takes office.
1647/48	The **Lustgarten** and an **Avenue of Linden Trees** are constructed.
1648	The **Thirty Years War** and its associated famines and epidemics decimate Berlin's population, now 6,000.
1659	Establishment of the Mark's library in the Cölln castle, opened to the public in 1661.
1664	The Mark issues an edict forbidding Lutheran and Reformed ministers from publicly abusing each other.
1671	Foundation of Berlin's Jewish community by 50 families driven out of Vienna.
1680	Cölln's medieval town wall demolished.
1685	Foundation of the **Berlin Stock Exchange**;
1688	**Friedrich Wilhelm** dies in Potsdam, his successor is his son from his first marriage, **Friedrich III**. Berlin and Cölln now have a population of 18,000.
1690	The lavish style of **Friedrich III's** court produces an expensive life style among Berlin's citizens; tea, coffee and cocoa come into fashion.
1696	**Gottfried Wilhelm Leibniz** founds the **Berlin Academy of the Arts**.
1700	The Gregorian Calendar is introduced into Protestant Germany; **Leibniz** becomes President of the **Science Society** (later Academy of Sciences); Berlin has 29,000 inhabitants.

1701	**Elector Friedrich III** crowns himself King of Prussia, and henceforth calls himself **Friedrich I**.
1709	Berlin and Cölln, Friedrichswerder, Dorotheenstadt and Friedrichstadt are united to form the royal residence of Berlin.
1710	Berlin's city constitution takes effect; the city wall is torn down and a customs wall with 14 towers erected.
1713	**Friedrich I** dies, succeeded by **Friedrich-Wilhelm I**, later the **Soldier King**.
1716	The trade ordinances of Berlin's business community exclude Jews from the Guild.
1717	Feudal service abolished; foundation of the Cadet Corps; introduction of compulsory schooling; Tiergarten opened to the public.
1721	Reform of Prussian justice system; French church built on Gendarmenmarkt.
1730	The "**Katte Affair**" shakes the Prussian Court: Crown Prince **Friedrich** attempts to avoid his father's military drill with the help of his friends **Katte** and **Keith**, the escape attempt fails and **Katte** is beheaded in front of the Crown Prince.
1739	**Friedrich-Wilhelm I** reforms the poor law, recognised paupers are supported, beggars forced to work.
1740	**Friedrich-Wilhelm I** dies, succeeded by **Friedrich II, the Great** ("I am the first servant of my State"); religious freedom forms the basis of Friedrich's settlement policy. Berlin becomes a center of enlightenment and new endeavors.
1745	In two wars against the Catholic Habsburg monarchy, Prussia captures Schlesien (Silesia).
1749	**Friedrich II** relaxes press censorship.
1753	Under **Friedrich's** orders the first industrial settlements are established on the **Cöllnischen Heide**.
1754	The rack is forbidden in criminal proceedings, Prussia acquires the Berlin Porcelain Factory and turns it into a monopoly under the name of the **Royal Factory**.
1768	The protection money which the otherwise tolerant **Friedrich** demands from the Jewish community rises to 25,000 thaler annually.
1770	Residences built on Unter den Linden.
1781	A new Prussian Code of Procedure is introduced.

King Friedrich Wilhelm I. visits the new buildings in Berlin's "Friedrichstadt". From the wall painting by Hugo Vogel in the Berlin Town Hall.

1785	"*Old Fritz*" dies; under his rule industry, in the form of factories, experienced a period of growth.
1788	King *Friedrich Wilhelm II* reintroduces press censorship, even though he is a promoter of business and art.
1789	*French Revolution*.
1793	First steam engine in Berlin.
1800	Berlin has 172,000 inhabitants.
1806	Occupation of Berlin by Napoleon's troops.
1808	Beginning of communal self-government after the fundamental administrative reforms of *Baron von Stein*.
1810	Foundation of Humboldt University by Wilhelm von Humboldt.

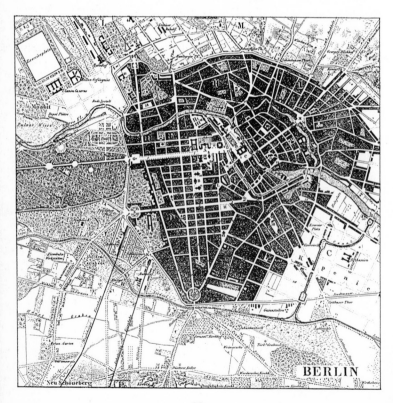

1813	The French leave Berlin, the **Wars of Liberation** begin.
1814	Jews receive full citizenship rights in Prussia.
1815	**Vienna Congress** begins **Restoration**, **German Confederation** founded.
1816	Political associations are banned, Germany's first locomotive cast in Berlin.
1819	Ministerial conference in Karlsbad forbids liberal, democratic and national movements; child labor in Prussian factories denounced by the municipal authorities.
1820	**Prussian Financial Reform** ends the tax autonomy of the communes.
1830	Berlin's municipal authorities introduce a dog tax.
1831	Cholera epidemic in Berlin.
1840	First horse-drawn omnibus service between Alexanderplatz and Potsdamer Bahnhof.
1844	The municipal authorities introduce a town gas works.
1847	Opening of the **United Regional Assembly,** the first Prussian Parliament, closed down in the same year. Revolts in Berlin over high prices for potatoes and grains.
1848	The **March Revolution** articulates the political demands of the citizens: freedom of the press, speech and association, reforms in policy, government and justice, establishment of parliaments, creation of a constitution; King **Friedrich-Wilhelm IV** ("The people all make me sick") is forced to set up the liberal **"March Ministry"**.
Nov 1848	Berlin beseiged. General von Wrangel's troops enter the city and disperse the **National Assembly** gathered in the Schauspielhaus; freedom of the press once again curtailed.
1849	**Friedrich Wilhelm IV** refuses the Imperial crown offered by the **Frankfurt Parliament**.
1856	**Association of German Engineers** founded in Berlin.
1858	Prince **Wilhelm I** liquidates his mentally-ill brother **Friedrich Wilhelm IV**.
1861	With the incorporation of Wedding, Gesundbrunnen, Moabit, Schöneberg and Tempelhof, Berlin doubles in size.
1862	**Otto von Bismarck** becomes Prussian Prime Minister.
1866	The **German War** between Prussia and Austria, long in the planning by Bismarck, leaves Prussia as the leading military power in Europe; the **North German Confederation** with Berlin is founded.
1870	**Franco-German War**.

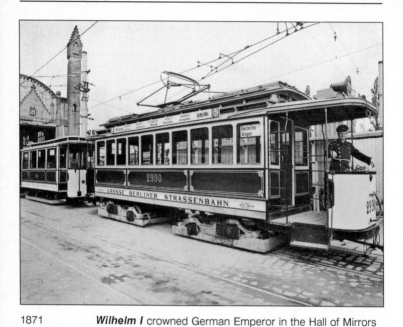

1871	**Wilhelm I** crowned German Emperor in the Hall of Mirrors at Versailles, the Imperial constitution takes effect, Berlin becomes capital of the German Empire.
1873	Collapse of the Berlin Stock Exchange ends the boom "foundation years".
1874	Press freedom is guaranteed by law, but not written into the constitution.
1877	Berlin's population passes one million.
1878	With the support of the Liberals and the Conservatives, the **Socialists Act** is passed: banning of the Social Democratic Party, the unions and their newspapers.
1881	Berlin separates from the province of Brandenburg and becomes an autonomous city.
1882	Berlin city railway opened.
1883	Medical insurance becomes compulsory in Germany with Bismarck's first piece of social insurance legislation.
1888	**Wilhelm I** dies, his successor **Friedrich III** governs for only 99 days; **Wilhelm II** becomes German Emperor and King of Prussia.

1890	Repeal of the **Socialists Act**; **Bismarck** dismissed.
1900	Civil Code takes effect, Berlin has 1,888,000 inhabitants.
1908	Berlin's U-Bahn runs for 14.5 kilometers.
1914	Following the assassination of the Austrian Archduke Ferdinand, the German General Staff demand a war in order to subjugate France (**Schliefen Plan**); the parliament (Reichstag) approves war credits with the support of the Social Democrats.
1917	Lack of provisions leads to mass strikes and demonstrations.
1918	**January Strike**: over a million German workers rebel; state of siege in Berlin; on 9th November **Scheidemann**, leader of the SPD, proclaims the **German Republic**; **Ebert** constitutes a provisional government which is recognised by the councils.
1919	German Communist Party founded in Berlin; **Rosa Luxemburg** and **Karl Liebknecht** are murdered; dissolution of the three-class electoral roll, elections for the national parliament; Versailles Peace Treaty, which Germany always regarded as a gagging treaty.
1920	The right-wing **Kapp Putsch** founders on a general strike; first elections for a City Council return a majority for the Social Democrats; horse-drawn buses introduced; **Greater Berlin** has 4 million inhabitants.
1922	The liberal Jewish politician **Walter Rathenau** is murdered by right-wing radicals; **Rapallo Treaty** is supposed to ensure a rapprochement between the German Republic and the Soviet Union.
1925	Reich President **Ebert** dies, his successor is the monarchist **Hindenburg**.

Karl Liebknecht

Rosa Luxemburg

Walther Rathenau

1927	The world-wide economic crisis begins on **Black Friday**.
1930	Government crises and the parties' inability to compromise leads to a permanant crisis in parliament.
1932	600,000 unemployed in Berlin; coup against the social democrat government of Prussia.
1933	**Hindenburg** names Hitler as Chancellor, the National Socialists are unable to return a majority in the March elections; Reichstag fire; **KZ Oranienburg** becomes the first concentration camp in the Berlin area; enabling act introduced, Social Democratic Party (SPD) banned.
1934	Power struggle between the Sturmabteilung (SA) and the Schutzstaffel (SS), Hindenburg dies, Hitler becomes German Chancellor and President.
1935	General military service and compulsory labor introduced; the **Nürnberg Acts for the Protection of German Blood** are passed.
1936	XIth Olympic Games in Berlin; **Carl von Ossietzky**, lying in a Berlin hospital after a long period of imprisonment in a concentration camp, receives the Nobel Peace Prize; the Air Force Ministry (Wilhelmstraße) is the first major building of the Nazi period.
1937	Berlin gets a new constitution; **Speer** develops a design for the transformation of Berlin into a new capital, **Germania**; Propaganda Minister **Goebbels** names 1237 as the year of Berlin's foundation.
1938	Exhibition of **"Decadent Art"** opened; Jewish street names altered; Jewish shops plundered during **"Crystal Night"**.
1939	Outbreak of World War II; opening of the State Chancellery.
1940	First British bombing raid; **Axis Pact** between Germany, Italy and Spain.
1941	Invasion of the Soviet Union; mass deportation of Berlin Jews begins.
1942	**Wannsee Conference** decides on the "final solution"; last sitting of the parliament.
1943	British bombing of Berlin intensifies; evacuation of Berlin's population begins; **Goebbels** speaking in the Sports Palace calls for **"total war"**.
1944	First daylight raid by the US Air Force; landing in Normandy; attempted **coup** against Hitler.

1945	Surrender; the Allies divide up the German Reich in the *Four Power Agreement*; return of the *Ulbricht Group*; *Potsdam Conference*.
1946	Berlin gets an interim constitution and a Municipal Assembly; the only free elections until 1990 take place in Greater Berlin; the KPD and the SPD are forced in the Admiralpalast to form the SED; rubble-clearance begins.
1947	A cold snap hits Berlin, shortages shut down thousands of factories; the Allied victors come to no agreement on the German question; the *Truman Doctrine* intensifies the Cold War; *Reuter* becomes Lord Mayor; U-Bahn returns to normal service.
1948	The East-West conflict intensifies, the Allies are divided, the departure of the Soviets from the Allied Control Council marks the end of the Four Power Administration; *currency reform* in the Soviet zone; SED intitiates the "*Town Hall Putsch*" Berlin blockade begins.
1949	Berlin's provisions can only be maintained through an *Air Lift*; West Germans have to give an emergency contribution to Berlin; the West German constitution takes effect; German Democratic Republic (GDR) established.
1951	*Reuter* becomes Governing Mayor; refugee stream from the GDR increases.
1952	The *German Agreement* makes the Federal Republic of Germany (FRG) a sovereign State; the GDR blocks all traffic to the Federal Republic, Berlin is not affected.
1953	Popular uprising in East Berlin (17th June) is put down by Soviet troops; first new stretch of U-Bahn constructed; *Ernst Reuter* dies in Berlin.

1956	The **National People's Army** is founded in the GDR; refugees from throughout the GDR come to Berlin.
1957	**Willy Brandt** elected Governing Mayor of Berlin.
1958	**Berlin Ultimatum** issued by the USSR demands that the Western powers leave Berlin.
1959	The **Berlin Ultimatum** expires uneventfully.
1961	Sector crossings to West Berlin are closed.
1962	The barbed wire along the sector boundary is replaced with a **Wall**; the Federal parliament passes **economic aid legislation**.
1963	**J.F. Kennedy** visits Berlin, four hundred thousand Berliners cheer him in front of Schöneberg Town Hall; West German citizens' visits to the GDR controlled.
1966	The **Extra Parliamentary Opposition** (APO) is founded; **Brandt** becomes Foreign Minister, **Heinrich Albertz** becomes new Governing Mayor.
1967	Introduction of GDR citizenship; in protests against the visit of the Shah of Persia, the student **Benno Ohnesorg** is shot by police; **Albertz** resigns, succeeded by **Klaus Schütz**.
1968	Attention focuses on the prominent APO member, **Rudi Dutschke**; GDR introduces passport and visa requirements for transit traffic.
1970	First **Four Power Conference** since the war.
1971	**Erich Honecker** becomes General Secretary of the Central Committee of the SED; the **Four Power Agreement** is signed, an agreement concerning transit traffic and improvement of travel between the two Germanies is signed.
1972	New travel regulations are introduced, the **Berlin Agreement** is signed.
1973	The Sports Palace is demolished; GDR doubles the minimum exchange requirement.
1974	FRG opens its **Consulate** in East Berlin.
1975	Berlin Christian Democratic Union (CDU) politician **Peter Lorenz** kidnapped by the **"2nd of June Movement"** and released in exchange for imprisoned comrades of this group.
1979	The GDR People's Chamber passes electoral legislation allowing East Berlin People's Chamber delegates to be elected directly.
1980	GDR increases minimum exchange to 25 DM; railway strike closes the S-Bahn.

1981   *Richard von Weizsäcker* elected Governing Mayor; *smog alarm* for the first time in West Berlin; squatting movement reaches a high point in West Berlin.

1984   The Consulate is overwhelmed with fleeing GDR citizens; the Berlin Traffic Authority (BVG) takes over the S-Bahn and begins restoration work; *Eberhard Diepgen* elected Governing Mayor.

1985   *Garden Show* in West Berlin.

1987   Separate *750th Anniversary* celebrations in both halves of the city; riots on 1st May in Kreuzberg.

1988   West Berlin is named *Cultural Capital of Europe*.

1989   Municipal elections return a SPD-Alternative List (Red-Green) coalition, *Walter Momper* (SPD) becomes Governing Mayor; opening of the Wall.

1990   The first free elections for the East Berlin Municipal Authority returns an SPD majority; all streets and roads between both halves of the city are opened, the Wall is almost completely dismantled; there will be elections for the whole of Berlin.

1991   The Election brings the conservative party, together with the social democrats, back to power, Eberhard Diepgen elected Governing Mayor for the whole of Berlin; Berlin becomes the seat of government.

Berlin's Districts (Area in KM² and Population)

Berlin

Reinickendorf
89.4   228 971

Pankow
78.5   135 276

(A)

Weißensee
39.8 102 338

(B)

Wedding
15.4 136 702

Prenzlauer Berg
10.8
169 445

Spandau
86.4   192 895

Tiergarten
13.4

Mitte
10.7
72 000   81 740

Friedrichshain
9.8
121 623

(B)

Lichtenb
26.2 18

Charlottenburg
30.3   145 564

Kreuzberg
10.4 127 393

Wilmersdorf
34.4 130 722

Schöne-
berg
12.3
134 610

Zehlendorf
70.6   85 161

Steglitz
32.0 167 559

Tempelhof
40.7
162 100

Neukölln
44.9 276 407

Treptow
40.6
114 749

Discovering Berlin:

The most interesting districts

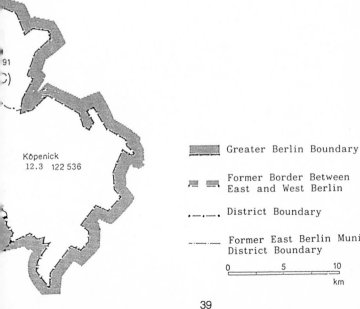

91

)

Köpenick
12.3   122 536

▨▨▨ Greater Berlin Boundary

≡ ≡ Former Border Between
East and West Berlin

._._. District Boundary

_.._.._ Former East Berlin Municipal
District Boundary

0   5   10
                          km

In the Heart of the City

Berlin's inner city draws visitors from around the world like a magnet. Berliners from both halves of the city and newcomers alike gather around the *Europa-Center* and the *Gedächt-niskirche*, between *Bahnhof Zoo* and *KadeWe*. This "capital in exile" has little of the cosmopolitan flair of other, comparable cities. Here you never see the elegance or charm of Düsseldorf, Munich or Hamburg, not to mention London's swing or Parisian *haute couture*. Of course these sorts of comparisons tend to reflect mere appearances rather than the real character of all these cities. But, after the destruction of the war and the building of the Wall,

Berlin never managed to preserve its character. The city's nerves were exposed and Berlin was vulnerable. Despite numerous attempts Kurfür-stendamm has never achieved world-class status, ultimately not really such a bad thing. The visitors who walk around the "ruined Church" meet locals as well as other tourists.

Europa-Center

Europa-Center was the name given by the city fathers to the tall, highly conspicuous building between Budapester Straße and Tauentzien. It celebrated its 25th anniversary in 1990. This multi-purpose building contains over 100 shops, various cinemas, theaters and restaurants, all under one roof. The revolving Mercedes star on top of the building is visible from a long way away. The success of this advertising campaign is indicated by the number of postcards picturing the building and its star sent throughout the world. If you would like to see the star at close quarters and at the same time enjoy a wonderful view over the city, you can take the elevator to the **Viewing Platform** on the 22nd floor (open daily from 9am, admission: 2.50 DM, Tel. 261 10 14).

The first steps in the city are made easier with a visit to the **Tourist Bureau** (Entrance Budapester Straße, open daily 7:30am-10:30pm, Tel. 262 60 31-33). For an administration charge of 3 DM you can arrange accommodation here. It is still advisable to enquire about accommodation in advance and in writing (Berlin Tourist Bureau, Europa-Center, D-1000 Berlin 30, FAX: 49 30 212 32 520).

Another means of getting a first impression of official Berlin is provided by the **Multivision Theater** (open daily, with sessions from 9am, admission 8 DM, Tel. 261 79 07) on the first floor of the Europa-Center. Berlin's history and present are shown in a slide show lasting around an hour. There is little critical perspective to be found here, but if you have no time for a city tour you will be well-served here.

At the basement of the Europa-Center in the **Irish Pub** the mostly young lovers of Guinness and Watneys assemble around trestle tables to make beery conversation amidst loud music. Here you can often expect to find standing room only.

If you stumble out of the pub after enjoying British and Irish beer, the **clock of flowing time** will seem like the product of some delirium. This oversized glass work of art, filled with phosphorescent water, marks the passing of each hour precisely. When the glass flasks empty on the hour, there are often long queues of people in front of the clock. It is best observed from the ground floor. You can also watch the swarm of people from *Tiffany's* with a refreshment alongside a colorful fountain.

The escalator to the first floor leads almost directly into *Mövenpick*, a branch of the Swiss restaurant chain. Here you can enjoy medium-priced food and drink all day long. In the *Daitokai* Japanese restaurant dishes are prepared freshly in front of you (open daily 12am-3pm & 6pm-12pm, except Monday, Tel. 261 80 99). The salmon is especially mouth-watering, if not exactly inexpensive.

If you need to find a stunning **tie** for your visit to the casino or an important rendezvous, let yourself be overwhelmed by the wide selection in *Harvey's* on the first floor.

From the ground floor of the Europa-Center pass the *French Cafe* and enter the so-called **Minicity**, a shopping complex with small fashion and souvenir shops.

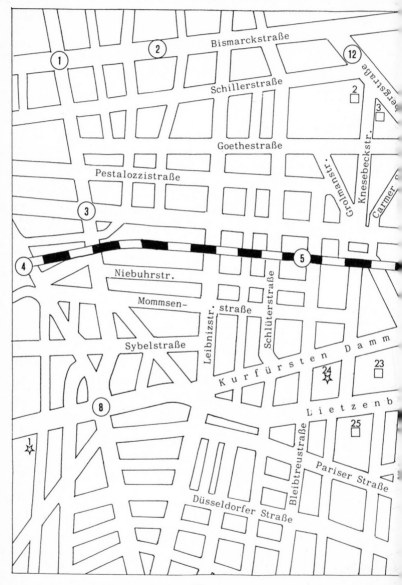

42

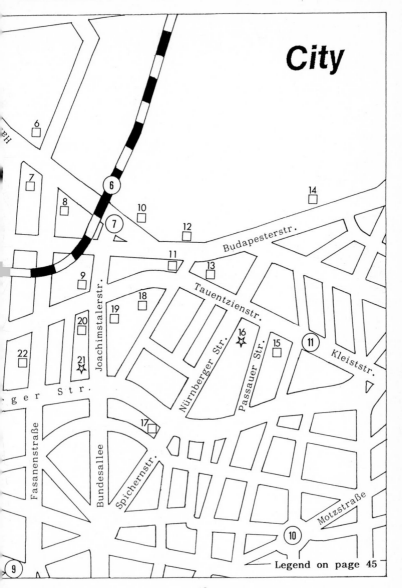

City

Legend on page 45

Among the wide selection of Kudamm cinemas, those in the **Europa-Center Filmtheater** deserve a special mention. Here there are still large screens (*Royal Palast*, five cinemas under one roof, Tel. 261 17 75), and comfortable seats (*Europa Studio*, Tel. 261 79 07).

Shortly before Tauentzienstraße, some steps lead to the four *Broadway Cinemas* (Tel. 261 50 74) which, despite being in the inner city, show more than just first-run films.

In October 1975 Berlin added another jewel to its metropolitan mosaic with the *Europa-Center Casino* (Tel. 25 00 89/0). Every day between 3pm and 3am gamblers can try their luck in an appropriate atmosphere. The largest sum won so far at roulette was 1.9 million Marks. For most visitors, an unattainable dream, but with the help of Lady Luck you may be able to supplement your travel budget playing blackjack, baccarat or even roulette (minimum bet DM 5, maximum DM 20,000). Entry costs DM 5, the minimum age is 21 years and, as they say, "the gentleman wears a tie". Identification should be carried. Naturally your bodily welfare is exquisitely cared for.

Breitscheidplatz

In front of the Europa-Center, on *Breitscheidplatz*, stands *Joachim Schmettaus's* **World Fountain**. Like much modern art, there was a great deal of controversy surrounding the fountain. Today it is a much-loved meeting-point for tourists and somewhere for Berliners working nearby to have their lunch. In summer the chairs of the *Restaraunt Mövenpick* (still offering some of the best ice-cream in town) are set up around the various parts of the fountain.

Care should be taken to avoid the skateboard riders jumping their self-made ramps or riding around the sharp curves. On Breitscheidplatz you will always find **street artists** from around the world who will play their music or put on some street theater for a few groschen.. And if you would like to have a caricature drawn of yourself, why not try one of the many charcoal

artists who wait here for customers. Bustle and confusion still dominate Breitscheidplatz.

The **Kaiser-Wilhelm-Gedächtniskirche** stands as a grotesque mixture of old and new, like a bulwark between the busy streets. The church was built in 1895 in honor of the not-so-peaceful *Kaiser Wilhelm I*. When World War II left little more than the foundations, the authorities were poised to demolish it. Popular opinion was against demolition, and in this case it was heeded: the ruins remained and a new building was draped around it. This fragment of what was once Berlin's tallest building quickly became known simply as the *Gedächtniskirche* (the Memorial

City

U-Bhf.
1 Bismarckstraße
2 Deutsche Oper
3 Wilmersdorfer Straße
7 Zoologischer Garten
8 Adenauer Platz
9 Hohenzollernplatz
10 Viktoria-Luise-Platz
11 Wittenbergplatz
12 Ernst-Reuter-Platz

S-Bhf.
4 Charlottenburg
5 Savignyplatz
6 Zoologischer Garten

1 Schaubühne /Far out
2 Kiepert (bookshop)
3 Renaissance Theater
4 University Quarter
5 Steinplatz
6 College of Arts
7 Berlin Stock exchange
8 Berlin Information Center
9 Café Kranzler
10 Staatliche Kunsthalle (State Art Gallery)
11 Kaiser-Wilhelm-Gedächtniskirche
12 Cinema-in-the-globe (Panorama Berlin)
13 Europa-Center
14 Aquarium
15 KaDeWe (Department store)
16 Dschungel Disco
18 Café Möhring
19 Ku'damm-Eck
20 Joe am Ku'damm
21 Ku'dorf
22 Käthe Kollwitz Museum
23 Ku'damm Karee
24 Big Eden Disco
25 Loretta im Garten

Church; namely, against war and its tragic consequences). Inside the new church, **classical music concerts** (Information: 24 50 53) take place in addition to church services.

In a neighboring building you will find the **Third World Shop** stocking products primarily from Africa. The steps of the Gedächtniskirche have also become a market-place for the **Street-Art scene**. Also some of the homeless community meet here, to acquire a few marks from passing "touris" for their daily beer ration.

Zoo

In the middle of West Berlin, only a stone's throw from the *Gedächtniskirche*, live almost 12,000 animals from around the world in **Germany's oldest zoo**. The buildings along Budapester Straße shield the extensive grounds from the hectic city traffic. A part of the gardens designed by *J. Lenné*, and built on the site of the *Royal Pheasantry*, the so-called Zoologischer Garten, was opened in 1844. At this time Berlin's development as a metropolis was still unimaginable, and the zoo lay outside the city. The collection of various animals in *Friedrich Wilhelm II's* menagerie, put together in 1795, formed the nucleus of the zoo. Exotic animals were brought from the Prussian colonies and displayed before the astonished Berliners. The animal houses were designed with great architectural care and an obsession for detail. The recently reconstructed **Elefantentor** (Ele-

phant Gate, entrance Budapester Str.) and the **giraffe and elephant house** are typical examples of the zoo's playful building style.

The Second World War inflicted severe casualties among the zoo's animals: out of 4,000, only 91 survived the bombing. While the neighboring *Tiergarten* park was being plundered for fuel in the cold post-war winters, the zoo was spared. In fact due to the Berliners typical love of animals it was rebuilt in this period. The range of animals to be found in the many animal houses and on the grounds, extended in 1987, is unique. The **nocturnal house**, with its fluttering and squeaking in artificial day-time darkness is highly recommended.

A further attraction in the zoo grounds, but also worth a separate visit, is the **Aquarium**. You can admire over 4,000 species in the *Crocodile Hall* and the tropical landscapes.

●The *Zoo* is open daily from 9am to dusk, latest 7pm, the *Aquarium* daily 9am-6pm.

The **Main Entrance** lies opposite Bahnhof Zoo. A second entrance lies on Budapester Str. beside the Aquarium. Admission to the Zoo is 7.50 DM, for the Aquarium 6.50 DM and in combination 11 DM. Children are half-price.

Budapester Straße

Budapester Straße used to be an extension of Kurfürstendamm, and thus of greater significance than today. The stretch between the Landwehrkanal and Breitscheidplatz is occupied by **large hotels**. The expensive shop-displays indicate that hotel guests are being catered for.

The spot where the *Grundkreditbank* has built its Berlin branch is of historical significance. Here, in 1919 on the corner of Kurfürstenstraße, the two Spartacists *Rosa Luxemburg* and *Karl Liebknecht* (together with *Wilhelm Pieck*) were interrogated and then murdered in broad daylight. On the Lichtensteinbridge there is a small **Memorial to Rosa Luxemburg**, whose body was thrown from here into the Landwehrkanal.

In 1990 Budapester Straße acquired a new attraction which should not be missed. *Panorama Berlin* (Budapester Str. 38, Tel. 262 80 04) is a **cinema-in-a-globe**; it breathes new life into the Berlin myth. The visitor stands in the middle of a film about the city and its people. The screen is the inner surface of a globe, so that the film is projected all around the viewer.

A few steps further leads to the *Linientreu* disco (Budapester Str. 42, Tel. 261 44 10), an apparently timeless relic of the 80s. Every day from 10pm onwards it attracts locals as well as tourists. The hard core of the resident disco scene still goes gladly to *Linientreu*. The music is harder and less oriented to the Top-10 than many of the other discos in the city.

Budapester Straße, continues on from here as a covered **Arcade**.

After the fall of the Wall and the subsequent stream of shoppers from Poland and Hungary, a number of cheap shops aiming specifically at this clientele opened up in this arcade.

The *Society* (Budapester Str. 40, open daily from 8pm, Tel. 261 61 16) is one of the many teenage discos in the heart of the city. It has no special character, but it is trendy. Despite extensive renovations, the neighboring fast-food stall remains unappealing.

The **Wohlthat'sche Bookshop** has the special feature of being open daily (except Sunday) until 10:30pm. The Berlin section is well stocked.

The **Staatliche Kunsthalle (State Art Gallery)** (Budapester Str. 43-44, Tue-Sun 10am-6pm, Mon to 10pm, Tel. 261 70 67/68) exhibits the work of international painters. The **Berliner Festspiele (Berlin Festival)** has an office at No. 48 (Tel. 25 48 90), which provides information about all the events taking place during the various cultural festivals.

From licorice to champagne, every flavor of ice-cream imaginable is available at *Henry's Eisshop* (No. 48).

Beyond the *Arcade* Budapester Straße turns into Hardenbergstraße. If you feel the urge to sample some German cuisine, you could try the Bavarian *Hofbräuhaus*.

Alongside the *Royal Palast* in the Europa-Center, there is the *Zoo-Palast* (9 cinemas, Hardenbergerstr. 29a, Tel. 261 15 55). Cinema 1 is one of Berlin's **most beautiful cinemas**.

Bahnhof Zoo

The merging of the two halves of the city has brought new life to **Zoologischer Garten** railway station as well as **Hardenbergplatz**, which runs in front of it. For decades the station was of little significance for long-distance travel. Before the Wall the most important connecting stations all lay in the eastern part of the city. **Bahnhof Zoo** served as the Central Station for the *Deutsche Reichsbahn*, the GDR railways. (The Deutsche Reichsbahn has been responsible for the railways in West Berlin until now.) One S-Bahn line runs through it, as well as occasional train traffic with West Germany and other countries.

For travelers who came to Berlin by rail, their arrival at Bahnhof Zoo was always a shocking first impression. Although it lay in the middle of the city, it had long been neglected and had decayed correspondingly. Travelers found the platforms old and dirty, the station hall was dark and the square in front of the station a playground for society's outsiders. The extensive renovations of the middle-1980s gave the station a modern and bright facade. The notion that the misery would also appear in a friendlier light was an illusion. The station halls and neighboring streets remain a collection-point for society's rejects. The dark side of an affluent society in the middle of the city. The fall of the Wall has only intensified the problem. The visa-free stream of East European citizens had the arriving trains from Poland, Rumania

and Yugoslavia bursting at the seams. Thousands of petty thieves and currency speculators, for whom the smallest profit outstripped what they could earn at home, spilled into the inner city. Black market traders, hands full of bundles of GDR marks, stood in front of the **Currency Exchange Office** on Hardenberg-platz. Their rates were always just a little better than the official ones. Those who did not deal in money went to one of the import-export shops which shot up like mush-rooms. Here they could buy tax-free goods which could be sold at home for many times the price. Polish sausage, Russian Vodka or smuggled cigarettes were also sold, all for hard Western currency.

Besides these trading activities, imported and home-made **crime** flourished around Bahnhof Zoo. Street prostitution, drug dealing and thieving are still the order of the day here. The so-called *"Hütchenspiel"* (hunt the ball game) has gone through a renaissance. Even when it seems obvious where the small ball is, be warned! The successful players are part of the team and serve only as bait. As soon as outsiders place their bets (100 DM), the ball is very cunningly removed, making it impossible to win!

This increase in illegal activity around *Bahnhof Zoo* should not, however, worry you too much. If you keep your eyes open, you have nothing to fear. This kind of misery, the homeless and the alcoholics, for whom Bahnhof Zoo is sometimes the last refuge, can be found everywhere in the Western world. In most big cities they are removed from public view, being concen-trated in ghettos, but this does nothing to change the problem. For the derelicts at Bahnhof Zoo the proximity to "normal" life is often the last barrier to total collapse.

•In the station building you will find a **Post Office**, which also offers a **night service**. Underground lies the **U-Bahn station**, with Lines U1 and U9. As mentioned before, directly beside the entrance there is a **Currency Exchange Office**.

Hardenbergstraße

Opposite Hardenbergplatz, before the railway tracks cross *Harden-bergstraße*, is the *Presse-Café* (Tel. 881 72 56). It's a round the clock meeting point for a quick beer or a bad coffee, when waiting for a train.

Behind the underpass the Ameri-can flag flies on top of a bare two-storey building. The so-called **Amerika-Haus** (Hardenbergstr. 21-24, Tel. 819 76 61) is a left-over from the early post-war period, when Berliners were keen on everything from across the Atlantic. Officially the building is a *US Information Center*, established to reinforce German-American friendship. In protest against American involve-ment in the Vietnam War, the building was often subjected to rock-throwing. Today the *Amerika-Haus* is still constantly guarded.

The **Berlin Information Center** (Hardenbergstr. 20, Tel. 310 04 10) does have a few brochures for individual travelers, but it primarily deals with group travelers and planning their programs.

If you are interested in seeing a hectic trade in stocks and shares, visit the **Berlin Stock Exchange** (Hardenbergstr. 16-18).

The *College of Arts Concert Hall* (Hardenbergstr. 33, Tel. 318 50) is used for classical and modern **concerts**. You should make sure you get a seat in the stalls, as the acoustics in the dress circle are not the best.

The **University Quarter** begins at Steinplatz with the *Technical University (TU)* and the *College of Arts (Hochschule der Künste, HdK)* (Tel. 318 523 74). The streetscape is correspondingly youthful. If you like cheap eats, there is the *TU Cafeteria (Mensa)* (Hardenbergstr. 34). In the *Old TU-Mensa* (Tel. 311 22 33) **Rock Concerts** or **Parties** of various sorts are occasionally held.

A cinema, theater and bar under one roof can be found in the **Kino/Café am Steinplatz** (Hardenbergstr. 12, Tel. 312 90 12). During the day one finds students escaping the cafeteria, in the evenings film or theater-goers. The **cabaret** *Bügelbrett* and the **puppet-theater** *Pfifferling* occasionally feature in the cinema.

The walk from the hectic Ku'damm to the *Café Hardenberg* (Hardenbergstr. 10, open daily 9am-1am, Tel. 312 33 30) is made all worthwhile if you sample the breakfast served here until 5pm.

Shortly before Ernst-Reuter-Platz there stands the beautiful state-run **Renaissance Theater** (Hardenbergstr. 6, Tel. 312 42 02). A unique event in Berlin's established theater world was the projection of advertisements on the curtain before it rose.

Berlin's largest selection of books, with a large English-language section, can be found at *Kiepert* (Tel. 31 07 11) on Ernst-Reuter-Platz.

Between Wittenbergplatz and the Gedächtniskirche

If you have just reached Wittenbergplatz with the U-Bahn (U1 & U2) and stepped out onto the busy street, it will be difficult to imagine that only a hundred years ago this was still a dirt road. It was around the turn of the century that the area attracted the well-to-do middle classes and became known as the *"New West"*.

51

Bahnhof Wittenbergplatz lay on the first inner-city rail link between Warschauerbrücke and today's Ernst-Reuter-Platz. The *"Old West"* ended at Nollendorfplatz. Here the above-ground railway had to be taken underground to spare the refined ladies and gentlemen from the "ugly" sight of this most proletarian means of transport. Bahnhof Wittenbergplatz was opened in 1902.

The price of land rose to such an extent that Tauentzienstraße turned from a residential area into a shopping street. Where there once stood residential apartments, emporiums shot out of the ground.

The most striking example is the **KadeWe** (Kaufhaus des Westens, Department Store of the "new" West), built in 1906/7. It was erected on a piece of land where recently built apartments had been demolished to make way for the store. The *KadeWe* was restocked so often that it was constantly regarded as too small. After suffering heavy damage during the war, it was rebuilt in 1950 as a symbol of the "economic miracle". The store boasts, if it cannot be found, it does not exist. Doubtless an exaggeration. Still, the range of goods on offer, presented in an exclusive atmosphere, is unique and worth a look.

Wittenbergplatz has been considerably cleaned up in recent years, with the introduction of grassed

areas with seats, and a fountain. **Snack stalls** with original Berlin fast food items, the twice-weekly **market** and some smaller shops enliven the square. It was built to generous proportions following the plans of its architect, *Hobrecht*.

The *standing café Einhorn* (Wittenbergplatz 5, open daily 10am-6:30pm, Tel. 24 63 47) serves vegetarian dishes. In Ansbacher Str. 29 Berlin's somewhat greying gay community meets with its recently arrived visitors in *Andrea's Kneipe* (open daily 11am-2pm, Tel. 24 32 57). It has been some time though since *Andrea's* was a real high-spot on the gay scene.

Between Wittenbergplatz and Breitscheidplatz **Tauentzienstraße** becomes purely a shopping street. Banks, insurance offices and furniture stores dominate the streetscape.

At No. 5 you will find the city branch of *Schuhtick*, with striking **shoe creations**. Directly alongside it *System Collection* sells unusual **jewelry** at affordable prices.

The disco *Yesterday* (Tauentzienstr. 8, open daily from 7pm, Tel. 262 31 54) is devoted primarily to young tourists.

Two further nightclubs in the area, admittedly on a completely different level, still enjoy a good reputation. The *Dschungel* (Nürnberger Str. 53, admission 10 DM, Wed-Mon 10pm-3am, Tel. 24 66 98) is already legendary. Who hasn't been caught here with someone in a compromising position?! Gossip depends on image, so the door-control is stricter than elsewhere. If you're in, you have to be *in*.

At *Cha Cha* (Nürnberger Str. 50, Tue-Sun 11pm-6am, admission 5 DM, weekends 10 DM, Tel. 214 29 76) the restrictions at the door are particularly daunting. Otherwise one can hear black music, when the trend allows it.

Ku'damm and Back

In darker days the Brandenburg Electors rode down today's boulevard to hunt in the nearby forests. The only evidence of hunting today are the fully-laden shopping bags of passers-by in search of a good bargain. **Ku'damm**, short for Kurfürstendamm, stretches from the Gedächtniskirche almost to the edge of Grunewald. A stroll through the collection of shops, street cafés, bars and mobile traders is well worth the effort. If you keep your eyes open, and look beyond the all-too touristy facade, you will discover some delightful attractions.

In Rankestraße, opposite the "ruined church", probably the best *Falafel Baker* (No. 3) in the city opens daily at 12am. Accompanied by cinammon tea and Arabian music you will be able to gather your strength for the Ku'damm tour. If you prefer Italian, there is the inexpensive self-serve *Avanti* (No. 2) restaurant. The *Eierschale II* bar (No. 1, Tel. 882 75 05) is open for thirsty visitors virtually round the clock. Jazz is played with Sunday lunchtime beers.

The following **walk** between the *Europa-Center* and *Lehniner Platz* includes many of the highlights, although only your own efforts to discover interesting things will complete the picture.

At the start of Ku'damm there are two **cinemas**. The *Marmorhaus* (No. 236, Tel. 881 15 22) has been divided into four smaller cinemas, and thus not to be recommended. In contrast the *Gloria-Palast with Gloriette* (No. 12, Tel. 261 15 57) is very good. A few years ago this traditional cinema stood in danger of demolition. It was to make way for the total reconstruction of the whole *Gloria-Passage* from the ground up. Luckily the architects had some vision and developed a concept which allowed the cinema to survive. In the process of renovation the projection and sound equipment was up-dated, making the *Gloria-Palast* one of Berlin's most modern cinemas.

In the **Gloria Passage** you will find some clothing stores and a poster gallery. High over Ku'damm, on the **Roof Terrace** of the *Hotel Pientka* (No. 12, 6:30am-8pm, Tel. 88 42 50) one can observe the hectic activity below. The self-service *Marché* restaurant (No. 14, Tel. 882 75 78) is a branch of the fashionable *Mövenpick*. The dishes are freshly-prepared and can be assembled according to your individual preferences. The prices are reasonable.

At house No. 16, **boxoffice Zanke** (Tel. 882 53 83), you can buy tickets for shows in the eastern part of town.

Café Möhring (No. 234, open daily 7am-12pm, Tel. 882 38 44), practically in the shadows of the Gedächtniskirche, is an ideal spot to enjoy coffee and cake on the pavement, and watch the world go by.

Kaufhaus Wertheim is not much different from other department stores; only the cheap fast-food stalls in the basement are worth a look.

Where Ku'damm meets Joachimstaler Straße an **oversized wall newspaper** with the latest news from around the world hangs above the heads of city strollers. Installed at *Ku'damm-Eck*, this popular source of information is financed by the advertisements it also presents. For a small amount you can also place a greeting for a few seconds.

Ku'damm-Eck has become somewhat run-down and seedy. The basement is devoted to games parlours and sex cinemas, and the other floors contain numerous small shops and two of the *Marmorhaus cinemas* (Tel. 881 15 22). Wax imitations of famous figures can be seen in the **Berliner Panoptikum** (3rd Floor, open daily 10am-11pm, admission 5 DM, Tel. 883 90 00).

Crossing Joachimstaler Straße, you virtually stumble into the chairs of *Café Kranzler* (No. 18/19, open daily 8am-12pm, Tel. 882 69 11), which are set up on the pavement at the first sign of sunshine. The "Kranzler" has for many years had a reputation for exclusive furnishings and good food. The balcony provides a fine view.

The name *Aschinger* also has a long Berlin tradition behind it. Here one used to be able to get the best pea-soup and beer at popular prices. *Aschinger am Ku'damm* (No. 26, Tel. 882 55 58) shares not only its name with its historic predecessor. In an atmospheric cellar-vault you get (and pay for) an excellent home-brewed beer. The menu leaves nothing to be desired.

The *Filmbühne Wien Cinema* (No. 26, Tel. 881 48 88) is a typical example of the annoying tendency to turn large cinemas into a number of much too small "intimate" cinemas. On the other side of the street the *Filmpalast* (No. 225, Tel. 883 85 51) is the positive counter-example. Modern equipment combined with a generous interior.

Käthe Kollwitz

In the same building there is *Joe am Ku'damm* (open daily from 10am, Tel. 885 90 10), a disco for the more sedate.

The **Lufthansa** office can be found at No. 220. Next door, on the balcony of the former Chinese embassy, why not make a selection from a small but good range of meals and cakes in *Café Leysieffer* (No. 218, open daily 9am-10pm, Sun from 10am, Tel. 882 78 20). The ground floor offers select pralines and other delicacies.

The disco in the same building has gone through a variety of names, the latest being *Pim's Club* (open daily from 11pm, Tel. 882 47 15).

King's Teegarten (No. 217, Mon-Sun 9am-7pm, Tel. 883 70 59) is a favourite address for tea drinkers. Almost **200 varieties of tea** can be sampled in a relaxed atmosphere on the first floor.

One further representative of the "better" **mainstream cinemas** is the *Astor* (No. 217, Tel. 881 11 08) on the corner of Fasanenstraße.

Both sides of Fasanenstraße are worth an excursion. The **Käthe-Kollwitz-Museum** at No. 24 (open Wed-Mon, 11am-6pm, admission 6 DM, Tel. 882 52 10) has a range of the works of this artist who portrayed Berlin so tellingly.

In the elegant *Café Wintergarten* (Fasanenstr. 23, open daily 10am-1am, Tel. 882 54 14) you can escape the Ku'damm frenzy to enjoy a good drink over an extensive range of newspapers.

Past the first-class **Hotel Kempinski**, which also has a cafe with street seating, one can find **curiosities** in the *Zille Flea Market*, shortly before the S-Bahn bridge.

On the other side of the street, at Fasanenstr. 79, is the **Berlin Jewish Community house**, with has space for exhibitions and other events (Tel. 883 65 48).

Back on Ku'damm the stroller is confronted by a rather complicated method of timekeeping. The **Mengenlehre Clock** on the corner of Uhlandstraße has four balconies, each indicates either hours or minutes. On the top are single minutes, then 5-minute intervals, followed by whole hours and then 5-hour intervals. A bit confusing, but logical!

The **Maison de France** (No. 211, Tel. 881 87 02) spreads French culture through occasional exhibitions and a bookshop stocking

French literature. The *Cinema Paris* (Tel. 881 31 19) shows international first releases.

Constantly concerned with polishing its image is the **Ku'damm Karree** (No. 206-208). Unfortunately it does not quite succeed. The interior is bright and sterile, with no atmosphere. The shops are almost all directed at the quick visitor, and the bars have no atmosphere. You could however have a look at the **Antique Market** or the **Teddy Bear Museum** (open daily, except Tue, 3pm-10pm, admission free, Tel. 881 41 71). In the *Sperlingsgasse* (at the exit to Lietzenburger Straße) there are a number of equally dreadful bars gathered under one roof. Whole sightseeing groups are catered for here. *Loretta im Garten* (Lietzenburger Str. 89, open daily 7pm-2am, Tel 881 68 84) has a comparable, if somewhat more youthful character. As the name suggests, a large beer garden which also offers grilled sausages. Further "attractions" are the youth disco *Flashdance* (open daily from 7pm, Tel. 883 52 08) and the small *Astor* cinema (Tel. 881 11 08). Exotic varieties of ice-cream are the specialty at *Café Eismann* (No. 203, open daily from 12am, Tel. 881 74 34).

Naturally in Berlin you will also find the strips of meat stuck between two halves of a bread roll, sold as a hamburger and tasting the same all over the world. *Burger King* on the corner of Ku'damm and Knesebeck-straße is open until late at night. A

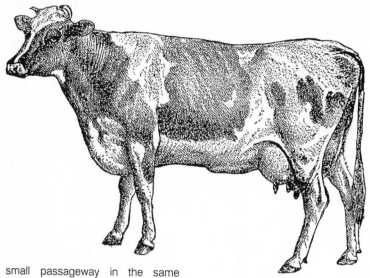

small passageway in the same building takes you to the small **Independent Cinema** *Lupe 1* (Tel. 883 61 06).

If you go to the *Big Eden disco* (No. 202, open daily from 7pm), you will be mixing with a very young crowd, few of them Berliners.

Ku'damm now continues as a boutique boulevard. Small, mostly exclusive stores entice you with their wares. One **Men's Store**, well-known for its continually striking window displays, is *Selbach* (corner of Bleibtreustraße).

Once again an excursion into the side street is worth your while. *Beiz* (Schlüterstr. 38, on Georg-Grosz-Platz, open daily from 6pm, Tel. 883 89 57) with its cellar-vault provides a good atmosphere with candle-light and muted music. The buildings in this part of Ku'damm have generally maintained or completely restored their original facades.

Two culinary specialties of different sorts lie side by side beyond the crossing with Wielandstraße. For those wishing to eat quickly there is the fast food outlet *Ku'damm 185*. This place can be said to take the 'credit' for making curried sausage respectable. The gourmets who turn their noses up here will prefer the nouvelle cuisine in *Bovril* (No. 184, Mon-Sat 12am-4am, Sun 6pm-4am, Tel. 881 84 61). Naturally the servings are small and the waiters arrogant.

A former porno-cinema, the *Hollywood*, has been turned into one of the most comfortable **Ku'damm cinemas**. (No. 65, Tel. 883 50 77).

In *Coupé 77* (No. 177, open daily from 10pm, Tel. 881 35 46) the dance floor belongs to the more mature disco generation.

Adenauer Platz (U-Bahnhof U7), at the crossing of Ku'damm, Wilmersdorfer Straße and Branderburgische Straße, has something for all ages. The atmosphere in the cafe' *Adlon* (Ku'damm 69, open daily from 10am, Tel. 883 76 82) is calm and restful.

The *Tolstefanz* disco (Brandenburgische Str. 35, open daily from 10pm, Tel. 892 77 83) should be approached with care, if at all, as it is patronised by a rough crowd. Recently it hit the headlines when a bouncer was shot on the door-step. There are better places in Berlin!

New Eden (Ku'damm 71, Tel 323 58 49) is less a disco than a **women's and men's (!) strip joint**.

Café Da Da Da (Ku'damm 73, Tel. 323 90 20) sounds suspiciously like German New Wave, and is thus fairly dated. The cafe itself is like that too, in the style of the early 1980s.

The Baghwan period and its boundless happiness still survives in *Far Out* (No. 156, Tue-Sun from 10pm, Tel. 32 00 07 23). Its great success seems to put its owners in the right, whether or not the profits end up in Poona. In contrast *Sky* (No. 156, Tel. 892 46 68) is relatively new to the Berlin disco scene.

Right beside these two dance-temples, Berlin's premier theater presents consistently stimulating productions. The **Schaubühne am Lehniner Platz** (Ku'damm 153, two auditoriums, Tel. 89 00 23), under the management of *Peter Stein*, puts on intellectual theater utilising all technical possibilities. In the associated *Bistro Universum* (open daily 7am-12pm, Tel. 891 30 60) one can discuss at length plays and actors.

Joachimstaler Straße

Joachimstaler Straße connects Ku'damm to Bahnhof Zoo. On one side **currency exchanges** and **peep shows** jostle with clothing stores and cheap supermarkets. Here it is primarily touristy and hectic.

The tavern *Holst am Zoo* (No. 1, Tel. 882 39 22) fits the area well. It's owned by the former president of the local football club *Hertha BSC*, and the bar is adorned with portraits of old football heroes.

South of Ku'damm there are a number of discos. For example, *First* (No. 26, Wed-Sun from 11pm, Tel. 882 26 86, restricted entry), *Sly* (Laser show, No. 15, open daily from 8pm), and *Ku'dorf* (No. 15, Mon-Sat from 8pm, Tel. 883 66 66), together with a number of bars of various styles all under one roof.

Charlottenburg

Charlottenburg is West Berlin's "city"; here both its cultural and its intellectual life pulses. However, life in this district is not hectic. Beyond the main streets lie quiet residential areas with their own independent social scenes. Charlottenburg borders on "green" districts such as *Tiergarten, Grunewald, Spandau*, and so compensates for its own lack of greenery by its proximity to these areas. Housing damaged in the war was generally restored, demolished buildings reconstructed, and a new residential area was established. The restoration of the equally-heavily damaged castles began in 1952. Today the **Schloß Charlottenburg**, built for the wife of *King Friedrich I*, retains all its former glory.

There is a concentration of business and cultural enterprises in the center of the city. The loss of a real inner-city with the rise of the Wall, led to a desire to turn the area around Ku'damm into an inner-city boulevard.

Three main streets traverse the district: Otto-Suhr-Allee, connecting with Hardenbergstraße; Bismarck-straße, extending to Kaiserdamm and Straße des 17. Juni; and Kantstraße, which leads on to Theodor-Heuß-Platz. Along these streets Charlottenburg offers the cultural and the culinary, each well worth discovering.

Ernst-Reuter-Platz

The island in the middle of Ernst-Reuter-Platz, with its meter-high **water fountain** and its seats, is a restful oasis amid the busy surrounding traffic. Four of the former and probably future most important streets meet here: Straße des 17. Juni and Bismarckstraße, Hardenbergstraße and Otto-Suhr-Allee.

Straße des 17. Juni, once *Charlottenburger Chaussee*, is a reminder of the popular uprising in East Germany in 1953. It leads through Tiergarten, connects Ernst-Reuter-Platz with *Brandenburger Tor* and goes as far as *Marx-Engels-Platz* in the Mitte district. On the right and left of this broad street stand the buildings of the **Technical University** (TU). In the TU's main building one can find notices about interesting events plastered on posts, and the inexpensive *Cafeteria*.

Charlottenburger Tor stands as testimony to the formerly well-to-do Charlottenburg population. It was erected in 1905 on the similarly-named bridge over the Landwehrkanal. Planned as a twin to the *Brandenburg Gate*, this ostentatious set of pillars, which marked what was then

Berlin's outer perimeter, was soon to lose its impressive shape. The current Straße des 17. Juni was widened extensively in 1937, and the gate was disassembled and the two halves re-built on either side of the new road.

Before the bridge one's eye falls automatically on the *Schleuseninsel* and the huge **Water Tank** of the *Waterworks and Shipbuilding Research Institute*. The tank, painted in a tasteless blue and pink, was built in 1974 and is used for testing model ships.

If you follow Straße des 17. Juni, behind *Charlottenburger Tor* you come to the **Ernst-Reuter-Haus**, built in 1939. Here one finds the *Senate Library* and the *Institute for German Studies*.

Berlin's **best flea market** takes place every weekend in front of the 200 m long building. Innumerable stalls offer a colorful hodgepodge of antiques, jewelry, art of all sorts, second-hand and designer clothing. Connoisseurs will be there early in the morning in search of a bargain. From around 9am, even before the breakfast cafes open, sleepy-headed crowds battle their way through the narrow passages. Everything that is not nailed down is for sale, and haggling is compulsory.

A few years ago a second, purely **Art Market** started in front of *Charlottenburger Tor*. This is also worth a visit. Both markets close around 3pm to make way for the Berlin street cleaners.

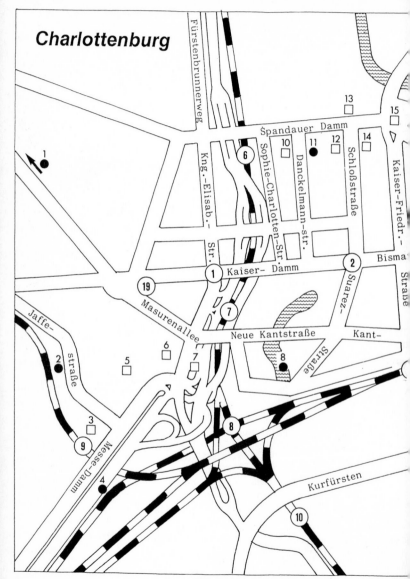

Charlottenburg

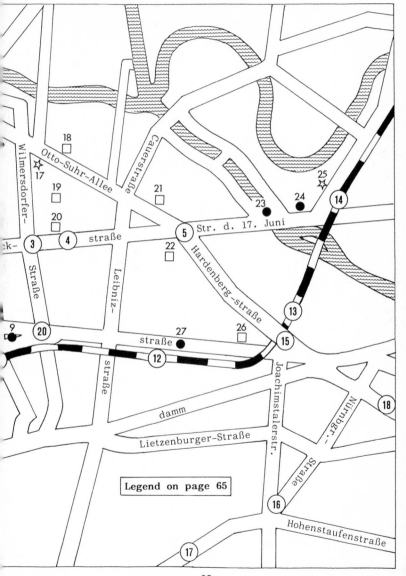

Tucked away in Wegelystraße 1, is the **State Porcelain (formerly Royal Prussian) Factory's** *Exhibition and Retail Pavilion* (open daily 9am-6pm, Sat 9am-2pm).

Otto-Suhr-Allee

The road connecting Ernst-Reuter-Platz and Schloß Charlottenburg, *Otto-Suhr-Allee*, has lost much of its former shine as a pulsating recreational street. Before the turn of the century the then-*Berliner Straße* had a magical attraction, especially in summer, for the capital's inhabitants. With its cafes, bars and chic stores well-to-do Charlottenburgers lingered here and allowed the lower orders to admire them. Seeing and being-seen was the currency. Today no one would dream of sitting in a garden tavern on Otto-Suhr-Allee. The street is now characterised by bumper-to-bumper traffic heading towards the freeway. Nonetheless, some buildings still retain their old charm.

Directly opposite the *Tribüne* theater is a Chinese restaurant called *Kanton* (No. 11). A few buildings further on (No. 25), the small elegant *Salue* restaurant offers, besides unusual opening hours and excellent food, an irresistable Wiener Schnitzel (Tue-Fri 11:30-4pm, Tue-Thu 6pm-12pm, Tel. 342 17 42). The **Charlottenburg Town Hall** (No.96-102) at the Richard-Wagner-Platz U-Bahn station (U7), was built in an art nouveau style and opened in 1905.

The ostentatious Spandau and Steglitz town halls are built in a similar style, which is not surprising as they were all designed by the same architect. The 88m high clock tower, visible from far away, is particularly impressive. On the first floor a **Memorial Table** commemorates the victims of German tyranny. Alongside it a fountain splashes. The **Press Office** (Tel. 34 30 33 02) distributes information and postcards.

The *Lipstick* disco on Richard-Wagner-Platz opens daily between 10pm and 5am exclusively for women (Sun, Tue & Thu men can also pass the strict door control). It is somewhat hidden away, with white doors and door-bell beside the entrance to a sports school (Richard-Wagner-Platz 5, Tel. 342 81 26). The modern interior and the usually comfortable atmosphere are what characterise *Lipstick*.

In the immediate neighborhood is the *Wendel* bar where they are proud of the 12 varieties of beer they have on tap. Old Berlin specialties are also served (beer from DM 5.20/0.4 l, open daily 4pm-12:30pm, Tel. 341 67 84).

From Otto-Suhr-Allee it is worth taking a short detour through Schustehrusstraße as far as Gierkeplatz. *Lavandevil* (No. 3, open daily 5pm-1am, Tel. 342 92 80), offers an exotic array of dishes (Egyptian, Persian and traditional), and on weekends the coarse jokes of the **Kappedeschle Puppetshow**.

West Berlin's speculative developers have played around with

Charlottenburg

U-Bhf.
1 Kaiserdamm
2 Sophie-Charlotte-Platz
3 Bismarckstraße
4 Deutsche Oper
5 Reuterplatz
15 Bahnhof Zoo
16 Spichernstraße
17 Hohenzollernplatz
18 Wittenbergplatz
19 Theodor-Heuss-Straße
20 Wilmersdorfer Straße

S-Bhf.
6 Westend
7 Witzleben
8 Westkreuz
9 Eichkamp
10 Halensee
11 Charlottenburg
12 Savignyplatz
13 Bahnhof Zoo
14 Tiergarten

1 Olympic Stadium
2 Eissporthalle
3 Deutschlandhalle
4 Avus
5 Fair Grounds
6 Broadcasting Tower/German Broadcasting Museum
7 ICC (International Congress Center)
8 Lietzensee
9 Stuttgarter Platz
10 Freie Theateranstalt Berlin
11 Klausener Platz
12 Antikenmuseum/Bröhan Museum
13 Schloß Cahrlottenburg
14 Ägyptisches (Egyptian) Museum
15 Gasthausbrauerei Luisen-Bräu (brewery)
16 Gierkeplatz
17 Lipstick Disco
18 Rathaus Charlottenburg (City Hall)
19 Stadtbad (swimming baths)
20 Deutsche Oper (Opera)
21 Schiller Theater
23 Art market
24 Flea market/State Porcelain Factory
25 Disco
26 Theater des Westens/Delphi/ Vagantenbühne
27 Savignyplatz

the small, striking building at *Schustehrusstr. 13* for many years. Only through the intervention of some committed citizans was it possible for the building, one of the last remaining examples of 18th century architecture, to be placed under a conservation order and saved from demolition.

On **Gierkeplatz** the **Luisenkirche** is tightly wedged between the surrounding apartment blocks. It was relatively late, namely 1716, before the church, then still covered in timber, could be used properly. Life around Gierkeplatz is colorful and lively. The majority of the buildings here have been conserved with sensible renovations.

Near the church square Behaimstraße branches off from Gierkezeile. At No. 21 you can take a vegetarian food break in the *Lützower Lampe* Café-Restaurant. The meatless menu is simple and economical (open daily 18-24, Tel. 342 61 55). Right beside it, in the *Cafétheater Schalotte*, there are often some interesting shows, either **cabarets**, performances by independent **theater groups**, or **concerts** (Tel 341 14 85).

Northwards Gierkeszeile leads back to Otto-Suhr-Allee, which ends shortly before *Schloß Charlottenburg* and continues as Spandauer Damm. The streetscape is now determined by the splendid castle buildings.

If you need to gather your strength

before the historical and cultural experience offered by the castle, you will be able to do so in the *Brewery Luisen-Bräu*. Apart from a really delicious beer on tap, they also serve good rustic, relatively economical buffet meals. Fresh beer is the main offering, which is why it comes in small glasses. But take care: according to an old tradition the beer will continue to be poured until the guest puts a cover over his glass! (Luisenplatz 1, open daily from 11am, Tel. 341 93 88).

Schloß Charlottenburg

If normally you are not interested in visiting showy castle rooms with stuffy interiors from bygone centuries, try and make **"Schloß Charlottenburg"** an exception. The palace park, which cannot be seen from the street, is partly landscaped and partly wild gardens. An inviting place for long walks.

As proof of his love the Elector *Friedrich III*, who later crowned himself King of Prussia, gave the original summer chalet, *Schloss Lietzenburg*, to his wife, *Sophie-Charlotte* in 1695. It took four years to complete the main building. As a consequence of his ever-growing desire for new forms of self-expression to match his new status as King, *Friedrich* commissioned more extensions.

The long east wing was the result and the park was landscaped on the same large scale as Versailles. In memory of *Sophie-Charlotte*, who died in 1705, the palace was further extended by the Prussian King. The

dome with Fortuna, the goddess of fortune, was placed over the main building and the orangery built.

The next ruler of Prussia, *King Friedrich II*, also had the palace extended by the best architects of the day. The eastern wing of the palace was built by the master builder and friend of the King, *Knobelsdorff*. Almost a hundred years later, *Queen Luise's Mausoleum* was built to *Schinkel's* design. This completed the palace as it looks today. The park was turned into an "English Garden" in the 19th century.

●The Palace (Luisenplatz, Tel. 32 09 11) can be visited daily, except Mondays, between 9 am and 5 pm. Besides the historical rooms, there are collections of porcelain, sculpture, paintings, and arts and crafts of the period. The Mausoleum can also be viewed.
●The combination ticket for all buildings, including guidance, costs DM 6 (concession DM 3).

Klausener Platz

Around *Klausener Platz* there lies what was once a densely populated workers' quarter. At the turn of the century, Charlottenburg was turned into an attractive and wealthy town through the development of industry. In 1877 the town was connected to Berlin and other industrial towns by the metropolitan railway ring. This supposed advantage of the Charlottenburg district led to a dramatic increase in population, and living conditions deteriorated accordingly. Today most houses have been completely renovated, and the desolate housing situation which dominated the area until the 1960s has been turned into a lively city environment. Older buildings have been preserved and the facades are testimony to the architecture of times gone by. A large part in this "careful" renovation was played by the squatting movement. In the 1980s they turned the problem of neglected buildings into daily headlines.

As part of the 750th anniversary celebration *Klausener Platz* was refurbished according to original plans from 1921. Today it is a well-loved meeting-point for locals, with large playgrounds and numerous benches.

The **Weekly Market**, Tue-Fri between 7am and 2 pm, around *Klausener Platz* is an ideal place to get to know the locals. Here you will also meet migrant (primarily Turkish) traders and customers, who have given the area a multicultural flavour over the last few years.

The **Freie Theateranstalt Berlin** (Klausener Platz 19, Tel. 321 58 89) puts on committed, politically informed plays.

The *Trio* restaurant (Klausener Platz 13, Tel. 321 77 82, Fri-Tue, 7-11.30 pm) offers a small but excellent range of dishes.

Wandering through the **Danckelmannstraße**, which connects Klausener Platz to Kaiserdamm, the small shops, Turkish greengrocers

and historical facades provide the right backdrop to a lively district.

It is well worth simply strolling through the streets of this quarter and absorbing the atmosphere. The old **Engelhardt brewery** in Danckel-mannstr. 9 is a relic of the industrial revolution. Production was moved to Kreuzberg early in the 1980s, and all that remains in Charlottenburg is distribution. A cultural utilization of old production sites has been demanded over recent years by various interest groups but rigid Senate policies have blocked this.

The *Dicke Wirt* pub in Danckel-mannstr. 43, offers elegant meals along with various types of wine. It's a popular meeting place for beer drinkers.

If you leave breakfast until 4 pm or only want to drink coffee or beer in a comfortable atmosphere, you will be at home in *Café Knobelsdorff* (Kno-belsdorff- / Danckelmannstraße, open daily 8 am - 12 am, Tel. 322 50 93). *The Art and Stout House* (Kno-belsdorffstr. 23) is a typical, some-what hectic, Irish pub. In summer the tables are set up as far as the street.

At Sophie-Charlotten-Str. 88 stands the **house of Heinrich Zille**. Zille captured the living conditions of the day with pen, camera and paint box. He lived in this house up to his death in 1929. In his honor, a Charlottenburg tavern collective has immortalised his name in the bricks and mortar of *Zille-Eck* tavern. The tavern-restaurant offers international meals surrounded by a number of Heinrich Zille's works. The atmo-sphere in the *Zur Linde* tavern (No.

Heinrich Zille

19, open daily from 4pm) is always friendly. The *Laternchen* at Horstweg 2, on **Sophie-Charlotten-Platz** offers food and drink until the early hours of the morning in a crowded interior.

From Sophie-Charlottenplatz (connection with U-Bahn Line U1) **Schloßstraße** leads back to Spandauer Damm. Here, well-kept apartment blocks, interspersed with luxurious greenery, provide examples of the imaginative facades of the 19th century. The former Officers Quarters of the *Gardes du Corps* now house the **Antikenmuseum** (No.1, small antiques from Greece and Rome, jewelry, mummies, open Sat-Thu 9am - 5pm, admission free, Tel.32 09 11); the **Bröhana-Museum** art from the Art Nouveau and Art Deco periods, (open Tue-Sun 10am - 6 pm, admission 3 DM/1.50 DM, Tel. 321 40 29); and the **Ägyptische**

Museum (No. 70, Egyptian art and culture from 500 B.C. to the Roman Empire, the bust of Queen Nefertiti, open Sat-Thu 9am - 5 pm, admission free, Tel. 32 09 11).

Despite the well-to-do surroundings, in terms of price *Pirandello* is a popular, highly recommended Italian restaurant.

Always well-patronised, especially in the summer months, is the *Zur Weißen Kastanie* garden tavern (Schloßstr. 22, open daily fro 2pm, Tel. 321 50 34). *Ristorante Don Camillo* (Schloßstr. 7, open daily except Wed, open 12am - 3pm and 6 - 11:30 pm, Tel. 322 35 72), where one can also eat in the garden, offers first-class Italian cuisine.

Bismarckstraße

From Ernst-Reuter-Platz, *Bismarckstraße* is the extension of Straße des 17. Juni. Functional buildings and shops dominate the streetscape.

The **Schiller Theater** at Bismarckstraße 110 (near the Ernst Reuter Platz U-Bahn station) represents Berlin's established theater culture. Classical and (less often) modern plays have been performed here since 1907. In the early years the *Schiller Theater Company* was maintained independently. Private donors from Charlottenburg's wealthy citizenry wanted to establish an institution which would give ordinary people access to high culture. This lasted for 25 years, until the National Socialists came to power, and their "equalization" of cultural bodies led to the dissolution of the *Schiller Theater Company*. Extensive war-damage meant that the theater could only reopen in 1951 after rebuilding on the old location. Ironically, *Gustav Gründgens*, controversial because of his involvement in the cultural activities of the Third Reich, became the first director of the new *Schiller-Theater*. The quarrels over the role of directors in so-called state theater continue to this day. Despite everything the *Schiller-Theater* and particularly the experimental **Schiller-Theater-Werkstatt** (workshop) are important parts of Berlin's cultural scene. Each is worth a visit. (Information and Ticket Reservations: Tel. 319 52 36). Both theaters can be reached with the U-Bahn and Buses 109, 145 & 245.

Another recipient of subsidies is the **Deutsche Oper Berlin** (Bismarckstr. 35 Tel.(recorded message) 341 44 49, Cashier Tel. 343 83 16), situated near the U-Bahn station of the same name. Without state support, each seat in this 1,700 seat temple of culture would cost at least five times as much. The opera house, re-opened after the considerable damage of World War II, sits comfortably among Bismarckstraße's austere buildings. Nevertheless, the *Deutsche Oper* enjoys an excellent reputation well beyond the city's boundaries.

Shortly before the Opera house, Krumme Str. branches off. In the 100-year-old **municipal swimming baths** (No. 10, open Mon-Sat, Tel. 34 30 32 14) one has to renounce modern comforts, but that makes a relaxed swim in the baths all the more worthwhile. The baths are decorated with Art Nouveau mosaics. A privately-owned sauna, with accompanying bar, opens Mon-Sat between 12am and 11 pm (16/20 DM without/with swim).

If you prefer a more modern swimming environment, the neighboring pool will suit you better (Tel. 34 30 21 41).

At the intersection of Bismarckstraße and Krumme Straße stands the 750th anniversary gift from the British government, a bust of Shakespeare. His name was also given to the square opposite the Opera. The tragic events which took place here on 2nd June 1967 would justify the name *Benno-Ohnesorg-Platz*. During a state visit by the then-Shah of Persia, a protest demonstration by Berlin students was violently dispersed by the police. The victim of this brutal police action became *Benno Ohnesorg*, killed by a police bullet. His death and the events of June 1967

dissolved the student movement. Berlin had been its stronghold.

One of Berlin's best-loved shopping streets is undoubtedly **Wilmersdorfer Straße**, which crosses Bismarckstraße. Not nearly as chic as Ku'damm, Wilmersdorfer Straße, mostly a pedestrian zone, presents itself as practical. No one saunters here, people buy their daily needs and leave. After closing time the street is dead and becomes the territory of skateboard riders.

Bismarckstraße keeps its name until Sophie-Charlotten-Platz (U-Bahn on Line 1), here it continues as Kaiserdamm. It's not only the narrow streets north of Sophie-Charlotte-Platz that have their own particular charm. Try the streets to the south with their small shops and taverns, and also the nearby *Lietzensee*.

At Suarezstr. 8, in the **Edelstein-werkstatt**, you will find unusual items of jewelry. The range of exotic gemstones is extraordinary.

The *Magazin* (No. 12, open Mon-Fri from 11am, Sat from 10am) provides the newest, and sometimes the oldest, **design ideas** - from knickknacks to furniture.

Directly opposite lies the *Vietnam*, a restaurant with economically-priced meals. Open on the weekend from 1 pm (Suarezstr. 61, Tel. 323 74 07). If you feel like Egyptian cuisine, you should try *Restaurant am Nil* (Kaiserdamm 114, open daily from 3 pm, Tel. 321 44 06). Viennese specialties can be found in *Eulenwinkel* (Kaiserdamm 4, 6pm-2am, Tel. 322 23 37).

At **Lietzensee**, south of Kaiserdamm (U-Bahn station on line U1) the densely populated Charlottenburg district becomes streaked with water and greenery. A playground, paths, swimming areas and the *Hotel-Restaurant Seehof* gives *Lietzensee-Park* the feel of an oasis amid a concrete jungle.

Exhibition Grounds

The *Exhibition Grounds* (Messegelände) stretch between Theodor-Heuss-Platz and the AVUS (Automobile Testing Track). The name is misleading, for here lies a real feast of culture, trade and sport. Here one of the city's landmarks, the 138m-high **Broadcasting Tower** (Funkturm), has loomed over Berlin since 1926. Both the platform and the *Funkturmrestaurant* (55 m. high, open daily 11am-11pm, Tel. 303 81) provide a magnificent view over Charlottenburg and part of the *Berlin Forest* (Elevator: 4 DM/2 DM).

The construction of the actual *Exhibition Grounds* began in the 1920s. The first halls were originally built for an automobile exhibition. The first radio exhibition took place here, in still very provisional surroundings, in 1924. From then onwards the Broadcasting Tower would continue to be used in its real capacity. In the following years the exhibitions grew rapidly. The only building to survive the war was the *Palais am Funkturm* with the connecting halls on either side. Today the *Palais* is used primarily for large balls.

The partially very modern halls of the 88,000 sq metres exhibition complex surround two open spaces. In the smaller space stands the Broadcasting Tower and at its foot the **Deutsche Rundfunkmuseum** (German Broadcasting Museum) (open daily except Tue. 10am-5pm) with exhibits from the history of radio and television.

The larger open space is set up as a summer garden. It offers those overwhelmed by the crowds in the halls the chance to rest themselves in a landscaped park. In the summer months concerts are regularly held in the **Open-Air Theater**.

The best-loved **Fairs** are the bi-annual *Broadcasting-Fair* (Funk-ausstellung) and the annual *Green Week*, once a pure farm fair, today a 10-day eating spectacular. The *International Tourism Exchange*, which takes place every year in March, has, since the opening of the border in 1990, been overwhelmed by a stream of GDR tourists. Other worthwhile exhibitions are the **Freie Berliner Kunstausstellung** (Free Berlin Art Exhibition) and the fashion shows of the independent designers. These designers turn the functional halls into board-walks for wild fashions.

As an extension of exhibition capacity, but also as a separate Congress hall, the controversial **International Congress Centrum (ICC)** was constructed between 1973 and 1979. The wildest analogies have been drawn of this shiny silver function building. Whether it is *"Megalomania Hall"*, *"The Charlottenburg Spaceship"* or *"The Congress Steamer"*, it seems that everybody either loves it or hates it. What is clear is that the construction became the greatest building scandal in Berlin's history. On completion the building had cost five times more than the original estimate. The ICC has cost the taxpayer a billion Marks. In professional circles the congress center enjoys an excellent reputation throughout the world. Over 80 congress rooms can house events of all sorts and sizes. In the large hall **Ballets**, **Musicals** and **Rock Concerts** are held. In autumn the ball season begins. If you would like to just have a look, you can join a guided tour through the buildings (Tel. Information, 30 38 31 75).

Messedamm begins at the ICC and later becomes Eichkamp. It runs along the AVUS to Grunewald. The multi-functional **Deutschlandhalle** (Messedamm 26, Tel. 30 38-1, Bus 219) is used for the most diverse types of events. The gigantic hall was originally built for the Olympic Games. The Deutschlandhalle was heavily damaged during the war, restored and reopened in its current form in 1957. Horse-riding events, tennis tournaments, boxing and wrestling take place here, alongside rock concerts, circuses and ice-skating events. One historical event which took place here was the *"Greater Berlin Rock Concert"* organised shortly after the opening of the Wall.

Directly beside it stands the **Eissporthalle** (Jafféstraße, Tel. 30 38-1), home of Berlin's premier ice-hockey team, *BFC Preußen*. Other sporting events and rock concerts also take place here. The hall offers space for over 6,000 visitors. Ice-skating is available in the hall in the winter months.

The **Berlin Oktoberfest** is set up every year on the parking lot in Jafféstraße. It's fun but it cannot be compared to the Munich event it is modelled on.

Opposite the Deutschlandhalle stand the grandstands of the former **AVUS** (Automobile Testing Track). Since the 1920s it has been the scene of spectacular car and motorbike races. The North Curve was one of the most notorious chicanes on German racing tracks. In 1967 it was smoothed out for safety reasons, and became a feeder for the Berlin-Nürnberg autobahn. Racing enthusiasts and automobile clubs were able to ensure that racing continued much to the annoyance of residents subjected to the noise. Berlin's former Red-Green Senate decided on environmental grounds to ban car and motorbike racing on the *AVUS* from 1991.

The Senate's decision, again on environmental grounds, to set a speed limit of 100 km/h on the AVUS led to rather grotesque protests. For weeks drivers agitated in demonstration marches and slow-moving car columns. After a few weeks, and the opening of the border, the protest was curtailed, another example of the "Berlin Wall tantrums".

What remains is the *AVUS* as an expressway through Grunewald to the former *Checkpoint Dreilinden*. It leads to western Germany, and can also be used for excursions to Berlin's surroundings (e.g. to Potsdam). Hitchhikers are no longer allowed on the road. They can only wait at the exit to Potsdamer Chausee.

On **Theodor-Heuß-Platz** (U-Bahn station on Line U1) an *"eternal flame"* burns. It was lit a number of decades ago by the former West German President of the same name. As it was intended to burn until the reunification of Germany, the square will soon be deprived of much of its attraction.

Olympic Stadium & Forest Stadium

The walk through the **Olympic Quarter** is best started at Steubenplatz (U-Bahnhof Neu-Westend, U1 or Bus 104). The connection to Theodor-Heuß-Platz is called Reichstraße. Passing through settlements of small houses the road leads over Olympische Straße to the complex of sporting arenas. Imposing and already impressive from a distance, the Olympic Stadium appears over the horizon.

From the **Olympic Bridge** you will get a view of the U-Bahn line, which runs above ground here, and was laid in 1936 to bring the crowds to the Olympic Games. The bridge is decorated with the flags of the nations which took part in those games. The broad forecourt in front of the stadium is used as a parking lot or, on quiet days, serves as a practice area for driving schools or skateboarders.

Passing the tennis courts, somewhat hidden in the greenery, you will pass the entrance to the *Hockey Stadium*. Continue to the right of the

Olympic Stadium and you will reach the entrance to the *Swimming Stadium*. In addition to international competitions the Swimming Stadium is also open in the summer to the general public (open daily 7am-7pm, admission 3 DM/1.50 DM, Tel. 304 06 76/8). The open-air pool is a favorite meeting point for sun-lovers.

The **Olympic Stadium** has two entrances. The *Eastern* or *Olympic Gate*, the main entrance, consists of two, 35 meter high columns, the *Prussian* and the *Bavarian* towers. Between both columns there hang the Olympic rings from the 1936 games. The cashiers are ranged along the entire breadth of the forecourt. The second entrance, the *Southern Gate*, was well-placed for the S-Bahn, today still out of service.

The stadium's original capacity of 100,000 was increased for the football World Cup in 1974.

In order to satisfy the National Socialists' desire for a stadium which would represent the "overwhelming power of the German race", the Nazi architect *Speer* became involved in the design. Throughout the stadium you can find traces of both the Olympic Games and the Nazis' megalomania. It is particularly noticeable on the Western side, at the so-called *Marathon Gate*, where huge sculptures were erected. Some, like the *"Goddess of Victory"* or the two *"Stewards"* which frame the entrance to *Maifeld*, still stand in the positions they were given by the Nazis. On the walls of the Marathon Gate the victors of the *"World Youth*

77

Games" are immortalised. The Olympic flame also burns here. Whether this will again be the site for an appeal to "the youth of the World" in 2000 is still unknown. The thought of a Greater Berlin Olympic Games seems to have a very special appeal for many politicians in the newly awakened metropolis. For the city, the estimated stream of over 2 million Olympic visitors would bring considerable problems with it, but would certainly also mean a good chance to improve the urban infrastructure. One can only hope that the more cautious and ecologically-informed plans will prevail.

The Olympic Stadium is rarely full. Once a year the West German Football Cup is played here. Occasionally rock groups will appear (recently the Rolling Stones), or the athletics will attract visitors to the all-seater stadium.

The **Maifeld** was planned as a parade ground and is today still used for military parades, such as for the British Queen's birthday parade. The occasional polo match is also played on the Maifeld.

Leaving the stadium through the *Southern Gate* in the direction of Reichssportfeldstraße, you will cross Jesse-Owens-Allee, named in honor of the black multi-medal winning U.S. athlete. *Jesse Owens* became the star of the 1936 Olympiad, and a thorn in the Nazis' side.

The **Riding Stadium** was built before the Olympic Games and serves today as a site for horse riding competitions.

The **Forest Stadium** (Waldbühne) is hidden away in delightful surroundings. During the Olympics it was used for gymnastics and boxing. In the 1960s the Rolling Stones so excited the audience that they demolished the whole theater. The Waldbühne was forgotten for some time after that. Fortunately that is all over now. The Waldbühne (approx. 20,000 seats) has been rediscovered as one of the best locations for **Open Air Concerts** (Rock, Jazz or Classical) and **Cult Film Nights**. Special buses run from the Olympiastadion U-Bahn station for such events.

From the **Belltower**, opposite the Waldbühne, you can finish off your tour with a final look out over the area (open April-October, daily 10am-5:30pm). The **Olympic Bell**, which now stands in the stadium near the *Southern Gate*, used to hang here. The bell in the tower is a replica of the original.

To get back to the inner city go to Theodor-Heuß-Platz with the U-Bahn or a bus, and from there, going past the Exhibition Grounds, go along Neue Kantstraße towards the city.

Kantstraße

Without doubt Kantstraße is one of Berlin's more interesting streets. It connects the Exhibition Ground area with the city (Bus 149), beginning at the ICC and going as far as Amtsgerichtsplatz as Neue Kant Straße.

The *Hinkelstein* tavern (Neue Kant-/Wundtsraße) does not have a particularly good atmosphere and is usually full, but it's still good for a quick beer and a snack.

Booked-out during exhibitions, but otherwise good alternatives to the Kurfürstendamm hotels, are the **Pensions at Neue Kantstr. 14:**

●*Hotelpension Am Kongreßzentrum* (45 DM/85 DM, Tel. 321 52 75)
●*Hotelpension Berolina* (55 DM/80 DM, Tel. 321 20 01/02)
●*Hotelpension Domino* (50 DM/90 DM, Tel. 321 20 01/02)
●*Hotelpension Richter* (50 DM/85 DM, Tel. 322 10 04, 322 50 68)
●*Hotelpension Seeblick* (99 DM/128 DM, Tel. 321 30 72)

The *Currywurst* stall near the District Court (Suarez-/Kantstraße) has been high on Berlin's fast-food hit list for many years. Apparently customers come from all over the city to eat curried sausage here.

Mylos (Holzendorffstraße near the District Court, open daily from 4:30pm, Sun from 12am) is decorated in the style of a modern Greek tavern.

South of the District Court, **Stuttgarter Platz** and the surrounding streets have acquired the reputation of being Berlin's new red light district. Here **Bars and Brothels** thrive. This densely-populated quarter has also become an area with an astonishing number of **Street Cafés** and **Taverns**. Here you will search in vain for the neon-lit establishments or hyper-modern interiors typical of Kreuzberg. Although some have new owners, most of the locations around the *"Stutti"* have a more traditional, but by no means stuffy atmosphere. Many small **Antique and Avantgarde Fashion Shops** encourage a stroll through the strikingly green streets. Occasionally you will find the remains of old buildings behind facades or entrances. Stuttgarter Platz can be reached from the Wilmersdorfer Straße U-Bahn (Line U7) or Charlottenburg S-Bahn (S3).

The *Schuldt & Söhne* in Trendelenburgstr. 14 (open daily from 4 pm, Sat & Sun from 3pm, Tel. 322 27 64) is a tavern in the old Berlin style with a small front garden. At the bar in *Nante 2* (Suarezstr. 38) hardened drinkers guzzle until they are legless and either fall over or sit out front on the terrace. In the *Stattcafé*(Suarezstr. 31, Mon-Sat 11am-1am, Sun from 10am, breakfast until 4pm!) there's almost a family atmosphere, especially on Sundays.

Klick is a mixture of cultural experience and a tavern atmosphere. The **Cinema** shows mostly commited films with a cult film session on Saturday (Windscheidstr. 19, Bus 110, 149, 204, 221, Tel. 323 84 37, admission 9 DM). In the *Klick-Kneipe* you can discuss the night's viewing in depth.

The **Borbone** supposedly has the best wine list on offer in any of Berlin's restaurants, together with excellent Italian cuisine. A tip for all genuine gourmets. Not cheap, but worth the price! (Windscheidstr. 14,

Mon-Sat 12am-12pm, Tel. 323 83 05). The interior of the *Palagonia* (Stuttgarter Platz 20, open daily from 5pm, Tel. 324 13 60) is even fancier. The food is also Italian - first-class, and a specialty is an entree buffet. The **Gasthaus Lentz**, without background music and with all the charm of a railway station, is the best-loved meeting-point on the Stutti. It gets very full in the evenings (Stuttgarter Platz 20, open daily 10am-2:30am, Tel. 324 16 19).

Feinschmiede (Windscheidstr 24,Mon-Fri 11am-6pm, Sat 10am-1pm) offers more to look at than to buy. But if you are interested in chair contruction, this is the place. **Men's fashion** with experimental designs can be found in *VETO* next door (No. 25, Mon-Fri, 2pm-6pm, Sat 11am-2pm). **Avantgarde fashion** at reasonable prices can be found in *Palto'* (Leonhardtr. 13)

Continuing on past smelly currywurst stands, the route zig-zags through the shadowy underworld back to Kantstraße. Beyond the crossing with Wilmersdorfer Straße (U-Bahnhof of the same name, line U7) the real attractions of Kantstraße begin, interesting shops and taverns, and also the occasional diversion into one of the sidestreets.

Formerly one of the best-loved spots for Berlin bands, *Kant-Kino* (cinema) is now "only" what the name suggests. Three **cinemas** under one roof - with the formula the smaller the cinema the more experimental the film (Kant 1+2, Kid, Kantstr. 54, Tel. 312 50 47, admission 6 DM/10 DM).

In Krumme Straße *La Batea* serves reasonably priced South American meals at sticky tables (Krumme Str. 42, open daily, Tel. 31 70 68).

Versandbuchhandlung Zweitausendeins at Kantstr. 41 is a treasure-trove for inexpensive **records and books**.

A worthwhile diversion from Kantstraße (under and beyond the S-Bahn bridge) at Leibnizstr 43, is the *Ristorante Mario*. A first-class Italian restaurant, with correspondingly high prices (open daily except Sat! from 12am, Tel. 324 35 16).

Chic, avantgarde **men's fashion** is on offer in *Veni Vidi Vici* at Leibnizstr. 40.

Safer sex has made it possible (necessary) - a whole shop full of condoms! Whether ribbed, or colored, dry or lubricated, whether flavoured with licorice or rum - it's in

Kantstraße 38 / Leibnizstraße
1000 Berlin 12 · Tel. 313 50 51

Condomi (Kantstr. 38, Tel. 313 50 51). Here every desire is fulfilled. For those with orientation problems in the dark, there is even a flourescent condom for sale. The times of secretive condom purchases are over, here you can satisfy your rubber desires to the full. One particular condom is displayed to the tune of Elton John's "I'm still standing", which says a lot about the fantasies of condom fanatics.

Abraxas is a Latin-American dance floor at Kantstraße 134. Not very large, but for years well-loved and unchanged (open daily except Mon, 11pm-5am, Tel 312 94 93).

One of the last representatives of traditional independent cinema is the **Schlüter**. The owners of this small **cinema** have a particular liking for the Marx Brothers and other black-and-white comedies (Schlüterstr. 17, admission 8 DM/7 DM, Tel. 313 85 80).

Dralle's provides cocktails and small snacks in a 1950s style (Schlüterstr. 69, 2pm-3am, Tel. 313 50). At the *Union Jack* 300 varieties of whiskey and Irish Guinness are on offer (Schlüterstr. 15, 7pm-3am, Tel. 312 55 57).

Along Kantstraße up to Savignyplatz there are a number of recommended cafés and taverns. One of these is *Mimikry* (Kantstr. 29, open daily 1pm-9am, breakfast 2pm-8am, Tel. 312 44 49), a favorite meeting point. For those with an appetite for oriental snacks, there's the *Der Ägypter* bistro (Kantstr. 26, Tel. 313 92 30).

In the same building *System Collection* offers amusing **jewelry pieces** at every price range. *La Culinara* (Kantstr. 32, Tel. 312 86 80) serves Italian meals between 5pm and 1am.

Between Ku'damm and Kreuzberg, in terms of style rather than geography, lies **Savignyplatz** (Bus 149, S-Bahn Line S3). It has its own mixture of chic and underground culture. During the day the two stretches of greenery which, divided by Kantstraße, form Savignyplatz, offer lunchtime resting spots for stressed bank workers and Poles taking a break from their shopping. Students from the nearby University also enjoy a second breakfast for

example at the *take away in front of Schuhtick* (flamboyant, but practical footwear). The selection is limited (no chips in sight), but the hungry queue tells the story: the curried sausage swimming in fat must have some special quality. Why not try it yourself.

No longer a secret, the *Ashoka* Indian fast-food restaurant at Grolmanstr. 51 serves tasty food until late at night.

Savignyplatz and its sidestreets are a treasure trove for **book lovers**. Just a selection: *Bücherbogen* (under the S-Bahn overpass. Art and photography books from all around the world, wonderfully suited to rummaging); *Politische Buchhandlung* (Carmerstr. 9, matches its name, a political bookstore); *Canzone* (Savignyplatz 5, literature and especially records from South America); *Lilith* (Knesebeckstr. 86, specialising in feminist literature); *Romanische Buchhandlung* (Knesebeckstr. 18, books in the Romance languages); *Regitz-Fachbuchhandlung* (Kantstr. 22, English reading matter).

With the new reading material under the arm you can now dive into the **Café and Tavern scene**. All of the following locations lie in the streets running off Savignyplatz.

Rost (Knesebeckstr. 29, 9am-2am, Tel. 881 95 01) opens early in the morning to offer a resting place to both the early risers and last nights left-overs. In *Cafetarium* (Knesebeckstr. 76, 10am,-2am, Tel. 883 78 78) things are more traditional. The

interior of *Restaurant Istanbul* (Knesebeckstr. 77, 12am-12pm, Tel 883 27 77) has all the atmosphere of a Turkish harem. Not cheap, but you will eat as if you are in Turkey.

The southern half of Savignyplatz also has a branch of the oldest profession. Whether the *Sophie Club* deserves its reputation as a luxurious brothel seems doubtful, the streetwalking representatives of this business are an adornment to an otherwise tame streetscape.

Life for the Berlin night owl would be unimaginable without the *Schwarzes Café* (Kantstr. 148, open continuously from Wed 11am to Mon 3am, Tel. 313 80 38). The cappuccino machine works round the clock and breakfast can be had at all times of the day and night.

Grolmanstraße and Knesebeckstraße both lead on as interesting streets from **the northern half of the square**. Between the two

streets, in the *Cour Carree* (Savignyplatz 5, open daily, 12am-1am, Sun 10am-1am, Tel. 312 52 38), you can enjoy French meals at reasonable prices. If the skies over Berlin allow it, you can sit outside at the garden tables. Less originally named is the *Shell* restaurant (Knesebeckstr. 22, 9am-1am, Tel. 312 83 10), named after the service station which used to stand here. But the similarities end there. In *Shell* there are no grease-stained overalls, but an assembly of the supposedly, intellectual elite. You should not expect large portions, but the food is certainly good. *CUT* (Knesebeckstr. 16, open daily 11pm-6am, Tel 313 35 11) tempts you with exotic cocktails in the atmosphere of a high-class bar. Although the service and the interior design in *Café Tiago* (Knesebeckstr. 9, open daily 8am-2am, Sun 10am-2am, Tel. 312 90 42) has long become an anachronism, its meals and cocktails are of a contemporary quality. The breakfasts and vegetarian meals are especially noteworthy.

The **northern side of Grolmanstraße** also offers some interesting cafés and restaurants. *Zwiebelfisch* (Savignyplatz 7, 12am-2am, Tel 31 73 63) is fancy, but nonetheless comfortable. *Florian* (Grolmanstr. 52, 6:30pm-3am, Tel. 313 91 84) with its German cuisine is a well-loved meeting point for the extroverts of the city's art scene. Naturally the prices are set a little higher, but what does it matter when you're dining with the stars of tomorrow? Next door, in *Café Savigny* (Grolmanstr. 53, 10am-1am, Tel 312 81 95) you can folllow a good meal with an excellent capuccino. If you would rather eat Greek food, then just over the street lies *Grolman's* (Grolmanstr. 21, 6pm-4am, Tel. 312 11 21), a regular haunt for the television and radio industry. An economical Indian fast-food place, the *Taj Mahal*, lies at the end of Grolmanstr. (No. 58).

Back to the southern side of Savignyplatz. The connecting arcade to **Bleibtreustraße** used to be a bargain El Dorado and a dope-dealers paradise. In keeping with the spirit of the times, the arcade has gone up-market.

At the crossing of Kant- and Uhlandstraße **Cinema, Jazz, Theater** and **Musicals** all jostle for attention.

The *Delphi* (Kantstr. 12a, admission 10 DM, Tel 312 10 26) shows cult films and interesting first releases. These keep the owners of this unusually large cinema in business.

In the same building the *Quasimodo* (open daily from 8pm, Tel. 312 80 86) is a **jazz cellar** of the old style - with a little luck you should experience some fine performances.

In the shadow of the *Theater des Westens* the **Vagantenbühne** (Tel. 312 45 29) wages a successful "David versus Goliath" struggle. Modern productions of the Classics are performanced here in the smallest of spaces. The audience sits close to the action and consequently has an intense theater experience.

This experience becomes an expensive luxury in **Theater des Westens**. Good seats cost around 70 DM. Higher above the stage it becomes less expensive, but also less comfortable. Still, it is worth a visit to this lovingly restored, traditional theater. Tickets can be bought from the small kiosk in the square (Tue-Sat, 12am-6pm, Sun 3pm-6pm, Tel. 312 10 22; performances Mon-Sat 10am-6pm, Tel. 31 90 31 93).

Schöneberg

From the "chic" part of Berlin's inner city we continue out of the city along Tauentzien/Kleiststraße to **Nollendorfplatz**. Then on to Schöneberg, one of the most densely populated districts. It has taken exactly 100 years for Schöneberg, then a sleepy village at Berlin's gate, to turn into one of the most interesting inner suburbs.

Around the *Nolle*, as the locals call Nollendorfplatz, the scenery is a mixture of old-world charm and uncompromising town planning.

Life is very hectic in this part of the city, dominated as it is by traffic.

Nollendorfplatz

Nollendorfplatz is the terminus of the short, purely Schöneberger U-Bahn Line 4 and also a stop on the notorious Line U1.

The most striking building in Nollendorfplatz is the *Metropol*. Huge neon letters on the historical, ornate facade invite you to Berlin's largest discotheque (Fri & Sat from 11pm, admission 10 DM, Tel. 216 41 22/ 216 27 87). It is also one of the best loved venues for national and international rock groups. In the same building the *Loft* (Tel. 216 10 20), which has a smaller stage, is kept for the lesser-known or more extreme types of music. In 1906 the

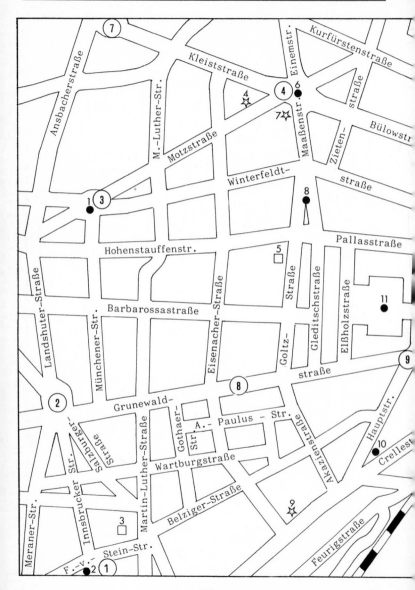

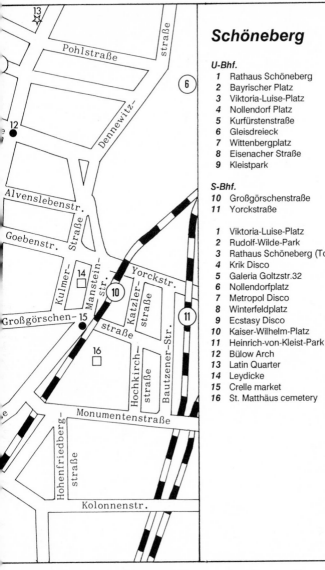

Schöneberg

U-Bhf.
1 Rathaus Schöneberg
2 Bayrischer Platz
3 Viktoria-Luise-Platz
4 Nollendorf Platz
5 Kurfürstenstraße
6 Gleisdreieck
7 Wittenbergplatz
8 Eisenacher Straße
9 Kleistpark

S-Bhf.
10 Großgörschenstraße
11 Yorckstraße

1 Viktoria-Luise-Platz
2 Rudolf-Wilde-Park
3 Rathaus Schöneberg (Town Hall)
4 Krik Disco
5 Galeria Goltzstr.32
6 Nollendorfplatz
7 Metropol Disco
8 Winterfeldplatz
9 Ecstasy Disco
10 Kaiser-Wilhelm-Platz
11 Heinrich-von-Kleist-Park
12 Bülow Arch
13 Latin Quarter
14 Leydicke
15 Crelle market
16 St. Matthäus cemetery

Metropol was built as a "new playhouse" and was used until 1930 as a theater. Later it became Berlin's largest cinema.

Café Swing (Nollendorfplatz 3-4, open daily 10:30am - 5am, Tel. 216 61 37) occasionally puts on great midnight concerts. Otherwise it's a tavern.

Winterfeldtplatz

The area around the *Winterfeldtplatz* was the center of events when Berlin's squatting movement was still in full swing. The houses worth preserving, in terms of their structural soundness, such as Maaßenstr. 11, 13 and Winterfeldtstr. 22, 24, 35-38 were intermittently squatted in.

There were also a number of occasionally ugly battles with the police. In 1982 in particular, the square was frequently filled with tear gas. Today there is hardly a trace of these upheavals. Most buildings have been modernised or torn down and replaced.

The colorful **Market** around Winterfeldtplatz prevails twice a week: Wednesdays and Saturdays. It is a social institution in the Schöneberg district, especially on Saturday. For years the countless traders had to put their stalls up somewhere else in the district, as the square around *St. Matthias Church* had to be re-covered with asphalt. The relationship between the stall-holders and their customers made certain that the market would

return to its old location. What Berlin's newspapers have lately described as the development of a "multicultural society" comes to life here. Primarily a varied food market, recently it has acquired an ever-increasing range of jewelry, art objects and fashion clothing. The diverse smells which delight the nose make the detour to Winterfeldtplatz well worthwhile. Garlic olives from the south of France, kebabs and falafel, herbs and spices from all over the world, smoked trout or the smell of fresh fruit and vegetables - all these make your mouth water. The cheese, vegetable and flower vendors all have the famous "Berliner Schnauze" (Berlin spiel) and use it regularly. For a visit on a Saturday morning you should allow plenty of time.

The best impressions of the "Winterfeldt-Feeling" are gained in the many **Cafés** which line *Maaßen-, Winterfeldt-* and *Goltzstraße*. Winterfeldtplatz offers an excellent variety of food, making it equally attractive after the market has closed and also in the evenings.

The first floor of *Eiscafé Berio* (Maaßenstr. 7, open daily 9am - 12pm, Tel. 216 19 46) offers good food, a wide range of ice-creams, and a fine view of the district.

Two interesting **shoe shops** lie almost directly opposite in Maaßenstraße. The *Schuhbidu* (No. 9) sells women's shoes in the latest designs and in various colors. *Zapato* (No. 14) sells modern styles for him and her.

In the *Sidney* corner café (open between 9am and 4am, Sat. until 6am, Tel. 216 52 53) they serve a breakfast called *Sidney Rome* consisting of croissants and fruit. In the summer you can sit in front of the café and admire the colourful crowds.

Perhaps the best falafel in town is produced at *Winterfeldtstr. 37*. It is served in a sandwich with either a mango or sesame sauce. Highly recommended! *Café Belmundo* (Winterfeldtstr. 36, open daily 9am-1am, Sat/Sun from 10am, Tel. 215 20 70) is somewhat off the track, hence the comfortable quiet atmosphere. Breakfast is served until 3pm.

The *Sexton* (Winterfeldtstr. 35, open daily 8pm-8am, Tel. 215 18 02) is an all night bar with more of a punk than yuppie clientele.

Lovers of Mediterranean cuisine have been coming regularly to *Alexis Sorbas* (Winterfeldtstr. 58, open daily from 5pm, Fri/Sat Greek folklore, Tel. 215 24 74) for years.

Männersache is a small shop at No. 46, which specialises in high-class **second-hand designer-clothing** for men.

Goltzstraße

Goltzstraße connects Winterfeldtplatz with Kleistpark. The street offers enough interesting cafés and taverns to pass a whole evening and half the night in.

Sand on the floor and palm leaves on the walls are the trademarks of

the *Slumberland* (Goltz-/Winterfeldtstr., Tel. 216 53 49). The day's problems are discussed here in an easy atmosphere. Open daily from 9:30pm. During market hours on Saturday the pavement outside *Slumberland* becomes a stand up beer garden between 11am and 5pm. Those who do not require liquid refreshment should make their way to *Habibi* (Goltzstr. 24, open daily 9am-3am, Fri/Sat round the clock) and try their falafel.

At the junction of Goltz-, Pallas- and Hohenstaufenstraße there are a number of small shops worth a visit. For example, the **import record shop** *Down-Beat* opposite the St. Matthias Church, specialises in black music.

Kaufhaus der Besten (Hohenstaufenstr. 68, Tel. 216 17 77) offers a clever mixture of **satirical books and postcards**, together with posters and other knickknacks.

Back on Goltzstraße the Indian fast-food joint *Rani* caters for the "gourmet in a hurry". Open daily between 12am and 2am with a

kitchen consisting of what seems like a thousand pots. They prepare very tasty Indian take-aways.

The **Galerie Goltzstr. 32** next door exhibits paintings and photographs (Mon-Fri 11am-6pm, Sat 11am-2pm, Tel. 216 73 48).

Café M. (Goltzstr. 33, open daily 9am-2am, Tel. 216 70 92) used to be called *Mitropa* and will soon revert back to that name. The *M.* is always overflowing, the Schöneberg set meets here for breakfast all round the clock. If you cannot find a place to stand in *M.*, take a short walk to *Café Lux* (No. 35, open daily 9am-3am, Tel. 215 96 74).

Across the street lies *Niemandsland* (No Man's Land). (No. 17, open daily 9am-2am, Tel. 216 65 15).

Bookshops, second-hand clothing and **antique shops** now dominate the street. Here typical Berlin life carries on.

Without any distinctive interior, but with a good selection of newspapers, *Café 3Klang* (No. 51, open daily 9am-3am, Tel 216 55 20) is a quiet meeting point. The *Gargano* restaurant (Goltzstr. 52, open daily 12am-2am, Tel 215 83 03) is one of the best restaurants in Berlin, with a large selection of pasta dishes.

From the end of Goltzstraße, **Grunewaldstraße** runs on to Kleistpark (U-Bahn station on Line U7). Solid rush-hour traffic passes along this narrow road. Away from this hectic activity, though, a quiet cultural scene has established itself in the sidestreets. **Vorbergstraße** is a particularly good example of why it is often worth diverting from the main roads.

No men please! The *Dinelo* is a women only bar (No. 10, Tue-Sun from 6pm, Tel. 782 21 85). Swabian cuisine is on the menu at *Wohlbold* (also No.10, open daily 6pm-2am, Tel. 784 67 35). The food is excellent and the prices reasonable. Even more economical, but not such good quality, is the drink and fast-food in *Estoril* (No. 11, open daily 6pm-2am, Sat/Sun 10am-3am, Tel. 782 57 26).

A **cinema** with an unusual selection of programs is the *Notausgang* (No. 1, admission 9 DM, Tel. 781 26 82). The owners of this tunnel-like cinema constantly manage to uncover old comedy classics. They are usually the first to show them in Berlin.

The neighboring *Feinbäckerei* (open daily 11am-3am, Tel. 784 51 58), a tavern in the old bakery style, has been around for years. The *Candela* is an Italian restaurant with nothing Italian. It's a café during the day, with food being served from 5

pm. The food is good, the prices reasonable and a table reservation is recommended (Grunewaldstr. 81, Tel. 782 14 09).

Avantgarde fashion can be found in *Biscuit* (No. 89, Mon-Fri 12am-6:30pm, Sat. 11am-2pm).

If you would like to know more about the district and its history, you should head towards the **Heimat-museum Schöneberg** (Schöneberg Local History Museum, No. 6-7, Mon-Fri 10am-1pm, Thur 4pm-7pm, Tel. 783 30 33).

Kleistpark

Until 1897 the **Heinrich-von-Kleist-Park** was the city's first Botanical Gardens. As living space in the district slowly became scarcer, the gardens were moved to Dahlem, the remaining green area was reduced and a park made of it. Today the attractively designed park seems out of place in the middle of the dense network of streets and roads.

The striking **Kings Columns** at the entrance to the park stood in Alexanderplatz as early as 1780. In 1910 they fell victim to the new town planning. Since then they have stood in the *Heinrich-von-Kleist-Park* and give the grounds a grand feeling.

The **Allied Control Council building** stands in the park grounds like a memorial to a dark chapter in German history. During the Nazi period it was the notorious People's Court which condemned thousands of people to misery and death. After the war, which also damaged the park, the Allied Control Council took over the building. The *Four Power Agreement* which regulated the relationship between East and West Berlin over the last decades was signed here. All the allied officials have now left the building, except those dealing with air safety. Over 500 rooms stand unused and empty.

It was the opening of the Wall which put the building back in the limelight. At the beginning of 1990 the allied "protective powers" met to discuss the changed situation of a united Germany and the correspondingly altered status of Berlin. One can only hope that the building, and with it the park, can be returned to civilian use.

On Kleistpark, at **Hauptstraße** 5 you can get breakfast in *Kleisther* until 5pm and various other small snacks and drinks until the early morning (open daily from 9am, Tel. 784 67 38). The *Anderes Ufer* (Hauptstr. 157, open daily 11am-2am, Tel. 784 15 78) has for years been a favorite meeting point for gays from all over Berlin. Being gay is not an entry requirement though.

Motzstraße

The district around *Motzstraße*, between Nollendorf- and Viktoria-Luise-Platz, was once an elegant residential area and home to the intellectual and artistic elite of the early part of this century. Personalities like *Albert Einstein, Rudolf Steiner, August Bebel* and *Kurt Tucholsky* all spent some creative time here. The higher-than-average proportion of Jewish inhabitants

Kurt Tucholsky

Albert Schweitzer

gave the district the nickname of the *"Jewish Switzerland"*, and made it a prime target for the Nazis. Little is left of the old buildings which made the district one of the best in pre-war Berlin. The damage during the war years was too great and new housing had to be built quickly after 1945. This is why functional buildings now dominate the streetscape.

Motzstraße (from Nollendorfplatz) with its small sidestreets is a good starting point for a walk through the *Bavarian Quarter*.

For **homosexuals** there is an *Information Center* and a *meeting point* (Tel. 216 60 00 and Mann-O-Meter 216 60 00). Favorite meeting points for gays are *Tom's Bar* (No. 19, open daily 11pm-6am, Tel. 213 45 70) and the *Pool* in the same building (Wed-Sat 11pm-5am, Tel. 24 75 29).

The *Krik* disco (No. 8, Tel. 216 93 55) opens at 11pm and only closes when the last person has gone home. If you get past the bouncers, you will be on one of the hottest dance floors in Berlin.

Pour Elle (Kalkreuthstr. 10/Motzstraße, Tue-Sun 9pm-5am, Tel. 24 57 33) is a **women only bar**. Here women keep to themselves except Tuesdays, when men can come along.

Night hunger can be staved off in the plush surroundings of the *Mau Mau* (No. 28, open daily 10pm-10 am, Tel. 213 27 02). A hint of gently swaying palms wafts from the Caribbean food served in the *Carib* (No. 31, Wed-Mon 3pm-1am, Tel. 213 53 81). Chicken and banana dominate the small, but excellent menu. A brief detour into Martin-Luther-Str. 11 is worth it for those who like good Indonesian food. In *Holland Stüb'l* (open daily 5pm-1am, Sun from 12am, Tel. 24 85 93) two people can feast on an Indonesian "Reistafel" for 65 DM. On Fuggerstraße, whether in the *Maharadscha* (No. 21, open daily 12am-12pm, Tel.

213 88 26) or in the *Maharani* (No. 18, open daily 12am-12pm, Tel. 213 40 22), good, well-priced food is served.

Motzstraße continues on to **Viktoria-Luise-Platz** (U-Bahn station on Line U4), which recently has been turned into a popular last resting place. The nearby *School of Fashion Design, Photography and Graphics*, and especially the surrounding cafés give the square a feeling that art and beauty are close at hand.

Hence the many mirrors in *Monte Video* (Motzstr. 54, Mon-Sat 8am-1am, Sun from 10am, Tel. 213 10 20), a fashionable café serving breakfast and light meals.

Hot leather nights in hardcore gay surroundings are what are promised in both *Dreizehn* (Welserstr. 21, open daily 5pm-5am, Tel. 24 23 63) and *Knast* (Fuggerstr. 34, open daily 9pm-5am, Tel. 24 10 26). Neither are far from Viktoria-Luise-Platz.

The *Arsenal* presents itself as the **cinema** of the *Friends of German Cinematography*. Behind this somewhat pompous name there lies an intelligent independent cinema with an excellent range of programs (Welserstr. 25, admission 8 DM, Tel. 24 68 48). Connoisseurs like to discuss the showings afterwards in the *Café am Arsenal* (Fuggerstr. 35, Mon-Fri 9am-1am, Sat/Sun 10am-2am, Tel. 213 58 26).

Motzstraße continues behind Viktoria-Luise-Platz with three more recommended taverns. In *Tomasa* (No. 60, open daily 9am-3am,

Fri/Sat to 4am, Tel. 213 23 45), with a decor verging on the tasteless, you are served large portions of tasty food. The menu is extensive and often truly exotic. The breakfast offerings (until 4pm) make it difficult to choose. More nostalgic is the *Schöneberger Weltlaterne*. You will still be enjoying old-fashioned charm here for some years to come (No. 61, open daily 11am-3pm, Tel. 211 62 47). The *Suppenkasper* (No. 63, open daily 9am-2am, Tel. 24 19 27) serves inexpensive country-style casseroles and light snacks.

Bülow- and Potsdamer Straße

To the right and left of the elevated railway Bülowstraße leads to the notorious **Bülow Arch**. During the day Bülowstraße is a sad and hectic residential road which, due to war damage, has lost much of the gloss of former days. In the twenties this gloss already had a somewhat lewd character. **Street prostitution** and **brothels** were and still are at home here. The very necessary "Safer Sex" discussion of recent years has played a large part in making prostitutes and their clients more visible and more sensible.

Potsdamer Straße also fails to qualify as a beautiful street, but its very particular atmosphere still makes it worth a look. If the "Potse" quarter fascinates you at first sight, you should take the time to study *Benny Härlin* and *Michael Sontheimer's* book *Potsdamer Straße, Sitten-*

bilder und Geschichten. In an easy and informative manner the authors bring a real piece of Berlin to life.

Ideally you should look up the *Mediencafé Strada* (Potsdamer Str. 131, open daily 10am-2am, Tel. 215 93 81), the affiliated **Bookshop** stocks more than just this work. The *Strada* is a positive example of "alternative" business enterprise. Formerly active in the squatting movement, the owners now wage the struggle against the establishment behind a well-kept bar. The squatting struggle resurfaced in the "Potse" in the early 1980s. At the peak of the *squatting movement* Numbers 130, 139, 157 and 159 were occupied. Through the sympathy of parts of the population and the tolerance of the then-SPD/FDP (German Social Democratic Party/ Free Democratic Party) Senate, the movement did achieve some limited successes. In the few months that the squatting lasted, they succeeded in bringing the issue into public debate and public consciousness. In particular the union-owned *Neue Heimat*, as the owner of many buildings left empty or threatened with demolition, was often caught in the cross-fire of criticism. A corruption scandal could no longer be kept from view and led to the resignation of the Senate and brought the CDU (Christian Democratic Union) to power. With little concern for possible losses, the new Senate began to clear all the squatted houses. It turned into one of the worst confrontations between

demonstrators and police since the student protests. In the course of a peaceful demonstration against the clearance of eight buildings, the situation escalated on the 22nd of September 1981. A crowd collected in Bülowstraße to express their rage at the clearance of one of the buildings. The then Senator for Domestic Affairs could not stop himself from holding a victorious press conference in front of the building concerned. As a "media encore", so to speak, the demonstration in front of the building was dispersed with brutal police force and the participants driven over the Potsdamer-/Bülowstraße crossing.

One of the demonstrators, *Klaus Jürgen Rattay* was hit by a bus and dragged along. He died of his serious injuries.

The cross in the asphalt in front of the Commerzbank is a reminder of this black day in recent Berlin history. For the rest of the remaining night there were pitched street battles between demonstrators and the police. The accumulated rage and grief of many Berliners exploded in destruction and violence, which the city government used as a rationale to clear more squats.

Potsdamer Straße takes on a seedy appearance as it heads towards Tiergarten. Brothels, dirty fast-food joints, gaming halls, videotheques and the heroin scene hidden in the side-streets have destroyed the road's reputation. The scenery has a provincial, rather than a metropolitan feel to it - an amusement district without any fun.

Perhaps this backdrop will change when Potsdamer Straße no longer ends at the now hopeless **Potsdamer Platz**, but returns to being one of the new Berlin's main roads. After all, Potsdamer Straße and its extension leads directly to the old federal highway B1 and on towards Potsdam.

Alongside normal café business the women's café *Begine* (Potsdamer Str. 139, open daily 6pm-1am, Sat/Sun from 4pm, Tel. 21543 25) also offers **literature and film events** by women for women.

Before the war Berlin's literary circle had its home in and around

the "Potse". Famous writers lived and worked here in the middle of the old metropolis. Except for the daily newspaper **Tagesspiegel** at No. 87, the "what's on" bi-weekly magazine **tip** (No. 89), and a few publishing houses (e.g. the *Rotbuchverlag*), the literary forces have almost completely vanished.

One particular meeting point on the "culture scene" lies beyond Potsdamer Straße. The *Einstein* (Kurfürstenstr. 58, open daily 10am-2am, Tel. 261 50 96), decorated in old coffee-house style, is reserved and the music subdued. A very different experience awaits the visitor to *Kumpelnest 3000* (Lützowstr. 23, open daily from 5pm, Tel. 261 69 18). The interior is a grotesque mixture of its days as a plush café and decor from the neon period. The music is generally House or Hip-Hop, but now and then German rockers from the 1950s are also played! In the middle of all this you can meet the locals over a Beck's beer.

Made in Berlin is the misleading name at Potsdamer Straße 106. Most of the **clothing** sold here is guaranteed not to be made in Berlin. One thing all items have in common: they are second hand and cost 25 DM per kilo. A pleasure and not just for the thrifty.

Quartier (Potsdamer Straße 96, Tel. 262 90 16, family owned since 1990) was reopened in August 1990 after extensive renovations. Under the leadership of local artists, concerts, cabarets, short films and variety shows have found a new venue here.

Live shows also occasionally take place in the modern *Miami Nice* (Potsdamer Straße 82, open daily from 9am, Tel. 216 66 56).

The Red Island at "schönen Berg"

What is left of the "Red Island" (so named because of the former communist and social democratic nature of the districts population)? At first sight, not much. There is a middle class atmosphere with no place for political slogans. People living in this harmonious, ethnically diverse neighborhood, hardly miss the lack of cultural attractions, preferring the evening visit to the local tavern.

Saturday is the best day for a tour through the area *between Kleistpark and Kreuzberg*, as that is market day in Crellestraße! Right next to the S-Bahn station (Line S1) you can see the ethnic diversity of life in Schöneberg. Most of the stalls are firmly in Turkish hands. Here you can learn all the rules of haggling and go home with the feeling that you've struck an especially good bargain.

After the bustle of the market, the quiet of a cemetery is a welcome contrast. Under the S-Bahn bridge archway, the **St. Matthäus-Friedhof** (cemetery) contains, alongside many others, the last remains of the *Brothers Grimm*. A memorial stone commemorates the would-be assassins of 20th June 1944. The bodies of the resistance fighters of *Count von Stauffenberg* were here for a short time, before they were exhumed and burned by the Nazis.

Aroma is a café, restaurant and photo gallery all in one (Hochkirchstr. 8, open daily from 7pm, Tel. 782 58 21). Always a little hectic, with good food and an interesting cultural program (films in Italian every Thursday), the *Aroma* presents itself as very Italian. In summer there are also seats in the quiet Hochkirchstraße.

Back under the S-Bahn **Großgörschenstraße** leads back to Kleistpark with a number of interesting taverns along the way. In *Flip Flop* (Kulmer Str. 20a, open daily from 8pm, Tel. 216 28 25) things are gay and easy. Nice atmosphere.

Two taverns lie opposite each other at the junction of Großgörschen-/Steinmetzstraße. They have survived for a number of years on the local loyalties of their mostly youthful neighbors. The *Gottlieb* (open daily 6pm-2am, Tel. 782 39 43) in particular has made a name for itself through its menu. The *PiPaPo* (open daily 9am-3am, Tel. 216 15 43) has hardly changed at all in recent years and so now seems a little alternative.

Indonesian meals (with many vegetarian dishes) are served amid traditional bamboo decor in the *Tuk Tuk* (Großgörschenstr. 12, Mon-Thu 5:30pm-11:45pm, Fri-Sat from 5pm, Tel. 781 15 88).

No list of "typical Berlin taverns" ever leaves out the *Leydicke* (Mansteinstr. 4, Tel. 216 29 73). A free seat is seldom found here. The interior of the *Leydicke* is as original as the waiter, who occasionally will also put a difficult guest in his place. This is all part of proceedings in this traditional distillery for fruit wine and liquors which, when drunk in large quantaties, have a devastating effect.

Along the S-Bahn tracks (Wannsee direction), divided at first by a broad stretch of wildly growing vegetation, and later by lines of housing,**Crellestraße** runs as far as Kaiser-Wilhelm-Platz. Beyond the Langenscheidtbrücke, which points the way to Kreuzberg, Crellestraße becomes part of a real working-class district. Old facades have been partly renovated and small stores still remain. But you should avoid being satisfied with such a glowingly romantic view and instead scout around the back courtyards and hallways.

Although the layout of Berlin's streets are hardly bicycle-friendly, it is still the best way to discover the city. The **Bicycle Center** (Fahrrad Büro) at Crellestr. 48 (Tel. 784 55 62) sells and rents bicycles in relatively good condition. After a tour of the "Red Island" or "Rote Insel" you will be able to recover in *Café Enorm* (Crellestr. 46, Tel. 782 04 57).

By the way: if you cycle from Kaiser-Wilhelm-Platz towards Kleistpark, you will pass over the hill which gave the district its name ("Schöneberg" means "beautiful hill"). It must have once been very impressive, but no one would think such a thing today.

Hauptstraße

The road from **Kaiser-Wilhelm-Platz** over Hauptstraße towards Friedenau leads through Schöneberg's historical center. This connecting road between Berlin and Potsdam was already of great significance as a trade route in the 17th century. The old Schöneberg city hall used to stand on Kaiser-Wilhelm-Platz. The central reservation which divides the two halves of Hauptstraße south of the square has miraculously been preserved from those bygone days.

Today this main artery is hectic and uninviting. The builders of the lovely **villas** which line the road would certainly never have dreamed that these beautiful 19th century buildings would be turned into Police Bureaus or youth drop-in centers. The farmers living in Schöneberg who made fortunes from the sale of their land as the capital grew, invested their wealth in inner-city housing and restaurants.

In those days Hauptstraße was a favorite excursion for Berliners. The most striking remnant of the old village days is the **church**, built in 1776 (Haupt-/Dominicusstraße).

A more recent addition to the area is *Ecstasy* (Hauptstr. 30, Tue-Sun from 11pm, Tel. 788 14 01), which serves as a venue for house, punk or hip-hop groups. If there is no concert in progress, you can dance to records.

The *Odeon* **cinema** (Hauptstr. 116, admission 10 DM, Tel. 781 56 67) is constantly under threat of demolition because of its location. This flat building does not fit in with the taller, more economical buildings along the rest of the road. As long as it survives, it will be devoted exclusively to films in their original language.

From the crossing of Haupt and Dominicusstraße you can see **Rathaus Schöneberg** in the distance, with its freshly painted facade. The city hall's forecourt was named in honor of *John F. Kennedy*. His speech, including the idiot board assisted words, "Isch binn ain Bärlina", touched Berliners so distressed by the erection of the Wall. If they had imagined at the opening of the city hall in 1914 that

99

forty years later the West Berlin Parliament would meet here, the interior decoration might have been a little more stylish.

As the two halves of the city gradually merge together it seems likely that the *"Red City Hall"* near Alexanderplatz will return to being Greater Berlin's seat of government. The Schöneberg City Hall will no doubt return to the second rank, "just" a district town hall.

The end of the Soviet blockade was celebrated in front of the Schöneberg City Hall, as is the annual May Day parade. A painful highpoint in recent history was the abortive attempt at self-adulation by the German Chancellor, *Helmut Kohl* on 10th November 1990. He was mercilessly whistled down by a unified Berlin crowd. He saved himself with an a cappela sing-along of the national anthem.

South of the city hall begins **Rudolf-Wilde-Park**, named after a former Schöneberg mayor. For Schönebergers, not exactly overwhelmed with green and open spaces, the park reaching as far as Wilmersdorf is a favorite rest and recuperation spot. The **golden stag** over the fountain at the entrance to the park is the district's coat of arms, and also a meeting point in the summer for couples. Quite a few durable relationships have started here....The lawn in front of the fountain has been significantly damaged by weekend footballers. It has been fenced in, but without success.

Under the bridge which divides the park lies the Rathaus Schöneberg U-Bahn station (U4). The park's hilly landscape, in summer covered with sunbathers, now stretches to Kufsteiner Straße.

The radio and televison station **RIAS** *(Radio in the American Sector)* broadcasts from the red building in Kufsteiner Straße. The future of RIAS after the fall of the Wall is uncertain, as its financing has not been secured. RIAS was founded on 21st November 1945 and since then has been financed by the US Senate. Its terms of reference explicitly included the "enlightenment" of listeners in the Soviet-occupied Zone.

After an extended walk through Schöneberg you can relax in the soothing atmosphere of the vegetarian restaurant *La Maskera* (Koburger Str. 5, open daily 5pm-1am, Tel. 784 12 27). The offerings include Italian wholemeal dishes and organically-grown fruit drinks.

Kreuzberg

Yorckstraße

Kreuzberg - no other district in Berlin has become so well known beyond the city limits. No other district is approached with so many pre-suppositions, or has so many romantic myths attached to it.

The district is made up of two administrative units. Unit 36 is poor, ill-reputed and in decline, unit 61 is somewhat better looking. Kreuzberg offers everything that goes to make up life in the city.

Many roads lead to Kreuzberg - the one from the city necessarily takes a number of detours, so logical was the planning of the East-West axis. What is now Bülowstraße was meant, according to the original plans, to run straight and to connect the inner city (from Ernst-Reuter-Platz) with a quick route to the city limits (Waltersdorfer Chaussee in Rudow). A huge industrial railway yard (*Anhalter Bahnhof*) stood in the way of the road. The railway

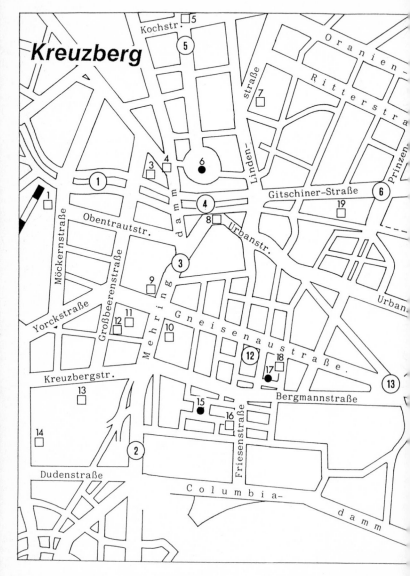

Kreuzberg

Legend on page 105

company, as owners of the area, saw no reason to sacrifice their property to such a road project. Hence the troublesome detour between Bülow-and Gneisenau-straße which leads under the S-Bahn bridges over Yorckstraße. Today the area is a wilderness covered in weeds, home to a variety of animals you would otherwise never find in a big city.

The Großgörschenstraße (S1) and Yorckstraße (S2 & U7) S-Bahn stations lie close to each other. The boundary between Schöneberg and Kreuzberg can also be reached by bus (Line 119).

A walk under the **Yorck bridges** is not enjoyable. Exhaust fumes from the cars rolling along the road all

day, together with grim-looking railway bridges, are only bearable from inside a bus. For bicyclists this spot on Yorckstraße is deadly.

Time and again the large bill-boards under the Yorck bridges are the targets of special artistic pro-jects. Whether empty spaces are filled up or existing posters "edited", the city's spray-can artists always manage to add some color to the grey walls.

The first bend in Yorckstraße is beyond the bridges, at the crossing with Bergmannstraße. Here the streetscape changes dramatically, and one of the most interesting "alternative-culture miles" in Berlin begins.

The **Berlin Puppet Theater** (Yorckstr. 59, Tel. 786 98 15) is not just for children. The classics, like *Shakespeare's* "A Midsummer Night's Dream", are also performed by the puppets.

For French cuisine in a simple atmosphere try the *Publique* (Yorckstr. 62, open daily 3pm-2am, Tel. 786 94 69).

"Kaffe Achteck" serves no drinks, on the contrary it disposes of them. In these cast-iron **pissoirs**, left over from the old days, men can relieve themselves in the middle of the traffic, e.g. at Yorck-/Hagelber-gerstraße.

Along the rest of Yorckstraße it is worth investigating some of the courtyards of individual houses. A good example of successful renova-tion is No. 74. Both courtyards now look bright, friendly and deliberately

green. Until a few years ago there were no inside toilets in these buildings. Today, like all over the city, even the attic has been extended. A crude contrast can be found at No. 76, where you can see how the living conditions are before any renovation has taken place.

For many years a true jazz tradition has been upheld in the *Nulpe* (No. 77, open daily 6pm-3am, Tel. 786 50 88). Jazz is played live every Saturday from 9:30pm. In *Al-Badaui* (Yorckstr. 15, open daily 4:30pm-1am) you will find some of the best Lebanese kebabs in the city.

The *Yorckschlößchen* tavern has been a steady favorite for many years (Yorckstr. 15, open daily from 9am, Tel. 785 17 70). There is live music on Sundays from 1pm. In summer the beer garden provides protection from the traffic. Given its rather out-of-the-way location, the *Splendid* (Hornstr. 23, open daily

from 7pm, Tel. 785 54 56) is almost a secret insiders bar. You can enjoy exotic cocktails or a good beer in this mirrored bar.

Nostalgic cinema freaks will find some movie delicacies in the **Berliner Cinema Museum** (Großbeerenstr. 57) on Mondays, Fridays and Saturdays. Only 25 "nostalgic" seats are available. As you cannot enquire about the program over the telephone, you should check either the city magazines or the daily press for details.

L'Etoile (Großbeerenstr. 60, Tue-Sun 6:30pm-1am, Sun from 10am breakfast buffet, Tel. 785 92 31) serves fine French food amid walls adorned with art. For lovers of

late breakfasts, there is *Café Mora* (Großbeerenstr. 57a, open daily 11am-1am, Tel. 785 05 85) with regular exhibitions on the white-washed walls. "Down the hatch " is the motto every day (except Sundays) until early in the morning in the *Bölkstoffkeller* (Großbeerenstr. 32, Tel. 823 98 38).

The iron gates between numbers 56 and 57 Großbeerenstr. lead you to the so-called **Riehmers Hofgarten**. This architectural beauty, 24 houses in Renaissance style, is the result of the successful battles of style the master builder *Riehmers* waged in the late 19th century. These battles were fought against proponents of a standardized style of building, and during a period of rapid industrial expansion in Germany. Riehmers' style, as it was realized in the *"Hofgarten"*, was regarded as wasteful and reprehensible. In the meantime the beauty of the complex has naturally been recognised, and since 1964 it has stood under a preservation order.

You feel as though you have been transported back into another era as soon as you feel the cobblestones under your feet. Authentic street lanterns and a striking amount of greenery line the way. An imaginatively constructed children's playground indicates that the apartments are large enough here to take in families with children. Civil servants and officers used to live here, but today it is only the most well-to-do who can afford an apartment in *Riehmers Hofgarten*.

It is almost a shock to re-enter hectic Yorckstraße opposite the Kreuzberg Town Hall. But this feeling soon vanishes, for it is not only Großbeerenstraße that has taverns and cafés.

In late 1950s style *Wirtschaftswunder* (Yorckstr. 81, open daily 4pm-6am, Tel. 786 99 99) serves drinks and chocolate marshmallows on kidney-shaped tables until the early hours of the morning. Right next door things turn Italian. In the *Café Centrale* (No. 82, Mon-Sun 6pm-3am, Tel. 786 29 89) you are shown to your place. The prices are reasonable.

The *Riehmers* dance bar has for years been known in trendy circles as *Café Quickie* (open daily 10pm-4am). The doorbell to the right of the entrance always manages to give the bouncer a fright, after which he selects the guests according to criteria known only to him. Apparently this ritual serves to maintain the balance between male and female dancers on the small dance floor. The atmosphere is nonetheless comfortable and the music usually well mixed - at times you can Salsa till you drop.

Riehmers is especially well-filled when the night performances in the neighboring **cinemas** are over. The *Yorck* and *New Yorck* (No. 86, admission 10 DM, Tel. 786 50 70) are two recommended cinemas under one modern roof.

Perlenstrand at Yorckstr. 89a offers, alongside innumerable pearls in all colors, finished **jewelry** and **designer clothing** (Mon-Fri 11am-6:30pm, Sat 11am-2pm).

Gneisenaustraße

Yorckstraße ends at the crossing with Mehringdamm (U-Bahn station U6 and U7) and the road continues until Südstern as *Gneisenaustraße*. This lively crossing has in the past been the scene of violent clashes between demonstrators and the police. In the middle of it stands the **Mehringhof**, which even in varied Berlin is a unique institution. A number of self-help projects have come together here under the roof of an old factory. The Mehringhof project began through the *Netzwerk Selbsthilfe (Self-Help Network)*, a "foundation for political and alternative projects". All those who feel they are not politically active enough, because of lack of time (or inclination), pay a monthly contribution to the foundation which then supports selected "alternative projects". Many of these projects are housed in the Mehringhof. The board at the entrance lists them all. There you will see, for example, the *School for Adult Education*, the *Libertäre Forum*

(organisation for a free socialism, Tel. 693 80 21), *Ökotopia* (natural produce store), the *Buchladen "Schwarze Risse"* (anarchist literature in a living-room atmosphere), or a *bicycle shop* (also rental, Tel. 691 60 27).

The *Mehringhof Theater* (Tel. 691 50 99) has established itself as a venue for various, usually first-rate, incisive cabaret groups. Here you will have to make sure you book in advance! The *Hans Wurst Nachfahren* (Tel. 693 37 91) are puppeteers who play their finger trade in the third courtyard. The *EX* tavern, due to its location and size is a favorite meeting place for many groups to the left in the political spectrum.

An offshoot of the Mehringhof is the **Berliner Kabarett Anstalt** (BKA, Berlin Cabaret Institute, Mehringdamm 34, Tel. 251 01 12) based in a former discotheque. The guest performances are usually iconoclastic and acerbic. Local performers also perform here.

The *Bermuda Dreieck* (Gneisenaustr. 5, open daily from 6pm, Tel. 693 89 36) is not a tavern for non-smokers. The air is thick with blue smoke, and the range of drinks is not overwhelming. *Mafalda* (Gneisenaustr. 8) serves Latin American specialties at reasonable prices. If you hunger for something without meat, why not try a tofuburger in *Natürlich Leben* (No. 16, Mon-Fri 10am-6:30pm, Sat 10am-2pm). When all other taverns are full, there's usually some space in *Malheur* (No. 17, open daily 4pm-4am, Tel. 692 86 28). It's not that the beer is worse here than anywhere else, but this tavern doesn't present itself as anything special.

The search for suitable headgear should lead you to **Hüte** *Kunst* (No. 19, Mon-Fri 11:30am-6:30om, Sat. 10:30am-1:30pm). This place offers a somewhat eccentric collection of hats.

Gneisenaustraße (U-Bahn station U7) is less spectacular up to the crossing with Zossener Straße. What can be recommended is *Hollyfood* (Zossener Str. 12, open daily 12am-10pm, Tel. 692 86 72) and its vegetarian offerings. Particularly noteworthy are the corn rolls with garlic sauce.

Functional 1960's appartment blocks, some with restored facades, others with new facades, dominate the rest of Gneisenaustraße. Fortunately the green central reservation offers something different for the eye. It is worth examining the living conditions in the side streets. Only after the crossing with Baerwaldstraße does Gneisenaustraße again become a commercial street, with charming antique stores, Turkish delicatessens, book stores, games halls and many service industries.

Südstern

The collection of taverns around *Südstern* (U-Bahn station line U7) begins with *Café Anfall* (Gneisenaustr. 64, Tel. 693 68 98).

In recent years a wide variety of cafés and taverns have been established here, in a relatively small area. Luckily Südstern lies off the

beaten tourist track and has been able to keep most of its original character. Your bodily needs are well cared-for, as the area contains some of Berlins best restaurants.

Wine from organically-grown grapes and fine vegetarian meals are served in a cool atmosphere in *Thürnagel* (Gneisenaustr. 57, open daily 6pm-12pm, Tel. 691 48 00). The comfortable *Notos* (Südstern 4, open daily 4pm-1am, Tel. 691 63 21) serves traditional Greek food amid an unconventionally bright decor.

The **Südstern Church** (formerly the Garnison Church from 1896) is no longer used for regular church services, but for a variety of other events. A small *Café* has been set up in a side wing as a youth meeting-point.

The *Ristorante Primo* (Südstern 3, open daily 12am-1am, Tel. 691 45 97), has a lovely summer garden, and an interesting menu, although the size of the portions has decreased since the restaurant's popularity grew.

Körtestraße is a narrow street leading towards Kreuzberg 36 offering a number of popular meeting points. *Wunderbar* (No. 38, open daily 9am-3am, Tel. 692 1 20) is loud and hectic. *Rampenlicht* (No. 33, open daily 9am-2am, Tel. 692 13 01), good for breakfast or sipping an evening cocktail, is the quieter but also slightly less exciting spot. *Tartuffel* (No. 15, open daily except Mon, 6pm-12pm, Tel. 693 74 80) is dedicated to the potato in all its possible culinary forms. The food in

Körte's (No. 5, open daily 5pm-2am, Tel. 691 66 26) is also hardly fancy, but it is served in a refined atmosphere.

Back to Südstern. From now on the road is called **Hasenheide**, named after the public **park**, which runs alongside it. The park does justice to its name with relaxing lawns, bicycle paths, a mini-golf course and a small animal reserve. In summer its modest open-air stage hosts small film and theater performances or rock concerts. You will get a good view of the area from **Rixdorfer Höhe** (Rixdorf Hill, made of rubble from World War II).

Diagonally opposite the *park* lies a restaurant where you are greeted in Turkish. The *Merhaba* entertains its guests with the delicacies of Turkish cuisine (Hasenheide 39, open daily from 4pm, Sun from 1pm, Tel. 692 17 13).

The *Apricot* restaurant (Hasenheide 48, open daily except Tue 5pm-1am, Tel. 693 11 50) specializes in French elegance. Here you are presented with haute cuisine (not just for Yuppies), in perfect style. It's not cheap, but prices are still reasonable.

A collection of *alternative culture* has been established at **Haus Hasenheide 54**. Dance workshops and theater performances take place in an old factory building (*Die Etage*, Tel. 691 20 95), while in the *Sputnik 2&3* **cinemas** a crazy mixture of diverse film genres are shown on their small screens (admission 8 DM, Tel. 694 11 47).

In *Heidereiter* (Hasenheide 58, open daily 10am-3pm, Tel. 691 30 82) trendy people have been meeting over cheap beers for years. A similar eternal flame, which has survived all the city's trends unscathed, is the *Sternling* (Südstern 14, open daily from 3pm, Tel. 694 25 37). Its interior looks as though the early 1980s are still with us.

Between Marheineke- and Chamissoplatz

From Südstern the initially quiet and comfortable **Bergmannstraße** leads on towards Kreuzberg.

No less than five **cemeteries** line the way to *Marheinekeplatz*. The graveyards, established in the 19th century, are the final resting place for a number of well-known families and personalities. The philosopher *Schleiermacher*, for example, is immortalised with a tombstone in the *Dreifaltigkeitskirchhof II*, the former Reichsminister *Stresemann* in the *Luisenstädtischen Kirchhof*. In a walk through the cemeteries you will see a number of neglected *Art Nouveau* tombs.

In Marheinekeplatz stands the **Passionskirche**, one of the few churches which takes on a cultural function for the neighborhood over and above its church services. Its name often appears on posters for concerts or lectures.

Despite strong competition the *Locus* tavern (Marheinekeplatz 4, open daily 10am-3am, Tel. 691 56 37) has for years enjoyed great popularity. Perhaps it's the Mexican dishes on its menu?

What is commonly referred to as the "Berlin Mixture", a feeling arising from the influences of diverse cultures and social classes, cannot be described, it has to be felt. One of the best opportunities for this is provided by a tour along the small gangways of the **Marheineke Market Hall**. This is pure Berlin! Whether you listen to the market cries of the fishmongers, bargain with the Turkish trader over the price of pistachios, or break out in a sweat over curried sausage and french fries, you will experience unvarnished Berlin at first hand.

Some original Berlin images are painted on the outer walls of the market hall. *Leierkastenmann, Wurstmaxe, Kohlenträger* and *Scherenschleifer* are part of old Berlin just as *Clochard* belongs under the bridges of Paris.

In Zossener Straße it is well worth visiting the *Grober Unfug* **bookshop** (No. 32). It has a gallery and English-language material on the first floor, and is a specialist store for all varieties of comics. The *Videodrom* (Zossener Str. 20, Mon-Sat 3pm-10pm) has concentrated its range of **videos** for hire on English-language films and splatter movies.

Bergmannstraße continues beyond Marheinekeplatz to Mehringdamm. The **houses** here have mostly survived in their original form. The front apartments are often 100 square metres in size, and some of the side and back apartments even have the old shared toilet on each floor. Many of the apartments around the courtyard are small, dark and usually still have coal oven heating. The small stores in, for example, Bergmannstraße, are vital to the many older people living in the area who find the trip to the nearest supermarket too much for them.

Naturally there are all sorts of second-hand stores, record shops and usually dreadful corner taverns. One of them is *Ambrosius* (Bergmannstr. 11, Tel. 692 71 82). The food is cheap and the atmosphere free. If you steer away from political discussions, you will be able to strike up some friendly conversations.

Directly opposite, *Ararat* (Mon-Fri 10am - 6:30, Sat 10am-2:30, Bergmannstr. 99a) deals in **art** and modern **kitsch**. For example, if you are looking for the ultimate **Mickey Rourke** postcard, you'll find it here.

Nostitzstraße leads up the hill to the area around **Chamissoplatz**. As a typical example of proletarian living conditions around the end of the 19th century, Chamissoplatz was regarded as worth protecting and renovating with the help of government subsidies. The so-called "block de-coring", i.e. the demolition of uncomfortable back and side wings, is the other side of the coin, as it destroyed much valuable living space. The quality of housing around Chamissoplatz has nonetheless clearly improved. The center of the square was remodelled as a playground and park. A great amount of energy was used up with the restoration of the buildings. Painstaking efforts were made to ensure that the facades were reconstructed down to the finest detail. In particular **house** 20 on **Willibald-Alexis-Str.**, with its striking back wing, is of great architectural interest.

The **Galerie am Chamissoplatz** (Chamissoplatz 6, Tue-Sat 4pm-7pm, Sun 2pm-6pm, Tel. 692 53 81) exhibits contemporary art.

The **Theater Zerbrochene Fenster** (Fidicinstr. 3, Tel. 694 24 00) next door, apart from performing its own productions, also provides a home for independent theater groups to present their work to the public.

Naturally a number of taverns have also established themselves around Chamissoplatz, to still the hunger and thirst of the district's inhabitants and their visitors.

The Italian menu in *Chamisso* in the treeless Willibald-Alexis-Str. (No. 25, open daily 6pm-12:30am, Tel. 691 56 42) is a favorite. The restaurant has a comfortable ambience. Things cut loose in the *Heidelberger Krug* (Arndtstr. 15, Mon-Fri 6pm-4am, Sat/Sun 10am-2pm, Tel. 693 78 34) until the early hours of the morning. If that is still not enough, you can try your luck in the *Schlehmil* tavern (Arndtstr. 25, open daily from 11am, Tel. 693 80 51).

The district tour through Willibald-Alexis-Straße leads to Friesenstraße, uninteresting in itself, but home to the **Junge Theater** (admission 15/20 DM, Tel. 692 87 35). This ambitious and well-loved theater does suffer a little from lack of space (no more than 100 seats). You will be mixing with a theater crowd over Swabian cuisine in *Kulisse* (Friesenstr. 14, Tue-Sun 4pm-2am, Tel. 692 65 06).

Viktoriapark

Kreuzberg Hill provides the best view of the district and a panorama over the former Wall area. This high point is reached after a walk through *Viktoriapark*.

You quickly discover the reason behind **Kreuzberg's** name - Hill of the Cross. Crowning the **National Monument** designed by *Schinkel* there stands the iron cross which gave the district its name in 1920. The monument itself is a memorial to the "glorious" wars of liberation, which also played a role in the naming of the surrounding streets. The graffiti on the recently restored monument indicates what little respect Kreuzbergers have for such

glorification of war. But otherwise the view over the city is very impressive. The waterfall is truly idyllic, and seems to flow as far as Großbeerenstraße. The hill's meandering paths let you forget the big city bedlam.

A walk over the *Kreuzberg* gives you a wonderful sense of its historical significance. Russian and Swedish guns stood here threatening the city's peace. When Napoleon approached the city, *Kreuzberg* with the help of the people was heavily fortified.

But a lot of pleasurable things take place on its slopes too. Where beer is brewed today (*Schultheiß-Brauerei* in Methfesselstraße) was, in 1828, the *Tivoli*. The *Tivoli* was the scene of some wild spectacles. Berliners

were attracted here by a permanent street festival with a beer garden and a huge slide. The tradition of beer-brewing has been upheld here since 1860. Unfortunately the large beer-halls of the former Tivoli brewery, also the site of vigorous political activity, have almost totally disappeared from memory. This is actually difficult to understand, as the Berliners have a great love of beery gatherings and open-air festivals. The annual late-summer *"Kreuzberger Festliche Tage"* will give a taste of that, but increasingly it is becoming more like a normal fair and less of a merry, people's festival.

A real beer garden atmosphere can be found in the *Golgatha* beside the Katzbach stadium. Even for strangers to the area, the *Golgatha* is not hard to find. You just have to follow the crowd. If you don't mind sitting on hard wooden benches, standing in a queue for your beer, and not being able to hear each other above the raucous conversation, you'll be rewarded with a real local feeling. In the summer months the former home stadium of the Kreuzberg Ballkickers is where you'll hear the hottest tracks laid down until 6 in the morning. The small dance floor is reminiscent of a steaming sauna.

The best and cheapest entertainment is still racing around on Kreuzberg's slopes. As soon as the weather warms up a little, the district's pleasure-seekers swarm over *Kreuzberg* and enjoy the day flying kites, playing ball, or barbecuing. If you're after a tan, don't worry, nobody will look twice at you, even if you end up sun-bathing beside a Turkish woman dressed according to Islamic law. Here no one bothers anyone else, you enjoy the cultural differences in peace.

The small **Animal Park** (at the Kreuzbergstraße entrance) is a rare opportunity, and not only for city kids, to see goats and geese at close range. At the foot of the small waterfall kids splash around in water which unfortunately is often dirty.

Wine is also grown on the Kreuzberg hillside, mainly for the sake of maintaining a historic curiosity. The wine is called *"Kreuz-Neroberger"* and 400 bottles are produced annually, and put aside for the enjoyment of VIPs.

On Kreuzbergstraße, the extension of Bergmannstraße, you'll find *Osteria No. 1* (Kreuzbergstr. 71, open daily from 8pm, Tel. 786 91 62), a tavern which has stayed unchanged and well-loved for years, and no-one really knows why. The prices are not high, but then the servings are also quite small. The *Villa Kreuzberg* **Youth Centre** (Kreuzbergstr. 62, Tel. 25 88 25 80) offers local young people one of the few places to meet other than taverns and discos. Local groups play music or perform plays in the small concert hall.

In a trip around Viktoria Park you can try out another favorite tavern, the *Orpheus* (open daily 4pm-3am, Sat/Sun from 10am, Tel. 785 77 34).

It offers small meals including pizzas at reasonable prices. The park entrance opposite the Orpheus leads directly to the *Golgatha*.

The turf at **Katzbachstadion** has seen quite a few generations of soccer players grow up. Early Berlin clubs used to play here before a full standing crowd. Today it's only the German-Turkish club *Türkiyemspor* which pulls that kind of crowd. They bring a breath of fresh air to the Berlin soccer scene and normally in front of thousands of enthusiastic, usually Turkish spectators.

Dudenstraße runs alongside Viktoria Park with little worth noting, towards **Flughafen Tempelhof**. The former "Tempelhofer Feld" was once used as an inner-city play and parade ground. That was before the central airport was built there in 1923. The National Socialists used the grounds for propaganda meetings. During the Berlin Blockade (1948/49) up to 1,300 airplanes (!) with supplies landed and took off here every day. The three arches of the **Air Lift Memorial** symbolise the three air corridors, which at that time signified the city's survival. On the pedestal of the **Luftbrückendenkmal** (Air Lift Memorial) stand the names of the air crew who lost their

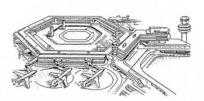

lives in this rescue operation. After the war and some provisional repairs, *Tempelhof* once again became an important international airport.

In 1975 it was abandoned, because of noise pollution and because Berlin's air traffic had grown beyond its capacity.

Möckernbrücke

The best way to Kreuzberg is undoubtedly on the *over-ground U-Bahn Line 1*. The play by the Grips-Theater, also made into a film, has become an eternal memorial to the open-air ride between Gleisdreieck and Schlesisches Tor. Out of the windows of the yellow train you'll get a good view of this part of the city, and especially of Kreuzberg's housing situation. The names of the stations are reminders of the former gateways through the old city wall (Hallesches, Kottbusser and Schlesisches Tor).

The over-ground *Möckernbrücke* station (where you can change for Line 7) lies directly over the Landwehrkanal, an arm of the river Spree. The canal flows between two streets, Hallesches and Tempelhofer Ufer.

You can see the wall mural of the **Museum für Verkehr und Technik** (Museum for Communication, Transport and Technology; Trebbiner Straße 9, Tue-Wed 9am-6pm, Thu-Fri 9am-9pm, Sat & Sun 10am-6pm, admission: 1.50/3.50 DM, Tel. 25 48 40)) from a long way away.

This over-sized museum was first opened in 1982 in the halls of a former market and cold-storage company. The constantly-growing exhibition halls and some open exhibition floors offer a good overview of the history of technical achievement in transport, communication, and energy. A "trial area" gives you the opportunity to explore technical problems in a number of experiments. At the moment the *Brandenburger Tor's Quadriga*, badly damaged during the 1989/90 New Year's Eve celebrations, is being restored in the museum. You can spend a whole (rainy) day in the museum, easily.

The area around Möckernbrücke station is fallow land, dominated by the former railway goods yard and the office buildings of the Post Office.

The **Theatermanufaktur** is currently based at Großbeerenbrükke (Hallesches Ufer 32, admission 12-24 DM, Tel. 251 09 41). Always struggling for its existence, the group has packed social criticism into accomplished theatrics for a number of years.

Hallesches Tor

The area around *Hallesches Tor* station has lost much of its original character through war damage and later modern buildings.

South of the Landwehrkanal stands the **Amerika-Gedenkbibliothek (American Memorial Library)**, opened in 1954 at the expense of the American people. With over 500,000 books and tapes for loan, the *AGB* is the most extensive public library in Germany. It stands as a service for every Berlin citizen, and at no cost (Mon 4pm-8pm, Tue-Sat 11am-8pm). The majority of its stock can be borrowed. The Berlin section in the library's cellar, which receives everything published about the city, has a particularly good assortment. For non-Berliners wanting to deepen their knowledge of Berlin, this section is a real find. After the opening of the Wall the loans and information sections were often in chaos. For a time the *AGB* had to suspend this service because of overdemand.

If you cross Blücherstraße and do a round-trip of the **Cemeteries**, you'll find the graves of some important Berliners. Personalities with reputations extending well beyond the city like *E.T.A Hoffmann, Glaßbrenner, Mendelssohn-Bartholdy, Lette* or *Schering* have their last resting-places here. During a relaxing walk through the rows of graves, you can day-dream about the achievements of the people buried here.

Opposite the graveyard entrance in Mehringdamm (another entrance is in Zossener Straße) stands the former **Kasernen vorm Halleschen Tor**, inaugurated in 1855 and home of a Prussian Dragoon Regiment. Today bureaucrats lie entrenched behind their files. Mehringdamm ends at the bridge of the same name.

In Stresemannstraße 29, the traditional people's theater, **Hebbel-Theater** (Tel. 251 01 44), has been reopened after years of restoration work. Stresemannstraße continues over Askanischen Platz (S-Bahnhof Anhalter Bahnhof, Lines S1 & S2), along the former border, to Postdamer Platz. Along the central reservation lie the remnants of the former city wall.

"Friedrichstadt" refers to the area bounded by the two main traffic arteries, Wilhelm- and Lindenstraße. The area is divided by Friedrichstraße, which kept its name during the division of the city. Wilhelmstraße is a fairly unattractive residential street and ends in the Mitte district at Otto-Grotewohl-Straße. The *Thomas-Weißbecker-Haus* (Wilhelmstr. 9, open daily except Mon from 10am, Sat/Sun breakfast buffet) has since 1 April 1990 had its own tavern with a garden.

The **Berlin Museum** (Tue-Sun 10am-10pm, admission: 1.50/3.50 DM Tel. 25 86 - 0) was built on the foundations of the former Supreme Court, destroyed during the Second World War. The extensive collection

of historic Berlin exhibits is only of real interest to those with a deeper interest in the history of the city and the Mark of Brandenburg. You can try out local specialties in the museum's *Weißbierstube* prepared supposedly in authentic old-Berlin style.

For nearly ten years there have been attempts to breathe new architectural life into the Friedrich-stadt area. The *Internationale Bauausstellung (International Building Exhibition)* produced some interesting apartment blocks in an otherwise drab street. They have a very futuristic look, but they are family-friendly and attuned to future needs. The central theme for the architects in the exhibition was the combination of living and working. In the pursuit of this aim, the infrastructure requirements of inner city living were somewhat neglected, and new leisure, educational and shopping facilties are only gradually appearing.

At the end of Lindenstraße the *Springer Verlag* skyscraper rises into the Kreuzberg sky. Built in the early 1960s as a striking, neon-lit "trade-mark of the free West", it houses the popular newspapers *Bild, BZ, Berliner Morgenpost* and *Die Welt*. On the top floor there is a "Visitor's Club" where visitors could get a good view of the border fortifications and the "evil East". The area around Kochstraße used to be the pulsating center of the German newspaper industry. Most publishers and printers were housed here. Today there are only two extremes left, the conservative *Springer AG* and the left-wing daily *"taz"*, still West Berlin's only national press organ. Apart from these there are also some book publishers in Lindenstraße.

Opposite the Springer building, the **Bundesdruckerei (Federal Printing Service)** prepares paper money and identification papers.

From the former *Checkpoint Charlie* border crossing, Friedrich-straße continues on to Mehringplatz. Nothing of the former high street is left now. On the contrary, the street seems in decay. The presence of the Foreigner's Police and the nearby Employment Bureau also gives the area a run-down feeling.

At **Mehringplatz** the old gloss of a bustling turn-of-the-century junction has been destroyed without trace by new, functional buildings. Not even the *"Friedrichssäule"* (Friedrich's Column), which has borne *Victoria, Goddess of Victory* since 1843, can bring the old days back to life.

Prinzenstraße

The next station in "deepest Kreuzberg" is *Prinzenstraße*. If you step out of the freshly renovated station hall into Gitschiner Straße, you'll hear, in the warmer months, loud squealing and splashing from **Sommerbad Kreuzberg** (Kreuzberg Summer Baths), or *Prinzenbad* for short. Really lovely grounds and a recently renewed swimming pool make it an ideal spot for summer enjoyment in the middle of the city (open daily, 8am-8pm).

Prinzenstraße runs south to cross the Landwehrkanal at the Baerwaldbrücke. At No. 1 the **Stadthaus Böcklerpark** offers one of the few meeting points for the kids in the district, notoriously poorly-served with leisure facilities. Regular concerts or readings take place here.

On both sides of the *Urbanhafen* (Urban Harbour) you can go for walks or sunbathe on the banks of the canal. Opposite, the rather ugly **Urban Hospital** disrupts one's view. Some fearless people use the somewhat polluted water for swimming. The old boats anchored in the canal have been turned into open-air cafes. The *Van Loon*, with a really good breakfast until 3pm, is especially recommended. A number of interesting cafes have also appeared on the southern bank of the canal. *Crimson* (Planufer/Grimmstraße) is patronized mainly for its front garden.

In Dieffenbachstraße Kreuzberg's night owls can meet for breakfast in *Rizz* (corner Grimmstr., open daily 10am-4am, Tel. 693 91 71) or in *Café Jedermann* (No. 18, open daily 9am-2am, Tel. 691 31 49). *Dieffenbach's* (No. 11, open daily 6pm-1am, Tel. 694 56 06) is one of the district's best restaurants. Here you'll eat at a reasonable price in a comfortable atmosphere.

The buildings which you'll notice from a distance on the *Fraenkelufer* (over the Admiral Bridge) were constructed during the 1987 International Building Exhibition. The district was named "Renewal Area Kreuzberg-South", where "careful city renewal" would be practiced for the first time. In the formation of new living areas, the emphasis was not only on the construction of new buildings, but also on the maintenance and renovation of old structures. Whether all this has ultimately benefited the local residents (rents have risen) is questionable.

Worth seeing is the very modern complex on the Fraenkelufer. The rear courtyards (Fraenkelufer 38) display a lot of greenery and angled balconies. Over time the inhabitants of this architectural "display case" have grown used to the camera-slinging tourists filing through the courtyard. At No. 23 you can buy ***crazy clothes and fashionable jewelry*** (Mon-Fri 10:30am-2:30pm & 4pm-6:30pm,sat 10:30am-3pm).

At the intersection with Kohlfurter Straße a sculpture of a punk and a fireman reminds you of the district's

wild days. In the early 1980s a number of buildings on Kohlfurter Straße (Nos. 40 & 46) were squatted in.

The *Kreuzberger Weltlaterne* (Kohlfurter Str. 37, open daily from 7pm, Tel. 614 91 51) serves paintings and Greek food.

In *Vierlinden* (Erkelenzdamm 47, open daily 11am-1pm, Sun from 10am breakfast buffet, Tel. 65 43 18) you can take a break over a beer or a coffee. Likewise in the *Kühler Grund* (Erkelenzdamm 49, Tel. 614 24 12) you can sit comfortably on the garden terrace and enjoy a small meal amid a colorful crowd.

Kottbusser Tor

The busy Skalitzer Straße leads past dreadful featureless apartment blocks to the square around the over-ground *Kottbusser Tor* U-Bahn station (Line U1 & U8). The "Kotti", as it is known locally, has been rather neglected. Many politicians would rather forget this part of the district. That they have been unable to do so is largely due to the frequent rebellions of the people living here.

Traditionally Kreuzberg is a typical working-class district, with a high population density, little open space and light industry. Added to that is the increased immigration of students and migrants seeking cheap rentals. Kreuzberg has, for example, the highest proportion of Turkish inhabitants in Berlin. This has led to

a particular cultural landscape, especially in the south-east *(SO 36)* of the district. Sadly, this is also accompanied by a potential for conflict. Despite, or perhaps precisely because of that, you should approach Kreuzberg with an open mind, without preconceptions, and with no (unfounded) anxiety. If you're interested in Berlin's counter-culture, you'll find *SO 36* of particular interest.

Through the pedestrian archways which surround the Kotti the route continues to **Dresdener Straße**. The architecture here gives you some idea of why violence can sometimes have its reasons. Dull concrete blocks with narrow corridors and small apartments are poor soil for a happy childhood. The punks asking for money ("haste mal'n paar Groschen?!") should be politely, but firmly refused. It doesn't really matter whether you give money or not, you'll still be followed with scornful remarks.

Dresdener Straße is not exactly spectacular, but this doesn't mean that it's asleep. It has, for example, two of the most interesting **independent cinemas**. In *Babylon (1 & 2)* you can still experience a cinema with atmosphere (Dresdener Str. 126, admission 9 DM, Tel. 614 63 16). The double program is worth particular attention.

For some time *Senso Unico* (Dresdener Str. 121, open daily 6pm-12pm, Tel. 65 65 20) has been right at the top of the in-list of Kreuzberg's trend-setters. It is probably

due to the excellent food served amid kitsch decor. Right next door is the less "trendy" *Gorgonzola Club* whose menu also offers some interesting items.

The Berlin rock group *Ideal* once sang *"Oranienstraße, here lives the Koran"*. The aromas coming from various kebab stalls and the bustle of vegetable and grocery stores indicates that this area, around **Oranienplatz**, is Berlin's real multicultural heartland. Oranienplatz offers one of the few green spots in this part of the city. Open-air concerts are often performed here in the summer. The square is always busy as it is connected to the hectic Oranienstraße.

Towards Moritzplatz is another typical Berlin tavern, the *Max und Moritz* (Oranienstr. 162, open daily 6pm-1:30am, Tel. 614 10 45). Traditional decor and fancy food.

The **Intimen Theater** (Oranienstr. 162, admission: from 15 DM, Tel. 65 10 00) brings many contemporary plays to the stage. Directly opposite there is a good selection of well-priced **second-hand literature**.

The **Kunsthaus am Moritzplatz** (Oranienstr. 46, Tue-Sun 12am-8pm, Tel. 614 55 77) presents the work of local Kreuzberger artists and others.

You can try on new and second-hand clothes first before buying on the corner of Oranienstr. and Luckauer Straße.

Pizzas arrive on the stickiest of tables in *Stiege* (Oranienstr. 47a, open daily 12am-3am, Tel. 614 68 16).

If the problems of the Third World concern you, you can get books, advice or just a cup of coffee in the **Bildungs- und Aktionszentrum (Information and Project Center)** (Oranienstr. 159, Mon-Fri 12am-7pm).

Heinrich-Heine-Straße (an extension of Prinzenstr.) at **Moritzplatz** (U-Bahn station Line U8) was rarely frequented in the past. However since the opening of the Wall the connection between the Mitte district and Kreuzberg has been used enthusiastically by car, bicycle and pedestrian. Along the former border the route now extends east, into deepest Kreuzberg. At some points there are still remnants of the Wall, but many stretches have seen the concrete replaced with wire fencing. Only with imagination will you get a sense of the oppressive atmosphere which the division of this part of the district produced for its inhabitants.

At the top of the street the *American Sector* ends officially, and an area, still legally free of the authority of the West Berlin police, stands on the other side of a fence. In Spring 1990 a tent city appeared in this former border area, inhabited by autonomes, former squatters and the homeless.

The popular *Henne* tavern (Leuschnerdamm 25, Wed-Sun from 7pm, Tel. 614 77 30), serves extremely tasty roasted chickens. They have become an institution in the district. *Henne*, named after the owner, seems a particularly fitting name. Orders are only taken until 8pm. If you can't find a seat, you can either wait or walk the short distance to *Zur kleinen Markthalle* (Legiendamm 32, Tue-Sat from 6pm, Tel. 614 23 56), where crispy chickens are also served. You can also sit in front of this tavern, dating from 1888, in its beer garden. Afficianados claim the chicken is even better here.

Leuschnerdamm runs parallel to the former "no-man's land" and then continues as Bethaniendamm to the River Spree. You can tell that the area has been left in peace for decades by the city planners. This made it possible for a variety of sub-cultural activities to develop here, which now feel endangered after the opening of the Wall.

One project which has in recent years been threatened with closure and even arson, but still survived, is the **Children's Farm** in Adalbertstraße. Donkeys, pigs, sheep and goats are kept here to bring a little nature into the lives of city children.

Between Adalbertstraße and Mariannenplatz caravans used to serve as homes for former squatters. Rock singer *Nina Hagen* spent part of her Berlin days here. The **St. Thomas-Kirche**, an imposing structure in early-Romanesque style, seems out of place looking from Bethaniendamm. However, the brick bulding, formerly West Berlin's largest church, has over the years served to lighten the scenery's Wall-dominated hopelessness.

At **Mariannenplatz** you can view the district's various characters both with pleasure and with slight shud-

ders. At the beginning of the 1980s the square was lavishly renovated, in accordance with the plans of the architect *Lenné*. The generous open spaces have become a relaxation spot for the locals, a Kreuzberg mixture of pensioners, punks, students and Turkish families. In Summer there are regular fairs and street parties. Occasionally a circus or an independent theater group will pitch its tent in the square.

Mariannenplatz is dominated by the architecturally beautiful **Art-house Bethanien** (Mariannenplatz 2, Tel. 614 80 10). The building, adorned with twin towers, used to be the Deaconess's Hospital. In the past the hospital employed some prominent staff (*Theodor Fontane* worked here for a short time as a chemist). After a fierce conflict over the appropriate use of the protected building, with some arguing for its use as a children's outpatients department, the Berlin Senate decided to devote the building to culture. The whole range of Kreuzberg's population finds social and cultural representation in the *Arthouse Bethanien*. The offerings range from film, through theater to music. There is a meeting place for the elderly as well as space for the cultural work of migrant citizens. You will always see notices for exhibitions or concerts in the *"Bethanien"* in the city magazines (Tel. 614 80 10, general information).

The flag of Berlin's squatters flew for the first time from the roof of the former nurses' quarters in the Bethanien Hospital. On 18 December 1971 homeless and unemployed youths spectacularly drew attention to their plight. They occupied the unused building and named it after *Georg v. Rauch*, who that year had been shot by police searching for terrorists. To everyone's credit, the **Georg v.Rauch-Haus** was not cleared by the police, but handed over to the occupants.

The **Galerie Manfred Beelke** at Mariannenplatz 23 (Tel. 611 57 33) brings art to the people. In Muskauer Str. 43 (Tel. from 5pm: 612 62 94) the **Hoftheater** presents plays with anarchistic charm and witty direction.

The white interior and the sophisticated menu reveals that the *Mundart* (Muskauer Str. 33-34, Wed-Sun 6:30pm1am, Tel. 612 20 61) is a high quality restaurant. The prices are generally acceptable, reservation is recommended. After a fine meal a good milk coffee can be enjoyed opposite in the *Café* (Muskauer Str. 23, open daily 11am-3 am, Tel. 612 67 07). If you've emerged late from under the blankets, you can breakfast here until 4pm.

At the southern end of Mariannenplatz stands a **Fountain** designed by the local artist *Kurt Mühlenhaupt*. The figures around the edge are firemen who quite possibly have put out a few fires in SO 36.

The area around Mariannen-, Waldemar-, Adalbert- and Naunystraße has often, particularly during periods of squatting, been a "battlefield" between demonstrators and the police. The main point of criticism for many inhabitants was and remains the program for urban renewal, especially its impact on the district's social structure. Certainly there has been a retreat from the policy of tearing old buildings down and replacing them with modern apartment blocks. Instead, facades were left standing and the rear parts of old buildings were demolished. This produced a lot more open space, but lost not only living space, but also the working areas used by light industries and small businesses. At first glance the district looks better, the facades of most buildings facing the streets having been modernised. Nonetheless, the inhabitants pay for this make-up job with higher rents.

An important function in the district is fulfilled by the **Frauenstadtteilzentrum** (Women's Center) *Schokoladenfabrik e.V.* (Naunystr. 72, Tel. 65 53 91). They offer advice on any sort of women's problems, and also a place just to drop in.

Mariannenstraße, with a mixture of renovated old and featureless new buildings, begins at the fireman's fountain. It is worth taking a look "behind the scenes" in the rear courtyards. In a former factory building (rear of No. 6), only women are served at the cafe tables. As an off-shoot of the *Schokoladenfabrik* (chocolate factory), the *Schoko-Café* (Mon-Fri 1pm-12pm, Sun 1pm-12pm, Tel. 65 14 64) is another meeting point for relaxing and reading a newspaper. The *Turkish Bath* (open daily 6pm-11pm, except

Sat, 1½ hours 8 DM, 2½ hours 12 DM, evening ticket, 15 DM) offers a relaxing opportunity to escape the stress of the city.

The *Rote Harfe* (Oranienstr. 13, open daily 10am-3pm, Tel. 618 44 46) at **Heinrichplatz** is open to anyone who wants to combine the intellectual scene with quaffing beer all night long. The cafe on the top floor is open until 8pm, offering good meals, excellent cakes and varieties of ice-cream. In the evening you can get good meals at reasonable prices. It's cooler in *Café Jenseits* (Oranienstr. 16, open daily 8am-2am, Tel. 65 29 01). Breakfast is served until the early afternoon.

Between Heinrich- and Oranien-platz you can begin discovering the most exciting street in this part of Kreuzberg. **Oranienstraße** has

something to offer right around the clock. During the day, usually after 10am, it presents interesting shopping opportunities, at night the action's in bars and dance halls.

While walking along Oranienstraße you shouldn't neglect the court-yards. The most diverse enterprises have sprung up on the huge factory floors of days gone by. Many artists rent cheap studios here, and the large spaces are often used as apartments.

Oranienstraße regularly changes in appearance. It is not only the facades which are decorated and freed from neglect. The stores also move with the times and are impos-sible to keep track of. What follows are just a few "eternal flames". You can discover the new trendy stores for yourself.

Near Heinrichplatz, in either *Buchhandlung 021* (No. 21, Mon-Fri 10am-6:30pm, Sat 10am-2pm) or the *Elefanten Press Galerie* (No. 25, Mon-Sat 11am-6:30pm, Sun 1pm-6pm, Tel. 614 90 36) you can find **literature** about the district or track down the latest novels. The second-hand **fashion store** *Stoffwechsel* (No. 32) sells new as well as used clothing. The dance halls *SOX* (No. 39, open daily 11pm-??, Tel. 614 35 73) and *Trash* (No. 40/41, Tue-Sun 11pm-5am) are not orientated toward the top-40. The music played here is typical of the scene here, hard and hectic. In *O-Bar* (No. 168), one of the most popular gay bars, heteros can also have a night out. The *Cazzo* bar (No. 187, Tel. 65 65 70) is known for good cocktails in a spartan interior.

Down Adalbertstraße and you are back to the Kottbusser Tor U-Bahn station. If the aroma of the Turkish grocery stores and fast-food stalls has given you an appetite, you can satisfy it with a traditional meal in *Beyti* (Adalbertstr. 10, all day long, Tel. 614 23 73). For a quick snack, the *Döner Kebab-Stand* under the bridge of houses is a good destination.

Görlitzer Bahnhof

From *Görlitzer Bahnhof* it is just a few paces to Kreuzberg's newest leisure facility. Here, on a former industrial estate *"Luisenstadt"*, where heavy industrial goods used to be processed, a park has appeared. **Spreewaldpark** fits well into its environment. No well-kept garden park, but a somewhat wild open space. The locals know how to protect such oases in their otherwise monotonous streetscape.

Before the park opened the **Spreewaldbad** was opened with a modern swimming pool (Tue-Fri 8am-10pm, Mon 2pm-10pm, women's swimming Mon 2pm-5pm, admission from 3 DM, Tel. 88 58 13/15).

The residential area around the Spreewaldpark is a typical example of the functional architecture of a growing worker's district. The area is not part of "representative Berlin", and therefore they've been frugal with renovation here. Many of the buildings in **Wiener Straße** have been left in the style of the late 19th century. The social structure of the relatively young population has allowed for the emergence of a number of cafes and taverns.

The *Wiener Blut* (Wiener Str. 14, open daily from 1pm, Tel. 612 66 56) is one of the newest "in spots". It has a rather "cool" atmosphere, but great cocktails. The *fsk* (No. 20 Tel. 611 70 10) is even more recent. In a cinema-tavern combination, films are shown and then discussed. The *Madonna* (No. 22, open daily 11am-2pm, Tel. 611 69 43) hangs over the tables, but otherwise there's nothing holy about this trendy cafe. In *Panama* (No. 23, open daily from 1pm, Tel. 611 81 37) you can have a good drink and ruminate on the rest of the world in an arty atmosphere.

Indispensable *jewelry* and other accessories for the inner-city outfit are sold in *Excesses* (No. 24, Mon-Fri 2pm-6pm, Sat 11am-1pm).

The interior of the *Casino* (No. 26, open daily 4pm-3am, Tel. 612 46 26) is spartan, but then the beer's cheap.

Known and loved as a disco with timeless dance music, the *Bronx* (No. 34, open daily 10pm-4am, admission free!, Tel. 611 84 45) will certainly still be here in ten years time, especially now it's suddenly in the center of Berlin.

The *Regenbogenkino* (Lausitzer Str. 22, Tel. 611 98 75) shows political films in a small room in the rear building of the **Regenbogenfabrik (Culture and Drop-In Center)**.

Over Lausitzer Straße you reach the Paul-Lincke-Ufer on the Landwehrkanal, the waterway used by both industrial and pleasure boats. At Kottbusser Brücke (bridge) the pleasure craft head towards Pfaueninsel, Wannsee or Tegel. On **Paul-Lincke-Ufer** you can breakfast until early in the afternoon in lovely cafes with front gardens. For example, the *Café am Ufer* (Paul-Lincke-Ufer 42-43, open daily 10am-12pm, Tel. 612 28 27) or the smaller *Café Übersee* (No. 44, open daily 9am-2am, Tel. 618 87 65; inside decorated with art, outside normal garden chairs). In the neighboring building *Exil* (No. 44a, Tue-Sun 7pm-1am, Tel. 612 70 37) has a front garden. It opens in the evening with specialties from the Alps Region at middle-range prices.

The **Wochenmarkt am Maybach-ufer** (Weekly Market) Tue-Fri (12am-6:30pm) supplies fresh fruit and vegetables, as well as diverse specialties from the Western pantry.

Back in Wiener Straße the cobblestones end at the Landwehrkanal, which marks the border with the Treptow district. At Glogauer Str. 2 the *Pike* disco (reached with Bus 129, Tel. 611 90 12/611 79 69) offers regular dancing and music. Along Görlitzer Ufer you can get to Schlesischen Straße/Puschkinallee, which lie close to Treptower Park (S-Bahn station).

Schlesisches Tor

Schlesisches Straße leads to the crossing near the terminus of Line 1, *Schlesisches Tor*. Here the Wall was a terminus not just for the U-Bahn. The pulsating life in the districts of Kreuzberg and Friedrichshain was also divided by the Wall. For the worker's in the West Berlin district the area near the Wall meant cheaper rents. Much was left unrenovated here. It was no accident that this densely populated area became a center of the squatting movement. The **Kerngehäuse Cuvrystraße** (No. 20-23) has remained in a former factory building, where self-managed working and living has been successfully practised for a number of years. In the same building the *Kiezpalast* offers culture to both residents and visitors. The *Ratibor-Theater* (Tel. 618 61 99) has been a fixture in Berlin's independent theater landscape for years, and in the *Kiezpalast* you'll find readings, music and cabaret performances.

In the Schlesisches Tor U-Bahn station the former **Kaufhaus Kato** has been converted into a performance space.

Here Turkish culture can be seen at every turn. Why not try the *Bagdad* Turkish restaurant (Schlesisches Straße 2, open daily 11am-12pm, weekends until 2am, Tel. 612 69 62) even if only for some tea. The food is also tasty and reasonably priced.

One of the first border crossings to be opened was the Oberbaumbrükke (Oberbaum Bridge). It is used as a traffic artery over the Landwehrkanal and on towards the Friedrichshain district, and also as an excursion route into Treptower Park. As an escape from the urban madness, the bridge is naturally inviting.

Following Köpenicker Straße you walk parallel to the "natural" border, the Spree River. Here you can track down some typical Kreuzberg institutions in the sidestreets. The **covered market** in Eisenbahnstraße is well worth a visit. The locals shop here for all their daily needs as well as making social contact. The **Theater Forum Kreuzberg** (Eisenbahnstraße 21, Tel. 618 28 05) is a small experimental theater. You can find more than films in the *Eiszeit* **Cinema** (Zeughofstr. 20. Tel. 611 60 16).

Today the *Alten Ballsaal* serves lamb and other specialties. The *Auerbach* (Köpenicker Str. 174, open daily 7pm-12:30am, Tel. 611 50 79) is perhaps a little expensive, but one pays for the ambience after all.

FÜR DAMEN: EIN PICCOLO GRATIS! IM TAUSCH GEGEN DIESE ECKE.

From Checkpoint Charlie to the Reichstag: all along the border
(Karen Meyer)

For 28 years **the Wall** was Berlin's greatest tourist attraction and the city's secret trademark. Today the remains of the Wall attract visitors like a magnet. The post-war period has finally come to an end in Berlin, where it lasted far longer than in the West German cities. Until recently the Cold War was still a reality along the Wall and especially at the heavily fortified border crossings, like **Checkpoint Charlie** (see map 1).

For West Berliners the Checkpoint was unloved, as it was barred to them as well as other West German citizens. It was set aside for foreigners, the Allies, Diplomats and - since 9 November 1989 - East German citizens. American soldiers above all did good business before the opening of the Wall, using the transit without customs control to buy up cheaply in the East. After the Wall's opening it was Soviet soldiers and border troops who traded uniforms, medals and party badges for hard currency. Almost forgotten now is October 1961, when Soviet and American tanks stood only a few meters from each other here in Friedrichstraße - the Americans

131

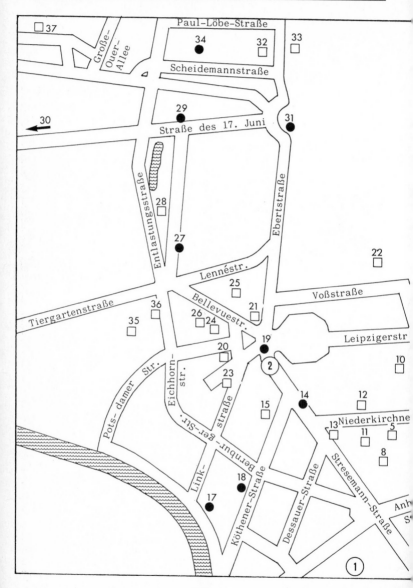

132

From Checkpoint Charlie to the Reichstag

S-Bhf.
1 Anhalter Bahnhof
2 Potsdamer Platz

U-Bhf.
3 Kochstraße

1 Checkpoint Charlie
2 Museum at Checkpoint Charlie
3 Bahnhof Kochstraße
4 Baroque building at the corner of Friedrichstraße/Zimmerstraße
5 Former Gestapo building/former College of Arts and Crafts
6 Former SS building/former Hotel Prinz Albrecht
7 Former Prinz-Albrecht Palace

8 Document Hall (Dokomentation Topographie des Terrors)
9 Anhalter Bahnhof
10 Former Reichsluftfahrtministerium (Imperial Air Force Ministry)
11 Martin Gropius Building/former Arts and Crafts Museum
12 Former Prussian Regional Parliament/ former GDR's Academy of Science
13 Former Folklore Museum
14 Air ventilator shafts of the S-Bahn
15 Haus Vaterland
17 Flea market
18 Monorail
19 Potsdamer Platz
20 Former Vox-Haus
21 Former Columbus-Haus
22 Bunker complex of the Reich Chancellery
23 Weinhaus Huth
24 Hotel Esplanade
25 Triangle between Bellevue- and Lennéstraße
26 Former People's court/former Wilhelm Grammar School
27 Siegesallee
28 Nissenhütte
29 Soviet Monument
30 Siegessäule (Victory Column)
31 Brandenburg Gate
32 Reichstag
33 Reichstag (Presidential Palace)
34 Platz der Republik (Königsplatz)
35 Philharmonie
36 Museum of Musical Instruments
37 Congress Hall

wanted to retain the unrestricted access to East Berlin laid down in the Potsdam Accord.

The simplest way to get to the former Checkpoint Charlie is on Bus 129, or with the U-Bahn, Line 6, alight at Kochstraße.

"Charlie" is not the name of a renowned GI to whom this was a memorial, but stands for "C" in the international alphabet code and indicates the third checkpoint after "Alpha" (Helmstedt/Marienborn) and "Bravo" (Drewitz/Dreilinden).

At Friedrichstraße 44 the private museum **Haus am Checkpoint Charlie** (2) documents the history of the Wall and the Cold War. The many photos and documents tell you of dramatic escape attempts and successful Wall crossings. One of the most tragic cases was that of *Peter Fechter*: the 18-year old bricklayer was shot in August 1962 when he tried to get through the Wall fortifications. He lay there, badly wounded, no one from East or West went to save him. Before the eyes of a crowd the young man bled to death. (*Museum am Checkpoint Charlie*, open daily 9am-10pm; a small cafe is connected to the museum).

The *Iron Curtain*, which brought the Cold War to the center of Berlin, cut brutally through the heart of the city. Lively streets like Friedrichstraße were turned into dead ends, traffic arteries were cut. Berlin had become Siamese twins. It had from now on a double life, two pulses - only a few underground veins remained open. One of them, U-Bahn Line 6, runs directly under Friedrichstraße. Until recently the train's arrival at **Bahnhof Koch-straße** (3) was met with the ominous message: "Last Station in Berlin West". The train traversed the city on a spooky trip, only stopping for Friedrichstraße, and then went without stopping past deserted stations guarded by lonely border soldiers. Even longer was the trip through East Berlin's underworld on Line 8. Since then, the dead stations in the Eastern half of the city have been reopened.

Friedrichstraße, one of the most famous and liveliest streets in Old Berlin, will need some time before it recovers from its imposed devastation. The Western part of the street, which leads to the middle of the historic center and in which the city's life pulses, became a dead end at both ends: in the north it was sealed off by Checkpoint Charlie, in the south by the reshaped Mehring-Platz. Many stores and taverns which had flourished before 1961 had to close down in the following years. The businesses that went bust included the famous chemist *"Zum Weißen Adler"*, founded in 1696, which was located from 1829 at the corner of **Friedrichstraße and Zimmerstraße** (4). The almost 250 year old baroque building which housed the chemist is one of the oldest buildings in the western part of the city. The various stages of

extension to the old building, eventually turning it into an apartment building, can be seen on the Wall in Zimmerstraße, and are marked in different colors. On the ground floor the *Café Adler* offers its guests mouth-watering cakes, Tue-Sun 10am-11pm.

In the streets running up to the Wall the commercial rents quickly dropped. Community action and self-help groups and artists moved into the cheap shop premises. The opening of the Wall spells the end for this counter-culture. Some of the tenants above the shops in Zimmerstraße must be anxious about being able to pay the next rent installment. These neglected apartments overlook the remains of the graffiti-adorned Wall. Near the border rents have increased by more than 100 per cent.

If you follow Zimmerstraße west, you come to the **corner of Wilhelmstraße** and an enclosed, open piece of land. You can step onto it through an opening in the fence. Here, close to the government quarter in Wilhelmstraße, lay the National Socialists (Nazi's) center of terror, the **Gestapo** (5), **SS** (6), and **Security Service** (7).

The buildings, heavily damaged during the war, were blown up in the post-war decade, the traces of history removed. In the 1950s there were plans to build a helicopter landing pad here. Later it was thought that Kochstraße could be extended as a highway through the area. Finally it was leased out to a rubbish-disposal firm and also became an area for driving without a license. Under pressure from anti-fascist groups, there was a nervous discussion about what to do with the area towards the end of the 1970s. During the 750th anniversary celebrations a provisional arrangement was agreed to, which remains unchanged to this day. The cellars and foundations of the building along the former Prinz-Albrecht-Straße (today Niederkirchnerstraße) were opened to the public. This ensured that this historical chapter was kept in full public view. The political and historical background to the terror which emanated from this area is represented in a **Document Hall** (8) (*Dokumentation Topographie des Terrors*, Tue-Sun 10am-6pm, admission free, catalogue in English or German, 10 DM).

In the 18th century a number of princely palaces with gardens sprang up along the north of Wilhelmstraße. In 1830 *Friedrich Wilhelm III's* son, *Prinz Albrecht* acquired the most southerly palace. He had the building converted by *Schinkel* and the park reconstructed by *Lenné*. Until 1934 it was put to a number of different uses. Finally *Reinhard Heydrich's* security service was located here, the information-gathering arm of the SS.

Niederkirchnerstraße (formerly Prinz-Albrecht-Straße), named after a resistance fighter, was first laid down shortly before the turn of the century. In 1905 the College of Arts

and Crafts was established, which the *Gestapo* occupied in 1933. From 1887/88 it was flanked by the Hotel Prinz Albrecht, which housed *Himmler's SS* from 1934.

In 1939, when the *Gestapo*, Criminal Police and Security Service were combined into the *Reichssicherheitshauptamt* (RSHA), roughly 3,000 people throughout the city were employed by the terror machine, half of them on this piece of ground. It was here where the Nazis genocidal policies were formulated: the establishment and running of the concentration camps and the organisation of the "Einsatztruppen" who were reponsible for the execution of hundreds of thousands of people in the occupied territories. For the opponents of National Socialism Prinz-Albrecht-Straße 8 was the most feared address in Berlin. The Gestapo did not "just" plan their terror from a distance in this former College of Arts and Crafts. Particularly intransigent or politically important opponents were brought to the building's prison and sometimes spent weeks being interrogated in the *Gestapo*'s rooms. The prominent prisoners included, among many others: *Georgi Dimitroff* (who came here after the Reichstag fire trial), *Ernst Thälmann,*

Kurt Schumacher, Theodor Haubach and *Erich Honecker*. The prison cells were in the south wing of the College of Arts and Crafts. The floor of the cells, (you can see where the walls ran around the narrow cells), was opened to the public in 1987. Today a provisional roof protects the broken remains of the foundations from the elements.

From the viewing platform you can see the large entrance of **Anhalter Bahnhof** (9) to the south-east - a sad remnant of the famous main railway station, built in 1874-80 by *Franz Heinrich Schwechten*. The station's barrel-roof - in its day the largest station roof in Europe - was constructed by the engineer *Heinrich Seidel*. Seidel was known to his contemporaries as the author of the novel *"Leberecht Hühnchen"*.

In its heyday the Berlin Anhalter Railway Station, which like other railways was privately owned until nationalisation at the end of the 19th century, saw 85 long-distance trains every day. *Borsig's* first locomotive, the *"Beuth"* departed from here in 1841. The station was central Europe's most important transport intersection, trains left here for Rome, Athens, Constantinople Brindisi, Nice and Paris. The arrival and departure of trains is a theme in innumerable contemporary novels and stories which were set in Berlin.

In 1952 the last train left from the war-damaged station. It was demolished between 1959 and 1962, although the structure was sound enough for it to be maintained. It had not been planned to leave the Anhalter Bahnhof's entrance stand-

ing, but after several quarrels among the demolishers it was decided to leave it as it was.

On the eastern side you'll see a monumental building clad in limestone tiles. The former **Reichsluftfahrtministerium (Imperial Air Force Ministry)** (10) was built in the 1930s by *Sagebiel*, who also designed Tempelhof airport. From the outside the building, made of massive square blocks, looks like the Nazi's ideal of a building to last till eternity. In reality the building was built with modern concrete techniques and later covered with the limestone tiles.

The *Martin Gropius Building* (11) which contains the **Arts and Crafts Museum** was completed in 1881 following the plans of *Martin Gropius* and *Heino Schmieden*. The facade of the late-classical construction indicates its intended purpose. The mosaics on the North-Western and Eastern facades represent epochs in art history. The frescos above the windows show various craft techniques which master artisans handed down to their apprentices.

When the museum in the Berlin Castle was discontinued in 1920, the collections in the neighboring museum, the East-Asian art collection and the Museum for Prehistory and Early History were all brought here. During the war the Arts and Crafts Museum suffered heavy damage, and demolition was often considered. In 1966 the ruins were placed under a preservation order, although without anything being done about the state of the building. The intervention of *Walter Gropius*,

Martin Gropius's great nephew, was responsible for providing the finances for the initial renovations. This at least prevented its total collapse. After the provision of a provisory roof, the Martin Gropius Building was still left to itself for a number of years.

Only in 1977 was building recommenced. The reopening of part of the building took place in 1981, and in the same year it caused a furore with the *Prussia Exhibition*.

The restoration work proceeded carefully in the 1980s. The main entrance was put on the southern side, as the territory of the GDR reached some distance west of the Wall to the steps. Today it houses the *Berlin Gallery*, the *Guild Archives*, and the *Jewish Section of the Berlin Museum*. The lower ground floor houses the office of the *Topography of Terror*. A number of major exhibitions such as *"Berlin, Berlin"*, *"Zeitgeist"*, and *"Horizonte"* have taken place here since the restoration was completed in 1987. The building is open Tue-Sun 10am-8pm, for special exhibitions until 10pm. Admission: 6/3 DM, 8/4 DM for major exhibitions. The restaurant on the lower ground floor offers new German cuisine and "healthy food", the meals are good, but not exactly cheap.

The **Prussian Regional Parliament** (12) was built opposite at the turn of the century, briefly housing the "People's Court" in 1934.

In 1886 the **Folklore Museum** (13) was built beside the Arts and Crafts Museum by *Hermann Ende* and *Wilhelm Böckmann*. You can see the

position of the building, demolished in 1962, if you follow the sidewalk on the corner of Stresemann- and Niederkirchnerstraße. The most famous part of the Folklore Museum was *Priamos'* Trojan Treasure, donated to the city of Berlin by *Heinrich Schliemann*. The treasure was laid out on red velvet behind a large round window and during the day the sun made the gold glisten. Today the treasure is missing.

The Folklore Museum was set up at a time when Germany had developed into a colonial power. All cultural artifacts seized from the colonies had to be taken to the capital's Folklore Museum, where a decision was then made about their eventual destination. In this way the best and most important pieces stayed in Berlin, which quickly became a center for ethnological research. Soon after its opening the museum was bursting at the seams, and in 1920 objects began to be placed in the *Martin Gropius Building*. During the Nazi era the racist teachings of the "super-race" were "scientifically" reinforced and presented to the public in lectures. The Folklore Museum, which was provisionally restored and served from 1955 as an exhibition building, was demolished in 1962.

If you go from the corner of Stresemann- and Niederkirchnerstraße north along the fragments of the Wall, you are following the old city boundary as it was until the middle of the 19th century. You will walk along the old *Ascanian Wall*,

begun in 1732, completed in stone in 1802, and dismantled in 1864. This toll wall led along Stresemanstraße and then north until the Unterbaumbrücke at the Reichstag. During the last 250 years the central district, as this area was known, saw only 100 years without a wall.

Shortly before Köthener Straße meets Stresemannstraße, you come across the S-Bahn's *air ventilator shafts* (14). In summer you can clearly see the cool, musty air which streams up from the tunnels. The North-South railway, here underground, which leads from Anhalter Bahnhof through Potsdamer Platz to Friedrichstraße was first built in 1935 by the National Socialists. It was meant to be ready for the 1936 Olympics. During the hectic building work safety measures were neglected, so that a part of the work between Potsdamer Platz and Brandenburger Tor collapsed, burying 19 workers. The line, which runs deep under the River Spree, the Landwehrkanal and the U-Bahn, was only fully completed in 1939. On 2 May 1945 the Nazis blew up the bulkheads to the Landwehrkanal and flooded the tunnel. This prevented the Soviets from driving undergound to the city center. The water flooded both the U-and the S-Bahn, drowning the many people seeking shelter there from artillery fire. After the war it took months to bury the dead and dry out the stretch of railway.

The **caravan park** (15) lying opposite sprang up a few years ago, when the *Tempodrom*, presenter of musical and cultural offerings,

erected its tent here. The *"Rolling Homers"* come from the most diverse social strata: artisans, teachers, actors, etc. They feel part of a village community and have managed to have the address, Köthener Straße 1-5, accepted by the authorities. They get water courtesy of the city, and they produce their own power with generators. The corporation to which the land belongs even accepts the settlement without any rent, so long as the area is not put to any other use. The fall of the Wall threatens the existence of the "Rolling Homers", since this land, originally on the city's fringe, has turned into prime real estate in the center.

The site where the "Rolling Homers" live today was from 1912 that of the **Haus Vaterland** (15a) - one of

Berlin. Potsdamer Platz

Berlin's most famous entertainment spots. Restaurants of various nationalities invited one to a culinary trip around the world. "Cowboy dances and Negro Jazz bands" ensured an authentic atmosphere; in other rooms there was Löwenbräu beer and folk dancing. The best loved was a regional specialty, the famous "Rhine Terraces". A huge panorama portrayed a Rhineland landscape, in front of which the tables and chairs stood as if on a terrace. On the hour realistic weather was simulated with lightning, thunder and rain. After the war the building was part of the GDR. A restaurant and a catering hall for war veterans was established in the war-damaged building. In the worker's uprising on 17 June 1953 the building was set alight by the rebels. In 1961 the GDR could not be bothered to erect a wall around the ruins, a fence would do. Officially the land could not be entered from the western side, so the ruins

became a desirable hiding spot for petty criminals, who could stay there undisturbed by the West Berlin police. In 1972 the area was handed over to West Berlin, and four years later the ruins of the *Haus Vaterland* were cleared away.

Until its demolition in the 1950s, **Potsdamer Bahnhof** (16) stood alongside the *Haus Vaterland*. The first Prussian railway between Potsdam and Berlin was opened here in 1838. Long-distance rail, U- and S-Bahn lines intersected at this point. Since the Wall was cleared away some of the bricked-up entrances to the U- and S-Bahn can now be seen. The railway station extended as far as the Landwehr-kanal, where today a *flea market*

142

(17) can be found. It was only after the demolition of the station that Bernburger Straße was extended through the site.

Diagonally across the site you can see the overhead rails of the *Monorail* (18), which stretch 1.6 kilometers between Gleisdreieck and Kemperplatz. The project, completely financed to the tune of millions of marks by the taxpayer, was an object of dispute right from the beginning. The main criticism was its limited capacity compared to the running costs and the position. The Monorail blocks the re-opening of the U-Bahn between Wittenbergplatz and Alexanderplatz, which was closed down after the building of the Wall. As this is the only U-Bahn line which links the city centers of East and West Berlin, the Monorail will soon be demolished.

"I can't find Potsdamer Platz" says the old man in *Wim Wenders'* film *Wings of Desire*. It's a common complaint. In fact it is difficult to find the square for anyone who returns to visit Berlin after a number of decades. The streets have changed, and where buildings used to stand there is now only sand and some tufts of grass. In the 1920s people spoke of *Potsdamer Platz* (19) as the busiest traffic intersection in Europe. Several bus routes led to the U- and S-Bahn, and more than a hundred trams crossed the square every hour. The first traffic lights in Europe, a traffic light with signals for five directions, was imported in 1924 from the USA and set up here.

Around Potsdamer Platz you could find a number of famous Berlin addresses. *Vox-Haus* (20) was where radio had its beginnings in Germany. It was demolished in 1969 with the removal of Potsdamer Straße. Also famous was *Columbus-Haus* (21), a modern nine-storey shopping and services center. In the 1950s the corner of Potsdamer Platz facing East had a huge piece of scaffolding carrying a neon sign. This sign transmitted the latest slogans to the East, which answered in turn with its own propaganda.

In the no-man's land north of the Potsdamer Platz checkpoint you can see a small hill. Under this hill lies the remains of the huge *bunker complex* (22) which used to be part of Hitler's Reich Chancellery. The real *"Fuehrer's bunker"*, however, has been demolished. Some thought will now have to be given to what is to be done with these remnants of the past. Until now they lay in no-man's land - the curious are already wanting to explore the area.

The *Weinhaus Huth* (23) is the only building which kept its position on Potsdamer Platz. Its existence was surrounded by controversey from the beginning. The Huth family overstretched itself with building costs of over 1.5 million marks for the new winery. The modern building method of using a steel skeleton stood the building in good stead during the war. The relatively minimal bomb damage was repaired with the help of its own employees.

After the war the building was sold to the Senate, which wanted to demolish it to make way for a highway. The plan was abandoned. Still, the tenants fear they will have to give way soon. *Daimler-Benz* has bought the 65,000 square meter area between the old Potsdamer, Eichhorn and Linkstraße, where the *Haus Huth* stands, and wants to build a service center.

The **Hotel Esplanade** (24), only a fraction of which remains standing on the corner of Potsdamer Straße and Bellevue Straße, was one of the noblest hotels in Berlin. The interior, with baths in almost all the rooms, was extraordinarily luxurious. There are now plans to establish a new film center for Berlin here, to house among others the *Deutsche Kinemathek*.

The *"Reichsgruppe Industrie"* met in the hotel during the last months of the war to forge plans for the reconstruction of the German economy after the war's end. At the same time people who apparently questioned the "final victory" were subjected to severe repression. Essential concepts for the post-war economy were introduced to the group by *Ludwig Erhard*, who later became Minister of Trade and Commerce under *Adenauer*.

The **triangle between Bellevue- and Lennéstraße** (25), which looking from the wall reaches right to Kemperplatz, belonged to East Berlin until July 1988. However, it was not surrounded by a wall, only a fence. In 1988, West Berlin pro-

posed building an entry to a planned freeway. Over the years the land had become home to a particular ecosystem. Many rare small animals and plants used the land free from human interference. Protests against the Senate's car-friendly plans grew, and finally *autonomes* and environmentalists occupied the triangle a few weeks before the hand-over to the West. The West Berlin police had no access to the squatter's tent city, as the land still belonged to the GDR. Attempts to drive the environmentalists from Bellevuestraße with water cannons and tear gas stopped when the GDR border police protested at their exposure to the teargas. On the morning of the hand-over the protesters faced a

tough police action, which they
escaped by climbing over the Wall to
the East. The GDR border guards
assisted them and rewarded them
with breakfast. Shortly after the first
West-East mass escape, the Senate
had the area levelled, but the new
Red-Green Senate no longer wants
to build the highway.

The *Wilhelm Grammar School* used
to stand beside the Hotel Esplanade, and counted *Walter Mehring* and
Kurt Tucholsky among its pupils.
Freisler's **"People's Court"** (26)
moved here in 1935, having been
established in 1934 in the Prussian
House of Representatives opposite.
The Court, which heard mainly
cases of "high treason", handed
down thousands of death sentences. The dispensation of justice was
arbitrary in the extreme, and their
were no appeals.

Siegesallee (27), built in 1878,
linked Kemperplatz with Königsplatz,
today "Platz der Republik". Between
Siegesallee and Entlastungsstraße,
hidden in the bushes, there stands
an old **"Nissenhütte"** (28), a British
military barracks. It was constructed
in Tiergarten as a refuge for the
homeless in 1945-49. In the early
post-war years Tiergarten was more
of a market garden than a park.
Most of the trees were cut down and
used as firewood, and in their place
people planted vegetables and
potatoes.

At the instigation of *Kaiser
Wilhelm II.*, Siegesallee was turned
into a boulevard adorned with 32
statues. The sight of the monumen-

tal figures, which represented the
rulers of Brandenburg and Prussia,
was to function as a lesson in
glorious history. The Nazis separa-
ted the statues, as they wanted to
broaden Siegesallee to make a
North-South axis.

The Nazis plans for the rebuilding
of Berlin as the world capital *"Germania"*, to be completed by 1950,
had Tiergarten at its center. For the
East-West axis Charlottenburger
Chaussee (Straße des 17. Juni) was
to be doubled in breadth. To make
space for the North-South axis,
which was to run in a straight line
from Tempelhof to Siegesallee in
Tiergarten, countless houses were
demolished. Ironically only one of
the planned show-pieces was ever
realised - the *Tourism Center*. The
intersection of the axes was to be
where the *Soviet Monument* stands

today. In the North, behind the *Platz der Republik*, *Hitler's* chief architect *Albert Speer* wanted to erect a "Great Hall", planned as the largest construction in the world. Around 180,000 people would have fitted into the 300 meter wide hall, the Reichstag would have looked like a toy alongside it.

The **Soviet Monument** (29) has stood at the intersection of the North-South and East-West axes since November 1945. It is a memorial to the more than 20 million Soviet victims of the war. The two tanks which flank the monument are meant to be the first to reach Berlin in April 1945.

The **Victory Column** (30) was erected in 1873 to commemorate the winning of the Franco-German wars in the same year. It stood on Königsplatz (Royal Square) until 1938. It was then moved by the

Gottfried Schadow

Nazis to its present location, the Grosser Stern (Great Star) square, as part of their plans for the East-West axis.

The **Brandenburger Tor** (31) was one of the fourteen city gates. Between 1788-91 it was built in its present form by *Carl Gotthard Langhans*, modelled on the *Propylaea* of the *Acropolis* in Athens. The *Quadriga* with the *Viktoria* was designed by *Gottfried Schadow* in 1789-93. Until recently Berlin's best-known construction was being renovated. The Eastern half of the city concerned itself with the gate, while the Museum of Communication, Transport and Technology in West Berlin renovated the *Quadriga*. The gate was re-crowned with the *Quadriga* in July 1991. The city's trademark has been renovated once before by East and West Berlin in co-operation. Between 1956-58 the GDR restored the war-damaged gate, and West Berlin dealt with the restoration of the *Quadriga*, although without the eagle and the iron cross. The latter has now been reattached.

Its four coaches had been removed before: Napoleon took the *Quadriga* to Paris as a victory trophy in 1806, in 1814 it was taken back and embellished with the Prussian eagle and the iron cross.

The Brandenburg Gate has experienced the most important events in German history: victorious troops marched in and out, defeated soldiers came back through it. The Kaiser took his carriage through the middle gateway, which was reserved

Emperor Wilhelm I., the victorious founder of the German "Reich".

From a painting by Ferdinand Keller.

festival was for the Berliners them-selves: half a million people from East and West celebrated together the first New Year's Eve after the opening of the Wall.

On the site of the former *Raczinski Palace* stands the **Reichstag** (32), completed in 1894 following the plans of *Paul Wallots*. On the 9 November 1918 *Philipp Scheidemann* declared the Republic from its balcony - while at almost the same time *Karl Liebknecht* proclaimed the *Socialist Republic* from the balcony of the castle.

After the famous Reichstag fire on 27 Febuary 1933, the Parliament moved to the *Kroll Opera House* (1852), a well known center of theater, balls and for a time the Royal Opera. The background to the Reichstag fire is still controversial. The Dutch anarchist *Marinus van der Luppe* was arrested that same night, and the Nazis blamed the commu-nists for the fire. Together with *van der Luppe*, four members of the Communist Party were accused, among them *Georgi Dimitroff*. The four were found innocent, but then brought to Prinz-Albrecht-Straße 8 to the Gestapo. *Van der Luppe* was executed. The fire provided the Nazis with an excuse for their first wave of persecution, which they legitimated through a so-called state of emergency. The basic rights established by the Weimar Constitu-tion were extensively overruled, and the death penalty reintroduced.

for him, when he went home from Tiergarten or from Charlottenburg. Only a few hundred meters further down the street stood the Berlin Castle. Finally, a grand funeral procession took the deceased *Wilhelm I.* through the gate for the last time. Just as impressive, but dreadfully gruesome, was the torchlight procession with which the Nazis celebrated their election victory on the evening of 30 January 1933. More jackbooted processions were to follow, and finally they had Charlottenburger Chaussee (Straße des 17. Juni) broadened as a parade avenue.

The 1 May 1945 was celebrated by Soviet and Polish soldiers under the Brandenburg Gate. The last great

Opposite the rear of the Reichstag you can see the **Reichstag Presi-**

dential Palace (33), which is connected to the Reichstag by an underground passage. It was never ruled out that the arsonist might have taken this route. Then it would have been done with the knowledge of the Reichstag President, *Hermann Göring* - and it would have been the Nazis' own people who were responsible.

Königsplatz *(Platz der Republik)* (34) was identified by Soviet troops in the final phase of the war as a victory target of great symbolic value. There were fierce battles for the area over a number of days. The image of a Soviet soldier flying the red flag from a corner tower of the Reichstag went around the world.

In 1957 it was decided to rebuild the Reichstag in a simpler form - without its dome - and it was completed in 1971. Today you can see the permanent exhibition *"Questions of German History"*. The Reichstag is used for meetings and conferences, and special sittings of the German Federal Parliament. The exhibition

"Questions of German History" opens Tue-Sun 10am-5pm, admission is free. In the Reichstag there are two self-service cafeterias and a restaurant.

North of the Reichstag, where the Wall stood until recently, there are a number of wooden crosses. They are in memory of those who, attempting to escape from the GDR, were killed trying to get over the Wall. The number of real victims is far higher than the number of wooden crosses.

A competent tour of the city's historical places starting at the Martin Gropius building and ending at the Reichstag is offered by *STATTREISEN e.V.* Group tours by arrangement, individuals according to schedule. Information Mon-Fri 10am-4pm on Tel: 395 30 78.

Wilmersdorf and Zehlendorf

The green districts of Wilmersdorf and Zehlendorf form an important part of Berlin's lungs. Wide areas of forests and meadows surround the broad arms of the Havel River and the small lakes. The suburbs of *Grunewald, Schlachtensee, Wannsee* and *Nikolassee* rank among the best residential areas in the city, and those who cannot live here, use the districts extensively for walking. The following section explores these districts all rich in beauty spots.

Dahlem

Dahlem, on the border between Zehlendorf and Wilmersdorf, is equated by most Berliners with "country life" in the big city. The

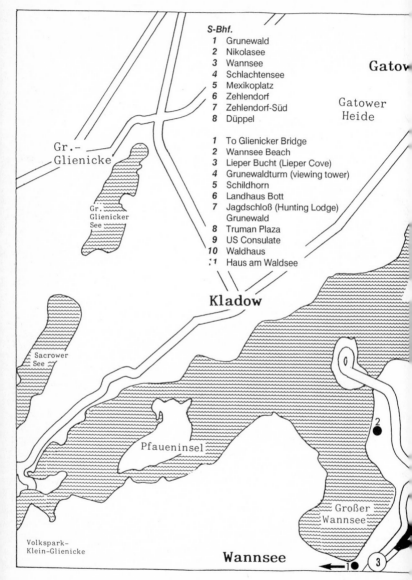

S-Bhf.
1 Grunewald
2 Nikolasee
3 Wannsee
4 Schlachtensee
5 Mexikoplatz
6 Zehlendorf
7 Zehlendorf-Süd
8 Düppel

1 To Glienicker Bridge
2 Wannsee Beach
3 Lieper Bucht (Lieper Cove)
4 Grunewaldturm (viewing tower)
5 Schildhorn
6 Landhaus Bott
7 Jagdschloß (Hunting Lodge) Grunewald
8 Truman Plaza
9 US Consulate
10 Waldhaus
11 Haus am Waldsee

Gatow

Gatower Heide

Gr.-Glienicke

Gr. Glienicker See

Sacrower See

Kladow

Pfaueninsel

Volkspark-Klein-Glienicke

Großer Wannsee

Wannsee

154

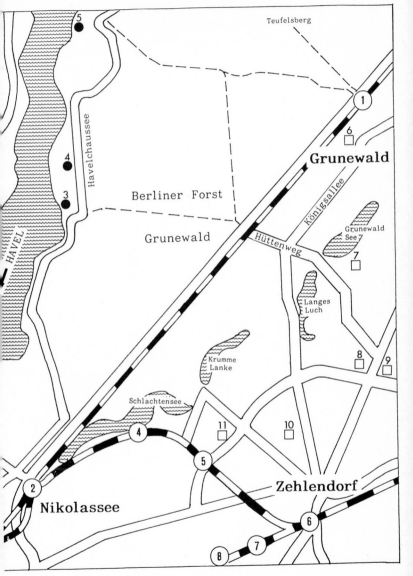

Teufelsberg

Havelchaussee

Grunewald

Königsallee

Berliner Forst

Hüttenweg

Grunewald

Grunewald
See 7

HAVEL

Langes
Luch

Krumme
Lanke

Schlachtensee

Zehlendorf

Nikolassee

U-Bahn station (Line U2) is called Dahlem-Dorf (Dahlem village), and is built in a timber frame style with a traditional thatched roof. Busy U-Bahn lines run through the area, as Dahlem is home to the *Free University* (*FU*).

A number of **museums of the Stiftung Preußischer Kulturbesitz** (Prussian Cultural Heritage Foundation) are located in Dahlem (admission free!):

Museum für Deutsche Volkskunde (German Ethnological Museum). Tue-Fri 9am-5pm, Sat/Sun 10am-5pm, Tel. 83 20 31. German cultural artifacts and their influence on the countries of central Europe are shown on the basis of everyday usage.

Museen für Indische, Islamische und Ostasiatische Kunst/Museum für Völkerkunde (Museums of Indian, Islamic and East Asian Art/Ethnological Museum). Lansstraße 8, Tue-Fri 9am-5pm, Sat/Sun 10am-5pm, Tel 8 30 11. Collections of the most important non-European cultural items are gathered under one roof. Traditional methods of production and applied arts are repesented in as much detail as religious rites and cultural artifacts.

Skulpturengalerie (Sculpture Gallery). Arnimallee 23-27, Tue-Fri 9am-5pm, Sat/Sun 10am-5pm, Tel. 8 30 11. Sculptures, icons and paintings with Christian motifs from the 19th century.

Kupferstichkabinett (Copperplate Engraving Gallery). Arnimallee 23-27, Tue-Fri 9am-5pm, Sat/Sun 10am-5pm, Tel. 8 30 11. A rich historical outline of drawing techniques in five rooms.

Gemäldegalerie (Painting Gallery). Arnimallee 23-27, Tue-Fri 9am-5pm, Sat/Sun 10am-5pm, Tel. 8 30 11. Extensive collection of national (*Dürer, Holbein*) and international (*Rembrandt, van Dyck*) paintings from every century.

Geheimes Staatsarchiv Preußischer Kulturbesitz (Prussian Cultural Heritage's Secret State Archives) Archivstraße 12, Mon, Wed, Fri 8am-3:30pm, Thu 8am-7:30pm, Tel. 83 20 31. Library, card and picture collection.

Before or after the art tour a good meeting point is the *Luise* (Königin-Luise-Str. 40, open daily 10am-1am, Tel. 832 84 87). You can get a good breakfast or enjoy the mildness of a lovely summer evening in the large beer garden. Just as much a garden restaurant, but a little less popular is the *Alte Krug* (Königin-Luise-Str. 52, open daily except Thu, 12am-11pm, Tel. 832 50 98). If all you want is cheap food, you should mix with the students in the *FU-Mensa* (Kiebitzweg 26).

Village life has still partly survived in Dahlem. It used to be Royal Prussian property, but today the **Domäne Dahlem** (Königin-Luise-Str. 49, Tel. 832 50 00, 831 59 00) is regarded as the "Property of Berlin". The *Dömane* preserves historic arts and crafts and is run by a non-profit making association. Domestic animals are kept in a number of stables, and grain is grown in small fields. An idyll in the middle of the city. But as so often happens, this idyll is also in danger. The Senate has plans to build sports fields for the Free University. It can only be hoped that the protests in favor of maintaining the Domäne last the distance.

In the *St. Annen* cemetery (Königin-Luise-Straße 55), row 28-3 contains the tombstone of Extra Parliamentary Opposition member *Rudi Dutschke*, who died on the 24 December 1979 from the effects of a murder attempt on 11 April 1968.

Zehlendorf

Zehlendorf lies in the old American sector of the "divided" city of Berlin. While the presence of the French and British "protectors" in West Berlin was seldom visible, the Americans always made their presence felt. On Clayallee (*General Clay* played an important role during the Berlin blockade) they have established a small settlement, with all the institutions needed to make life in Berlin bearable for Americans.

From the **Oskar-Helene-Heim** U-Bahn station (U2) it is only a few steps to Truman Plaza. From this point on the dollar reigns. The facilities, which include a cinema, burger joints, hot dog stands, a huge shopping center and an army post office, are reserved for soldiers and their families. The quarter gives you a glimpse of the "American way of life". Fans of the area come to the annual **Deutsch-Amerikanischen-Volksfest,** a popular fair which

takes place each year at the expense of a different US state. Another favorite event is the **Rodeo,** held here in the summer. Now that the reunification of the two German states has made the presence of the Allies superfluous, it will be interesting to see whether these events remain in the city's calendar.

Opposite Truman Plaza lies the *US Consulate* (Clayallee 170, Mon-Fri 8:30am-11:30am & 1:30pm-3pm, except Wed afternoon, Tel 832 40 87) and the *US Mission.*

You can't miss the transmission tower of the *AFN (American Forces Network)* rising in Zehlendorf's sky. From here soldiers serve soldiers with sounds and information from home. The program includes a regular language course (*German phrase of the day*) and a midday cooking recipe. For Berliners, especially in the surrounding areas, *AFN's* round-the-clock music was a well-loved addition to the air waves. Older Berliners in particular were reminded of secretly listening to "enemy broadcasts". Meanwhile *SFB, RIAS* and private radio stations with similar formats have pushed *AFN* down the ratings list.

Stepping out at **Onkel-Toms-Hütte** U-Bahn station (U2) a rewarding experience awaits you at the *Waldhaus* restaurant (Onkel-Tom-Straße 50, open daily 5pm-1am, Tel. 813 75 75). The grilled sausage and steaks in its lovely beer garden are a little expensive, but the atmosphere helps you overlook that.

The final station on Line U2 is **Krumme Lanke.** The **Haus am Waldsee** (Argentinische Allee 30, Tue-Sun 10am-6pm, Tel. 807 22 34) lies in a very beautiful location, and regularly holds excellent art exhibitions. Fischerhüttenstraße leads past Waldfriede Hospital to the huge forested area of Grunewald.

Grunewald

Beside the well-used *AVUS* expressway runs the environmentally sensible alternative S-Bahn Line 3. This line connects the inner city with the south-western forest areas. The first station "in the countryside" is *Grunewald*. It marks the transition from the residential areas to the pure forest areas. The S-Bahn's carriages are large enough to carry a bicycle, giving you the opportunity to explore

Grunewald in comfort on a saddle. The paths are often very rough, so it is inadvisable to take a bicycle with thin tires. It is possible to hire bicycles and tandems from the S-Bahn station, at the Schmetterlingsplatz exit. Weekends and holidays between 10am and 7pm (Tel. 811 58 29). Longer-term hire is also possible.

The Grunewald S-Bahn station is an ideal starting point for a tour of the Berlin Forest. If you head westwards, you can get to *Teufelsberg* over a number of routes. In the east there are the first villa areas and then the chain of lakes leading to Wannsee.

From under the *AVUS* Neue Schildhornweg begins at Schmetterlingsplatz and leads over a fairly even surface to *Teufelssee*. The striking chimney-stack which disturbs the wooded skyline belongs to the former **Wasserwerk am Teufelssee** (waterworks), which was put out of commission in 1969. The building was erected as early as 1871. From here the southern districts of Berlin were provided with drinking water. Today *Ökowerk* (Tel. 305 20 41) has moved into the old boiler-house and holds regular presentations on environmental protection. Teufelssee is naturally also a popular lake for swimming. On sultry summer nights there are often swimming parties held there.

From the lake it is a short distance to **Teufelsberg,** the highest point in Berlin. The hill is made of rubble from the Second World War. This part of war-damaged Berlin was set aside after 1950 as an 85 hectare park and has been continuously planted. Teufelsberg is not only visited by hikers, but in summer by kite flyers and model airplane pilots too. In winter tobogganers and skiers hurl themselves down at what is in Berlin terms "breakneck" speeds. Berlin's typical delusions of grandeur have not left Teufelsberg untouched. In connection with the 750th anniversary celebrations, a world cup ski competition took place on Teufelsberg. Attracted by fat fees, the best skiers in the world came down the artificial snow brought here specially on the day. But for an excursion site with a wonderful view over the city and plenty of greenery, Teufelsberg is still a justified favorite.

If you set aside half a day, you can enjoy an excellent walk from Teufelssee along the **Havel River beach.** Schildhornweg leads, well-signposted, as far as Havelchausee. Schildhorn is a small picturesque island, favored by Berliners as a weekend retreat, and

for its good food. The *Schildhorn* (Am Schildhorn 4a, open daily 10am-12pm, Tel. 304 04 63) is certainly one of the most beautifully-located restaurants in Berlin. The old traditions of bringing your own chair, and coffee being brewed at your table are long gone. The prices are well-adjusted to the well stuffed wallets of the clientele who find their way here. Beside the restaurant there are some particularly attractive, spray-painted remnants of the Wall.

If you feel like having lunch or drinking coffee on a *pleasure boat,* then the *Alte Liebe* (open daily 11am-11pm, in winter 12am-11pm, Tel. 304 82 58) is for you. This unseaworthy pleasure barge has lain for a number of years tied to a post, out of operation. It waits for guests wanting to enjoy the evening sky over the Havel. The post lies north of Schildhorn.

Along the shore of the Havel you should not overlook the path south towards the *Grunewaldturm* (open daily from 10am). The architect responsible for this viewing tower, erected in 1897 and originally called *Kaiser-Wilhelm-Turm*, also designed the *Kaiser-Wilhem-Gedächtniskirche* in the city. The view is worth the climb.

Only a few minutes away lies the *Lieper Bucht* with a lovely sandy beach and the little *Lindwerder Island*. There is a restaurant on the island where you can refresh yourself (open daily from 10am, Tel. 803 65 84).

Going back to the Grunewald S-Bahn station, you can start to explore the Berlin forest in a southerly direction. First you will have to cross an elegant villa quarter. The beauty of the buildings on the right and left of Fontanestraße and later *Königsallee* invite you to linger a little. The so-called villa colony of Grunewald was founded in 1890 and quickly became the favored residential area of the well-to-do. As Berlin's inner city became a business district and the quality of life decreased, the city's rich moved to the edge of Grunewald. Villas were built close together, one ever more ostentatious and well-appointed than the other. This has led to the developmet of an elite quarter, in which the inhabitants keep to themselves and spend their time among their own kind. The "Rot-Weiß" tennis club, founded in the early days, is a good example of this elitism. Every year the stadium at *Hundekehlesee* hosts the German international women's tennis championship. Those who are or want to be "in" meet in *Landhaus Bott* (Königsallee 56, open daily from 10am,Tel. 826 15 23).

Königsallee leads north directly to Kurfürstendamm and southwards to Grunewald itself and its lake. The paths are well sign-posted, so it's easy to find one's way.

At the *Naturschutzgebiet Hundekehlefenn,* a nature reserve, you can leave the busy Königsallee and travel along a small canal as far as the northern end of *Grunewald*

Lake. Circling the lake takes, depending on your walking speed, roughly an hour. Unfortunately the waters and their surroundings have suffered considerably in recent years. The reason lies primarily in air pollution, which has also affected the trees in this area. This aside, the Grunewaldsee is where many people go for their summer walks. A number of dog bathing spots make bathing in the muddy water even less attractive. Nude swimming is permitted at the so-called "Bullenwinkel" (bull corner).

The *Jagdschloß (Hunting Lodge) Grunewald* has also seen better days. It was built in 1542 in the Renaissance style and since then has often been rebuilt and extended. The museum, with a considerable painting gallery, can be viewed Tue-Sun between 10am and 6pm (Admission: 2.50/1.50 DM, Tel. 813 35 97). Close to the lake you can enjoy a well-earned rest in the beer-garden at *Forsthaus Paulsborn* (Tue-Sat 11am-11pm,Sun 9am-11pm, Tel. 813 80 10).

Crossing Hüttenweg, you will now have reached the swampy *Naturschutzgebiet (Nature Reserve) Langes Luch.* The sound of machine gun fire, which echoes through the forest regularly, comes from a training ground belonging to the US Army. The Army often holds simulated battles on its military reserve.

Again you have to cross a street and continue along Rietmeisterfenn, until you reach *Krumme Lanke* and finally *Schlachtensee*. Both lakes can be circled along beautiful paths. But it is also worth making the occasional detour into the thick Berlin forest. If you've had enough, you can head citywards from either Krumme Lanke U-Bahn station (U2) or Schlachtensee S-Bahn station (S1).

On lovely summer days, especially in the school holidays, fun-seeking city folk crowd into the Nikolassee S-Bahn station (S1 & S3) and escape towards **Wannsee Bathing Resort.** As you step out of the station and follow the crowd, you'll notice the many gleaming motor cycles and their riders, who meet at the stand up "Spinnerbrücke" cafe. The path through the forest is called Wannseebadweg and leads to the bathing resort (open daily 7am-8pm, adults 3 DM, concession 1.50, Tel. 803 54 50).

The bathing resort is a Berlin excursion site as essential to the city as Müggelsee in the East. Hundreds of beach umbrellas and deck chairs stand on a 1,000 metre stretch of sand. Music blares from portable radios and everywhere smells of potato salad and *Piz Buin*. The Wannsee terraces are good for loitering and a cool beer. If you want to put aside the very last piece of cloth while sun-bathing, you can disappear behind a fence which protects you from voyeuristic eyes. The completely fearless even go in the water...

Wannsee

Once again an S-Bahn station is the ideal departure point for an exploration of this area. *Wannsee* is the terminus of Lines S1 and S3. From here trains and buses also travel towards Potsdam and other excursion sites. But above all this is where the steamboats depart for their trips on the Wannsee and the Havel. Voyages to Potsdam (past Kladow, Pfaueninsel, Moorlake and the Glienicker Bridge) are also offered in cooperation with the *Weißen Flotte* (White Fleet). The waterway to the inner city, either to Kottbusser Bridge in Kreuzberg or to the Kongresshalle, can be used by taking the Landwehr canal journey. Information about departure times and tours can be obtained from the following shipping companies: *Heinz Riedel* (Tel. 691 37 82, 693 46 46), *Bruno Winkler* (Tel. 391 70 10, 391 70 70) or the *Stern- und Kreisschiffahrt* (Tel. 803 10 55, 803 87 50).

A pleasure spot always has a garden restaurant. At Wannsee station it is the *Loretta am Wannsee* (open daily 9am-1am, Tel. 803 51 56). It has a huge beer garden, but you can also sit inside and be served some fancy food (very good baked camembert).

Volkspark Klein-Glienicke (Little Glienicke Public Park) - Glienicker Brücke (Glienicker Bridge)

Bus No. 6 connects Wannsee station to Berlin's outer suburbs and Potsdam. For decades **Glienecke Brücke** was characterised as the "Brücke der Einheit" - Unity Bridge. This title was only rightfully restored after 9 November 1989. Many Berliners and Potsdammers use the now open route over Glienecke Lake to visit the other side. The volume of traffic during the initial euphoria at times produced chaotic situations, with long waits and endless traffic jams. Before the opening of the Wall only representatives of the "protective powers" and occasionally spies being exchanged could pass over the bridge.

The **Volkspark Klein-Glienecke** is part of an architectural concept with the *Schloß Sanssouci* in Potsdam. From a number of viewpoints you can see as far as Potsdam. For a long period the park, established between 1824 and 1850, was neglected and its significance unrecognised. The **Schloß Klein-Glienecke** stood on this spot, until it was rebuilt according to the wishes of *Prince Karl von Preußen* in 1826. The landscape gardener *Lenné*, among others, was responsible for the layout of the park. It is well worth taking an extended walk through the expansive grounds. As soon as you walk through the richly decorated gate you will be captivated by the park's atmosphere. The fountain with the golden lions and the surrounding colonnades remind you of their Italian models. The castle at the moment can only to be viewed from the outside. But it cannot be too long before the castle's interior restorations are complete and it is made accessible to the public.

The casino in Rococo-style is just as interesting as the "sailor's home" or the hunting lodge (the association for former drug addicts *SYNANON* - a pottery workshop with shop - is housed here). It is worth taking time to discover the park's full beauty.

Just a short walk along the Havel brings you to the departure point for the trip to **Pfaueninsel** (Peacock Island). Heavy smokers should secure their dose of nicotine before leaving, as the island is a nature reserve and smoking is strictly prohibited. The reserve is especially well protected and cared for. The island's peacocks have absolute "right of way" on all the paths. To avoid frightening them you are not allowed to leave the established paths.

Lenné once again had an artistic hand in the layout of the island park, but his influence was only felt after 1822. Before that the romantic little island was acquired by *Friedrich Wilhelm II* and he had it fashioned for his entertainment. The castle looks like a ruin. This impression was deliberate, corresponding to the romantic fantasy of the royal mistress.

Back to reality, you can either turn into the *Wirtshaus zur Pfaueninsel* tavern (Tel. 805 22 25) or let Bus No. 66 carry you to Wannsee.

Accommodation:
●*Hotel Alte Fischerhütte* (Fischerhüttenstr. 136, 1-37; 50/80 DM; Tel. 801 70 92)
●*Hotel Haus Leopold* (Fischerhüttenstr. 113, 1-37; 70/120 DM; Tel. 813 29 64)
●*Hotel Forsthaus Paulsborn* (Am Grunewaldsee, 1-33; 90/140 DM; Tel. 813 80 10)
●*Landhaus Schlachtensee* (Bogotastr. 9, 1-37; 115/165 DM; Tel. 816 00 60)
●*Studentenhotel Hubertusallee* (Delbrückstr. 24, 1-33; 50/60 DM, 35/40 DM for students; Tel. 891 97 18)
●*Appartements Schlachtensee* (Eiderstedter Weg 43b, 1-37; 80/120 DM; Tel. 801 76 66)

Spandau

In the beginning there was Spandau, then came Berlin - no matter how trite this remark may be, it's true!

The historical fact that Spandau's town charter precedes that of Berlin gives this district a special status. Today it is unusual to see Spandauers as separate from the Berlin population, although they themselves will occasionally assert it proudly. In fact the 201,915 inhabitants (31/12/87), among them 18,583 foreigners, on the west bank of the Havel are well integrated with Berlin life.

Spandau is happy to see itself as the real capital of the area. Close contacts exist with Nauen, until 1988 linked as a partner town. Since the opening of the border, the links with the 48 municipalities beyond the Spandau forest, apparently never completely severed, are being carefully restored.

The atmosphere of Berlin's second largest district (in terms of geographical size) conveys a noticeable sense of history. This historical presence can be felt more here than in any other district. Three stone buildings rise above the inner city and remind you of the old days: the *St Nicholas church* on Reformationsplatz, the town hall, and the citadel, a typical example of the High Renaissance.

The partly restored old town is worth visiting not only for the historically-inclined. Nonetheless a few **historical remarks** here. The

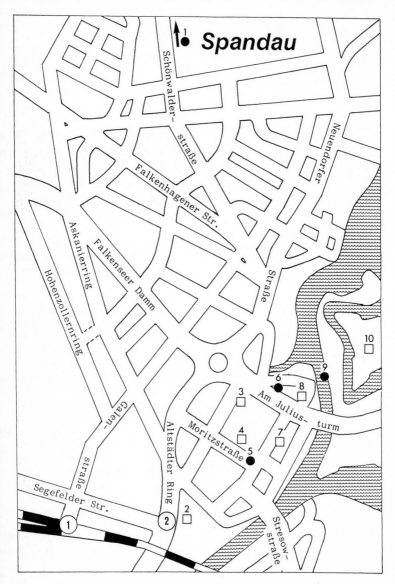

Spandau

area occupied today by Spandau was settled very early, largely because of its strategic location. It lies at the intersection of the two rivers, the Spree and the Havel. Archaeological finds indicate human habitation long before the beginning of written history. During the extensive trading activity of the *Mark of Brandenburg* in the 12th century, "Spandow", as it was then known (until 1878), lay on the trading route to Poland. Spandau acquired the rights of a town in 1230.

As the significance of the two trading settlements Cölln and Berlin increased over the centuries, so that of Spandau sank. The double town was equipped with economic power (lobbying is not a new problem). It soon controlled the supplies to the whole surrounding area and ultimately all of the foreign trade. Spandau was left only with the route to the fortress and garrison town.

With the commencement of the *citadel* in 1557 Spandau, the site of former castles and fortresses (since

the 13th century), was given a purely military function. The unfortunate citizens of the surrounding towns had to finance the building of the citadel. It was built in the style of a "neo-Italian fortress art". The first serfs moved in in 1580. To this day Spandau has not broken free of its status as a garrison town, almost all the units of the British "protective power" are stationed in Spandau.

The *Thirty Years War* (1618-1648) extracted new sacrifices from the Spandau population. Not only did they have to pay increased war taxes, they also had to provide private accommodation for soldiers. Today you can still see in some houses in the old town the attic constructed for the accommodation of soldiers. Over the course of the *Thirty Years War* the Spandauers suffered great hardship. On top of the war deaths there came the Great Plague, which reached its dreadful climax in 1637. On the order of the

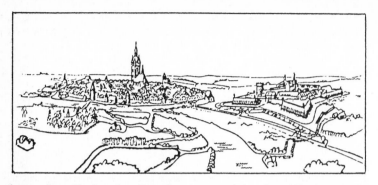

then ruling Elector the Spandau Council was forced to nail up the houses of plague victims and mark them with white crosses.

Spandau's history from then on continued to be closely connected with a war economy. Existing plans to extend the citadel were never realised, but the local **armaments industry** with powder and arms factories laid the foundations of Spandau's industrial character. (The height difference between the upper and lower Havel was enough to produce the water power required for heavy industry.)

A regulation forbidding building on the open space surrounding the citadel, as well as Spandau's status as a fortress town, established in 1873, led to an increasing isolation from its surroundings and especially from Berlin. The arms factory, from 1854 under the control of the State, continued production until 1919. Further armaments factories arose. Weapons production around the citadel increased as a result of the First World War. With the loss of the

war and the demobilisation regulations laid down in the Treaty of Versailles, these factories moved towards "peaceful production".

A cry of dismay arose from the Spandau population when the town was made part of Greater Berlin in 1920. People found it a great injustice that the tax income of industrial Spandau no longer flowed into their own treasury, but into that of Greater Berlin. Against all protests Spandau became Berlin's 8th municipality. Today most Spandauers are happy this step took place, as they would otherwise have become part of the GDR and would have led a very different life.

The years after the *First World War* were marked by massive unemployment and housing shortages. Emergency projects like the construction of parks had to be undertaken, as civil production could not reach the previous levels of activity of the armaments industry.

The 1929 world economic crisis was a considerable setback for the successful interventions of the

Social Democrats, who governed from 1921. In the elections to the district parliament in 1929 the *National Socialists* (Nazis) almost achieved an absolute majority of seats. With their seizure of power in 1933 the life of the Spandauer changed once more.

The district's infrastructure became an important factor in the development of the *Third Reich*. Arms production received new blood. Forced labour and concentration-camp prisoners were often used as workers. Pure **industrial quarters** arose, like *Siemensstadt*, where a large proportion of Berlin's production is still located. Naturally these industrial areas were prime targets during the air raids of the *Second World War*. The dismantling of Spandau's industrial sites after 1945 caused just as much damage as the bombing during the war. The destruction of large residential areas and transport routes were, alongside the supply of water, gas and electricity, the main problems of the post-war years.

In summer 1945 Spandau was put under the control of the British. Once again the existing military infrastructure could be put to a new use. Extensive rebuilding programs for the location of industrial sites and the reconstruction of residential areas again made Spandau the largest industrial district. It also had the most forested and leisure areas in West Berlin. This economic strength and the fact that the district is essential for Berlin's energy supply and rubbish disposal has given Spandau a new self-confidence.

The population is more stable here than in other districts, the fluctuation in inhabitants is minimal, once a Spandauer, always a Spandauer. The fact that the district is often seen as a cultural desert bothers almost no-one, you can always go into town for frenetic city life. In addition the extension of U-Bahn Line 7 in 1984 provided a fast connection to the inner city districts.

Politically Spandau is governed by an absolute majority of the *SPD* in local government. Not insignificant is the number of radical right-wing *Republicans*, who gained 6.7% of the vote in 1989.

Tour of Spandau's Old Town

"Rathaus Spandau" is the terminus of U-Bahn Line 7. Directly opposite the station is the town hall (Carl-Schurz-Str. 2-6) with its busy, modern forecourt. The town hall marks the southern end of the old town. From here buses travel to the outer districts and to the Spandau Forest. More recently buses have been able to travel to Spandau's partner town, Nauen and also Falkensee, beyond the former border.

The **town hall** was built between 1910 and 1913 *"by the citizenry under the rule of Kaiser Wilhelm II"* as the inscription on the town hall's coat of arms explains. The ostentatious building says something about the affluence and also the arrogance of Spandauers before the First World

War. The 72m high tower of the seat of government is no longer accessible to visitors. It would provide a good view over the old town. Towards the end of the Second World War the town hall suffered heavy damage and was rebuilt in the 1950s. The work of local artists is presented in the exhibition hall (2nd floor). Directly beside it you can plan the rest of your tour over a model of the old town.

Information about sights and Spandau itself is available in the *Pressestelle Bezirksamt Spandau* (Spandau District Information Center) (Room 160, Tel. 33 03 24 03) during office hours.

German food is served in the *Ratskeller* at the southern end of the town hall (Tue-Sat 10am-12pm, Mon 4pm-12pm; Tel. 333 39 78).

Leaving the town hall square, following the so-called 'Mühlengraben' (mill ditches), you will get to the remains of the old town wall. The wall used to circle the whole of the old town. It was first built in 1319 and, in contrast to more modern walls, always fulfilled its function.

Carl-Schurz-Straße connects the town hall with Reformationsplatz. What used to be Klosterstraße and Potsdamer Straße were renamed after *Carl Schurz*. Schurz was an important figure in the revolution of 1848 and later in America's struggle for freedom. Today it is one of the two important shopping streets in Spandau's old town.

The medieval town center and its historic (timbered) buildings from the 18th and 19th centuries are treated with great care. As well as war damage, irresponsible town planning has sacrificed many former houses and shops. But there is still evidence of architecture worth protecting, such as the baroque **Burger** (citizen) **House** at No. 16 in the pedestrian zone leading to St Nikolas' Church. House No. 31, at the intersection between Carl-Schurz and Moritzstraße, was the corner of the former **Spandau Workhouse.** In 1581 a palace was built here, which was transformed in 1686 into a workhouse by the *Great Elector*, and used as such until 1897. This was also where the poet *Gottfried Kinkel* was held for his revolutionary activities. At No 41, which originates from the second half of the 17th century, rustic meals are served in the *Räucherkammer* (open daily 11am-11pm, Tel. 333 44 08).

In recent years **Reformationsplatz,** with **St Nikolas' Church** looking out over it, has been the site of extensive restoration work to maintain its historic character. The gothic church was built in the first half of the 15th century, on the spot where a church is said to have stood as early as 1200. The year 1539 marks the conversion of most Spandauers to the Protestant faith, which the then *Elector Joachim II* followed. A statue is dedicated to him in front of the church.

In the more recent past, before and during the Nazi regime, *Martin Albertz*, brother of the former go-

verning mayor, was pastor of the parish. As a member of the *Confessional Church*, which constituted the opposition to the Nazis' assimilation of the Church, he was often imprisoned.

St Nikolas' Church was robbed of its high tower (once 77.5 meters) by an air raid in 1944, and given a provisional new covering. On the first floor of the tower there is a small exhibition on the history of the church. Inside the church the baptisimal font is particularly worth viewing. It dates from the year 1398 and shows four evangelists carrying the bronze basin on their shoulders. The Renaissance altar dates from the year 1582, but the organ is much younger (1956).

In the process of assessing Reformationsplatz for new building work, a number of discoveries from Spandau's early days were made. **Reformationsplatz No. 3** stands on the foundations of a Dominican monastery from the 13th century. Through a glass panel you can see the remains of the monastery's wall some 2 meters below street level. Before the monastery's cemetery was built over it yielded a skeleton and some Slavic jewelry from the 12th century. Today you can absorb the historical character of this spot in the *Altstadt-Café*.

Continuing along Carl-Schurz-Straße, you will find a lively establishment in the **Kant-Gymnasium** (High School). The *Volksbühne Variante* (performances: Tue,Sat 8pm, Tel. 333 43 73) presents mainstream plays, but for a mature audience.

Straße Am Juliusturm divides the busy and partly modernised area of the old town from the more northerly areas of **Kolk** and **Behnitz.** Small angular houses, cobblestone pavements and quaint little bridges make up this area's charm.

If you cross the seven-lane road, you end up on **Hoher Steinweg.** At No. 7, the former fire station, lies the *Restaurant Kolk*. At the end of the street there are the remains of the old town fortifications from the first half of the 14th century.

Opposite, in the *Vladi im Kolk* restaurant (Hoher Steinweg 5, Tue-Sat 4pm-11pm, Sun 11:30am-10pm, Tel. 336 61 85), you can eat in a historical atmosphere at reasonable prices.

The Hoher Steinweg runs into a small street called **Damm**. *Elector Joachim II* had a fishing village built here for the inhabitants from the area designated for the citadel. Some houses have been restored and look as good as new. The original fishing rights granted by the Elector are still in force today.

At the end of the Damm lies **Spandauer Schleuse** (Spandau Sluices). These were put into operation in 1910 and since then have connected the Upper and Lower Havel. Every year almost 40,000 boats and ships queue up for the sluices, which operate for 17 hours a day during the summer months. Along the Havel you can walk or cycle along newly-laid paths.

In **Behnitz street**, with a view over the sluices, stands a late baroque house, built in 1770. The composer *W. Heinemann* lived for a number of years here.

Built in 1847/48 as a Catholic church in the style of a basilica, the **St. Marien Church** lies at the end of the small Behnitz cul-de-sac.

Spandau's oldest section, **Kolk**, is commemorated in the name of an angular cobblestone street. Pastel colored house fronts alternate with more historic facades. The *Kolkschänke* at No. 3 is an old soldier's tavern, built around 1743.

Past the painted houses the route leads via a small meadow back to Straße Am Juliusturm.

Continuing along Havelstraße, and past Reformationsplatz, you will reach **Breite Straße**, another pedestrian zone in the old town. To reach Breite Straße by U-Bahn, exit at the Altstadt Spandau station. The **Second World War** has left its enduring mark here, as almost 50% of the historic buildings were destroyed. This means that at first glance Breite Straße looks very modern. You would never suspect that **No. 32** is the oldest residential property in West Berlin. After extensive debate the late Gothic building was faithfully restored and in the future it will be used as a cultural center.

No. 20 is worth seeing for its classical facade and the so-called bat windows. It also houses the *Bistro Bonaparte*, a French restaurant (open daily 12am-12pm, Tel. 333 17 09). The bistro acquired its name because Napoleon once spent a night in the house. The menu regularly includes a *Huhn Marengo* (Marengo Chicken), prepared as in Napoleon's day.

To the right and left of this lively shopping street many small alleys branch off. One of these, Wasserstraße, meets the Havel. It offers a view of the loading cranes along the shore and the industrial areas on the other side of the Havel. The Lindenufer promenade is ideal for walks along the Havel. A memorial plaque is a reminder of the darker days in Spandau's more recent history. At Lindenufer 12 stands the Jewish community's synagogue, erected in an oriental style in 1895. During the pogrom of 9 November 1938 the synagogue was set alight and destroyed. Four years later it was completely demolished.

Fischerstraße runs parallel to Breite Straße. **Fischerstraße No. 26** was built in 1760 in a baroque style and, like the two neighboring houses, only recently restored. At No. 28 a small passageway leads to an old courtyard. The *Galerie und Goldschmiede Spandow*, housed in a former stable, prepares the finest **jewelry** (Mon-Fri 10am-6pm, Sat 10am-1pm).

For a typical Berlin snack it is worth visiting the *Kupferpfanne* at Marktstr. 3. The meat rolls are called "hamburgers", but the interior is traditional, like the service.

Marktgasse (previously Nagelgasse, and before that Strippe) contains timbered houses from the early 19th century as well as Art Nouveau-style houses.

In recent years Spandau's old town **Marktplatz** (market place) has almost been restored to its old self. Most of the old buildings were destroyed by air raids, but as early as the 1950s a start was made on reconstructing the intersection of Moritz- and Mönchstraße. The old tradition of an open-air market was also revived. The "Land- und Bauern-Markt" enjoys as much popularity in late summer as the annual Christmas Market with many cultural offerings and arts and crafts stalls.

Historical Tours of Spandau's old town are available between May and October (every Thu and Sat at 4pm, they start in front of St. Nicholas's Church at Reformationsplatz; information Wed 9am-12am and Thu

12am-2pm on 333 30 00; tickets are on sale 30 minutes before the start of the tour, adults 5 DM, children 2 DM).

Accommodation
in the old town:
● *Hotel Herbst* (Moritzstr. 21, 1-20, 80/140 DM; Tel. 333 40 32/33)
● *Hotel Benn* (Ritterstr. 1a + 15, 1-20, 55/73 DM; Tel. 333 10 61)
● *Hotel Altstadt Spandau* (Wasserstr. 4 + 8, 1-20, double from 140 DM; Tel. 333 62 64 or 333 45 88)

close to the old town:
● *Pension Spandau West* (Staakener Str. 87, 1-20, 48/85 DM; Tel. 333 60 21)
● *Hotelpension Kallmeyer* (Seegefelder Str. 75, 1-20, 60/85 DM; Tel. 333 22 72)

The Citadel

Leaving the old town along Straße Am Juliusturm, you will see the huge *Spandauer Citadel* fortress from far away. Over the citadel bridge and then through the gatehouse, you enter the historic inner courtyard of the fortress, built in the style of the high Renaissance. This Brandenburgian/Prussian fortress with four bastions was built between the years 1590 and 1594. It stands at the confluence of the Spree and the Havel.

In the course of time the citadel has served many purposes. It has been a fortification against Berlin's attackers; state prison; shelter for the Royal family; storehouse for the

treasure given by France to Prussia as war reparation, and during the Second World War as an army gas laboratory. The Nazis' stores of poison gas have recently brought the fortress back into the headlines. There are fears that there are still undiscovered stores, and the installation, especially the *Bastion Brandenburg*, was temporarily closed to the public. The search has since come to an end, but because of restoration work not all the citadel's buildings can be viewed.

The **Juliusturm** (Julius Tower) has become Spandau's trademark. From its viewing platform, 30 meters high, you get a wonderful view over the old town and, on a clear day, to Berlin. Between 1874 and 1919 the tower held the war reparations, 120 million marks in gold coins. Early in the 1980s the *Bastion Königin*, with the **Zeughaus** (armory), was restored. The **Stadtgeschichtliche Museum Spandau** (Spandau Historical Museum), which presents the district's history, is housed in the **Palas**, an old Gothic building. On weekends between 10:30am and 3pm there are tours of the whole site. They explain an important part of Berlin's history in a not too-tiresome way. The citadel can also be visited every day 9am-5pm, except Mon.

An evening meal in the *Zitadellen Schänke* (open daily except Mon 10am-12pm, Tel. 324 21 06) is a particular delight. The meal is served in historic vaults.

The grounds which surround the citadel moat invite you to a walk or a visit to the **Freilichtbühne** (open-air theater). The theater offers mainstream and children's entertainment and music performances.

Town Forest

The **Spandau Forest** covers 1,163 hectares or 4.5 sq. miles. The two forest areas Hakenfelde and Radeland used to be divided from neighboring Nauen by the Wall. Now people from all over Berlin come here for their Sunday stroll. This forest is immeasurably important for the rest and relaxation of the city's population. With its **nature reserves,** *Teufelsbruch, Großer* and *Kleiner*

Rohrpfuhl and the *Kuhlake* it is one of the most beautiful of Berlin's excursion sites. Pines make up 60% of the trees, followed by oaks (20%) and larch trees (5%). The variety of plants and animals (75% of bird varieties in Berlin) is the highest of all Berlin's forest areas.

Until the end of the 18th century pigs grazed in the forest. Even today it is possible to come across a wandering wild pig or red deer. To be quite sure of seeing something you should begin with a tour of the wildlife preserve at the Hakenfelde gamekeeper's house.

Berlin's generally high level of pollution naturally doesn't spare the Spandau forest. A large proportion of the trees are damaged by pollution. To limit the impact of air pollution, the Berlin Senate introduced the so-called *"healthy forest program"* in 1983. In this program the type of tree appropriate to a particu-

lar location is selected carefully. A stable mixture of trees is encouraged, and early, moderate and repeated reforestation is undertaken. All this doesn't prevent air pollution, but it is hoped that it will limit the future damage by increasing the trees' resistance. Throughout the forest the representatives of particular types of tree are indicated with colored markings. They have been selected according to their degree of representativeness and are under special, scientific observation.

The following suggestions for hikes through the Spandau forest are taken from a publication put out by the Senator for City Development and Environmental Protection, ***Berliner Wanderblatt Nr. 5:***

A hike through forests and fields
(red tree markings):

From the final bus stop on Line 54 it is only a few steps to the **Wildlife Preserve** by the Hakenfelde gamekeeper's house. If you follow the red (and for half the distance, the green) tree markings, the 9km round trip will open up the many varied features of the Spandau forest.

Along the **Kuhlake** the path is very broad and continues north for some way. The Kuhlake, together with many ditches in the forest, used to be important for the drainage of the forest. Today it is the other way around: water pumped into the Kuhlake from the Havel preserves

the Radeland area, which has lain dry for decades. It ensures the necessary supply of groundwater. This part of the Spandau forest is one of the great "reservoirs" of Berlin's water supply.

Very soon the forest fades away - it opens out into an ever-wider meadow, which the Kuhlake snakes through. At the edge of the meadow there are woods of pine, oak and birch.

The small birds one comes across include the *Eisvogel*, which long ago made this area home. In spring you cannot avoid hearing the "concert" of countless frogs.

Very abruptly, the Kuhlake disappears again into the forest. Oaks, birches, linden trees, maples and elms together with many coniferous trees make a dense roof over your head. At a watering-hole the drainage ditches swing to the east and west away from the Kuhlake. The Kuhlake flows through richly varied woods to the North. In spring thousands of wood-anemone cover the forest floor here.

Soon you will see some benches under some old birch trees, this is a good place to take a rest. It is only a few meters further to the northern outskirts of town. Our path takes us back to the south through corn fields and meadows and then disappears into a dense pine forest and meets a bridge over the drainage ditches. Then begins a dense, dark spruce forest. Subsequently it passes by the newly-established ponds of the Kuhlake system. This area cannot be entered, as waterbirds and other animals - especially amphibians - are being encouraged to settle here. Along the way there are a number of benches at the edge of the lake. The last stretch is governed by pine forests, in part impenetrable and thus protective of the wildlife. Eventually the view to Kuhlake opens out, and after crossing a few dunes and small hills you return to the starting point.

A hike from Oberjägerweg to Kuhlake

A hike designed for car drivers. It starts from the parking lot at the intersection of Schönwalder Allee and Oberjägerweg. This 6 km long round trip runs first to the north, through a dense pine wood along a narrow path to the fields surrounding the forest. Then through an oak forest to the Kuhlake.

From here the path, now marked in red, continues north. After the pine forest which follows the bridge over the cross ditches, a connecting path leads eastwards to the Kuhlake. After a short distance south, the path turns at an old oak tree to the east. Through a varied forest you soon return to Oberjägerweg.

On all walks you should at all times observe the following:

●Smoking is only allowed in the forest between November and the end of February!
●Nature reserves are never to be entered, the only exceptions being specially marked paths!
●To protect the plants and animals you should not leave the paths!

Zigzagging through the center (Mitte)
(*Lutz Göllner*)

It is easy to find Paris or Rome more beautiful than Berlin. This is partly because most of the historic buildings in these other capital cities have been left standing.

Berlin, this artificially constructed capital of a German Empire which did not exist until 1871, has destroyed itself three times. The building boom of the foundation years turned Berlin into one of Europe's largest capitals, but it also destroyed many

historic locations. And what the bombing raids of the Second World War left standing was soon taken care of by the building programs of both East and West Berlin in the 1950s.

Paradoxically it was *Karl Friedrich Schinkel*, Berlin's chief architect in the period after the wars of liberation, who most effectively destroyed old Berlin. Even then, as the fortress moats at Lustgarten were being filled in, the building boom of the foundation years was just a process of elaboration. Architecture inspired only by history. Suddenly there were buildings in Berlin which looked like Roman temples. Style became something exchangeable.

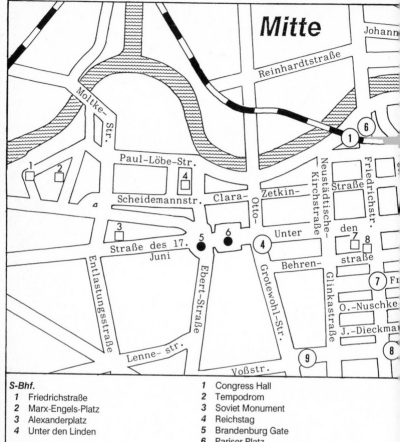

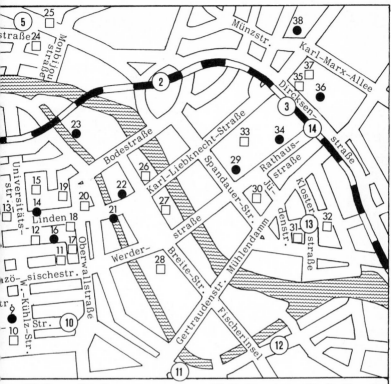

17	German State Opera	**32** Zur letzten Instanz (The Final Appeal)
18	Opera Café/The Crown Prince's Palace	**33** St. Marienkirche
19	New Watch/today War-Memorial	**34** Television Tower
20	Armory/today Museum of German History	**35** Department Store Central
21	Marx-Engels-Bridge	**36** Alexanderplatz
22	Lustgarten	**37** Hotel Stadt Berlin
23	Museum Island	**38** Scheunen Quarter
24	Main Post Office	
25	Synagogue	
26	Berlin Cathedral	
27	Former Palace of the Republic	
28	Former Parliament Building	
29	Neptune Fountain	
30	Red City Hall	
31	Old City Hall	

The old, beautiful Berlin can still be found in the Mitte district. It was from this district that the twin city of Berlin and Cölln grew, and also where the arrogance of the *German Reich* manifested itself most clearly. Here, between Potsdamer and Alexander Platz was where life raged in the 1920s. On the edges of this former city the Nazis set up their terror stations. These were to form the architectural foundations of the planned capital *Germania*. And here too was where the communists erected monuments of exemplary hideousness.

As I said, it is easy to find a beautiful quarter in Paris or Rome. In Berlin you have to search for such spots, but then that does give them some charm. Perhaps the visitor will agree with *Heinrich Heine*, who described the view over the old center from Unter den Linden: "Really, I know of no more imposing sight, as that looking from the Hundebrücke towards den Linden...one magnificent building after the other."

A roundtrip

The roundtrip begins at **Alexanderplatz.** Once upon a time this was the pulsating center of city life, day and night. Sadly where the market halls and the main police station once stood, today stands a huge lump of concrete. Surrounded by the new *Hotel Stadt Berlin* skyscraper and the square-shaped *"Centrum Warenhauses" Kauf am Alex* (Central Department Store), the square

generates one thing: boredom. **Karl Marx Allee/ Frankfurter Allee** joins Alexanderplatz from the northeast, and is totally Stalinist in architectural style. During the day there are crowds of people, but at night you get the feeling you've wandered onto the set of a bad science-fiction film.

Named after *Tsar Alexander* in 1805 (on the occasion of a friendship pact between Prussia and Russia), this square has never had the big city elegance of the other squares in the Mitte district. The Berlin doctor and writer *Alfred Döblin* described it particularly well in *Berlin Alexanderplatz*. The novel's fragmented montage style finds its architectural equivalent in the combination of U- and S-Bahn stations. The station is

where *Franz Biberkopf*, the "hero" of German history, pursued his shifty business. Even professional Berliners can get lost here.

If you're thirsty already, you can turn into the *Hotel Stadt Berlin* (Alexanderplatz, hall bar: open daily 10am-12pm, life bar: open daily 10pm-5am, Tel. 9-21 90) where there are some reasonable bars.

North of the Alex lies the **Scheunenviertel (Scheunen quarter)**, which used to be a little like the *Marais* in Paris. Still outside the city gates in the 19th century, it offered intitial shelter for refugees from the countryside. Towards the beginning of this century increasing numbers of eastern Jews, fleeing from the Polish pogroms, came to the thriving capital. They also found shelter in

the Scheunenviertel. But at this time the new working class suburbs of Kreuzberg, Neukölln and Prenzlauer Berg were being built. This left no room for this living ghetto.

Only a stone's throw from the Kaiser's city palace and the grand boulevard Unter den Linden, the inhabitants of the Scheunenviertel lived in impoverished conditions with appalling hygiene. The city authorities had long regarded the ghetto as a thorn in its side. At the same time, the alleys and courtyards offered ideal hideouts for all sorts of shady enterprises. With the foundation years came the beginning of its gradual demolition. Its inhabitants underwent a remarkable symbiosis: in front of butchers offering kosher meat, Berlin's prostitutes loitered; beside Jewish betting shops, infamous Berliners pursued their underworld activities.

In the "Roaring Twenties" the quarter began to change its character. The former gangster taverns were now frequented by artists like *Bertold Brecht, Gustav Gründgens, Marlene Dietrich* and *Claire Waldoff*. The popular song "Mummy, the man with the coke is here" had a completely different meaning in Scheunen.

Underneath the S-Bahn bridges you come to the second, larger part of the Alex, which no longer has anything in common with the historic Alexanderplatz. The bombing during the Second World War turned the area into an open field, whose only historic reference points are the Gothic Marienkirche (St. Marien Church) and Red City Hall.

The **Fernsehturm** (television tower), was erected in 1967-69 and is 362 meters high. It is a prime example of the concrete-plated

184

buildings typical of the former-GDR. Other examples stretch right and left from *Marx Engels Forum* as far as Spandauer and Jüdenstraße. The tower has a viewing platform and a restaurant at 204 meters. If you like, you can go up in the lift at an inflated price and eat expensive second-rate food (November-March open daily 9am-11pm, April-October 8am-11pm; last trip: viewing platform, 10:30 pm, Telecafé 10 pm, Tel. 9 212 33 33; time limits: viewing platform 30 minutes, Telecafé 60 minutes).

The **Marien Church,** built in 1250 was a part of the city extensions at the New Market. It was once surrounded by a maze of alleys, which were bombed away during the Second World War. Restored after the war, sculptures and paintings from other destroyed churches in the city were brought here. Particularly worth seeing is the Confessional Cross, which is set up inside the church's main entrance. The Berliners had to erect it in 1324, to remove the excommunication order imposed on the city by the Church. It had been imposed after a Church provost wanting to acquire political influence was helped into the hereafter (Mon-Thu 10am-12am, 1pm-5pm, tour at 1pm; Sat 12am-4:40pm; Sun 10:30am service, followed by tour).

Between the Marien Church and Red City Hall stands the **Neptun-brunnen** (Neptune Fountain), built in 1891, which once adorned Schloß-platz. The four women who sur-

round the fountain symbolise what were then Germany's main rivers, the Rhine, Elbe, Oder and Weichsel. Berliners affectionately refer to this ensemble as "the only women who could hang on to the edge."

Red City Hall is so named because of its color, and not the politics pursued here until 1990. The building was erected in 1861-69 to replace the old city hall, which had become too small. A frieze of 36 terracotta panels portraying Berlin's history to 1871 runs around the building. In the *Rathauskeller* (City Hall Cellar) you can eat a good, reasonably priced lunch (Rathausstr. 15-18, open daily to 12pm, Tel. 9-212 53 01). The heraldry room displays the coats of arms of all 23 Berlin districts, including the 12 in West Berlin and the three newly-created East Berlin districts. The 1,000 employees of the municipal authorities have to be satisfied with roughly 250 rooms. In compensation though they can use their breaks to visit the hairdresser and beautician in the same building. For nostalgia fans: Red City Hall is one of Berlin's few government buildings which still has a *paternoster*.

Behind the city hall, standing on Mühlendamm is the **Old City Hall,** originally built as an additional communal administration building. Until 1948 the Greater Berlin Municipal Authorities met here. During the blockade the Socialist Unity Party (SED) orchestrated the so-called "City Hall putsch". This resulted in the retreat of the West Berlin representatives and the formation of a separate East Berlin city government. Behind the old city hall to the east lie the only remains of the former Berlin city wall and the legendary (hence surviving) tavern, *Zur letzten Instanz* (The Final Appeal) (Waisenstr. 14/16, Mon-Sat 4pm-12pm, Tel. 9-212 55 28).

A visit to the **Klosterstraße U-Bahn station** is recommended. The patterns of the wall-tiles in the entrance halls are modelled on the "Processional Road of Babylon" in the Pergamon Museum. The whole station has been superbly renovated. One of the entrance halls has paintings of historic Berlin views (ironically all of them from the Western half). On the platform there are pictures of old types of transport as well as an old 3rd class U-Bahn carriage.

Behind the old city hall, going right and under Mühlendamm, you cross Spandauer Straße. At the corner of Eiergasse begins the **Nikolaiviertel**, popularly known as "socialist Disneyland" or "Honeckerland". As part of the 750th anniversay celebrations in 1987, the old SED leadership employed building workers from all over communist East Germany to build this structural monument.

Another socialist version of "old Berlin" can be found on Husemannstraße in Prenzlauer Berg. No wonder people from the capital were unloved in the rest of East Germany: while houses in Leipzig and Dresden fell to ruin, whole colonies of builders worked in this quarter (the term

"quarter" seems a gross exaggeration for the 40,000 square meters around the Nikolaikirche).

The main attractions are the cosy historical taverns around the Kirchplatz. At the entrance to Eiergasse stands the *Paddenwirt* (Nikolaikirchplatz 6, Mon-Sat 12am-12pm, Tel. 9 -21 71 32 33). If you go around the church you'll come to the *Nußbaum* (Am Nußbaum 3, open daily 11am-12pm, Tel. 9-212 36 37). Around the corner in Poststraße you'll find the *Gerichtslaube* (Poststr. 28, public bar open daily 11am-12pm, Tel. 9-21 71 32 02), formerly a part of the old city hall. Heading towards Mühlendamm, beside the **Handwerkmuseum** (Handicraft Museum) (Mon 1pm-7pm, Tue-Fri 10am-7pm, Sat 9am-1pm) you'll find *Rippe* (Poststr. 17, Tue-Sun 11am-10pm, Tel. 9-21 71 32 35).

If you don't feel like eating and drinking, a visit to the **Nikolaikirche** (church) is recommended (Nikolaikirchplatz, Tue-Sun 10am-5:30pm, Tel. 9-21 71 31 46). This is Berlin's oldest building, dating to around 1200. The current structure of this late-Gothic church was completed in 1470. *Karl Friedrich Schinkel* renewed the interior of the nave in 1817. Damaged during the Second World War, it has been restored perfectly and is now one of the "outdoor exhibits" of the *Märkisches Museum*. On 29 June 1990 the President of the Federal Republic of Germany, *Richard von Weizsäcker*, was awarded honorary citizenship of Greater Berlin here.

On the corner of Poststraße and Mühlendamm stands the **Ephraim Palace.** *Veitel Heine Ephraim, Friedrich II's* banker, built this house in the 18th century in the Roccoco style. The house was demolished in 1935, but the original facade remained in West Berlin until 1983. For the restoration, the facade was reinstalled, facing a different direction. In the building there is a cafe (Poststr. 16, Tue-Sun 10am-7pm, Tel. 9-21 71 31 64) and a restaurant (open daily 11am-12pm), both decorated in the baroque style. There is also a museum with constantly changing exhibitions (Tue-Sat 9am-5pm).

Going north along the River Spree, which is at its narrowest here, crossing Werderstraße and over the Rathausbrücke (City Hall Bridge),

you get to **Marx-Engels-Platz.** The central building in this square, how could it be otherwise, is the **Palast der Republik** (Palace of the Republic), the seat of the former-GDR parliament. A visit to this parliament is worthwhile if you would like to feast your eyes on the dreadful wall murals done in the "socialist realism" style. People only have ridicule left for their former government's pompous self-congratulatory building. The mirrored exterior reflecting the sunset does look quite good, but a visit to the restaurant inside only sends shivers down a visitor's spine.

Although the Berlin City Palace, the largest baroque building in Northern Germany, was only lightly damaged during the war, it was blown up in 1950. Socialist historiography has always been like this: the **Marstall** (Royal Stables) south of the Palace only owes its survival to the fact that the "Revolutionary Committee of Workers and Seamen" had a meeting there in November 1918. There is, incidentally, a very good restaurant in "Am Marstall", the *Schwalbennest*, popularly known as "Negerbusen" (Negro Bust) (Marx-Engels-Forum 23, Mon-Sun 11am-12pm, Tel. 9-212 69 19). It is vastly superior to the one in the Palast der Republik.

On the southern side of Marx-Engels-Platz stands the **Staatsratsgebäude der DDR** (Parliament Building), a new 1960s building, the facade of which incorporates the portal of the former city palace. From its balcony *Karl Liebknecht* is said to have proclaimed the *Free Socialist Republic* on 9 November 1918.

Going westwards takes you over **Schleusenbrücke,** with pictures of old Berlin set into its railings. Two of the images are of the artist *Kurt Schumacher*, who was murdered in the Plötzensee workhouse in 1942 for being part of the resistance group *Schulze-Boysen*. Left of the Werderschen Market stands a gloomy building with a sandstone facade reminiscent of Nazi architecture. Built in the 1920s, it first housed the Reichsbank, then it became the *SED's headquarters*. Today it contains only the *PDS* and other parliamentarians. The cash for Germany's monetary reunion was also kept in this building under tight security.

Directly opposite, in the Friedrichswerderschen Kirche (church), there is a museum devoted to Berlin's most important architects: the **Schinkelmuseum** (Werderstraße, Mon-Sun, 10am-6pm, Tel. 9-208 13 23).

Unter den Linden (Under the Lime Trees)

Oberwallstraße leads north to Berlin's supreme boulevard: **Unter den Linden.** The history of Berlin, Prussia and Germany is generally manifested most clearly here.

The eight groups of figures on the railings of **Schloßbrücke** (bridge), today Marx-Engels-Brücke, are also creations of the Prussian master builder *Karl Friedrich Schinkel*. At the opening of the bridge in 1823 the

Karl Friedrich Schinkel

189

Karl Joseph Lenné

Berlin landscape architect *Karl Joseph Lenné* finally restored the square to a park. The large granite bowl was erected in 1830, and it was returned to this position after the park's partial reconstruction. In 1894 *Wilhelm II* decided to finally destroy the park and to erect the new **Dom** (cathedral), a monumentally hideous building. Although it was heavily damaged during the war, in 1975 a start was made on its restoration. With the help of the German *Evangelical Churches*, the cathedral was restored in a simpler, but no more beautiful shape. The history of the Berlin cathedral and its predecessor is documented in a small exhibition (Mon-Sat 10am-5pm, Sun 12am-5pm). From 1991, when the restoration will be complete, the cathedral tomb with the stone coffins of the Prussian kings will be reopened to the public.

cast-iron railings did not exist. The crowd pressed against the wooden railings and 22 Berliners drowned in the Spree.

Beyond the Kupfergraben (a small arm of the River Spree) the now destroyed **Lustgarten** once lay. The Lustgarten had a richly varied history behind it. Constructed as early as 1573, it was left to run wild during the *Thirty Years War*. In 1647, after his return from Königsberg, the *Great Elector* had the garden rebuilt. Later it developed into Berlin's first *botanical garden*. In 1713 King *Friedrich Wilhelm 1*, later the Soldier King, turned the Lustgarten into - how could it be anything else - a drill square. The square was constantly encroached upon, first by the cathedral on the eastern side, then by the museum to the north. The

Museum Island

The Spree and the Kupfergraben surround an island, at the southern tip of which once stood the town of Cölln. In the middle stood the royal palace with the Lustgarten, and the northern tip was divided off by a moat. In 1822 the moat was filled in, and two years later work began on building the first museum. The idea behind the layout of the buildings was to adapt the Lustgarten architecturally to the symbols of Prussia. The City Palace stood for the monarchy, the Cathedral for the Protestant Church, the Armory for military power and the Old Museum for the Arts. In 1841 the development of the northern part of the island into *Museum Island* began at the order of King *Friedrich Wilhelm IV.*

Directly behind the Lustgarten lies the *Alte (Old) Museum,* one of Germany's first buildings devoted solely to being a museum. Built in 1824-28 in the classical style, it is definitely *Schinkel's* most significant work. Once it held the royal collection of Greek and Roman art. *Schinkel* bore this in mind, having the portico supported by 18 Ionian columns. Completely burnt out during the war, the Old Museum was reopened in 1966. Today it contains the 20th century section of the National Gallery, a small room of copperplate engravings, and a collection of drawings. The Old Museum also houses the *New Berliner Gallery* with changing exhibitions (Wed-Sun 10am-6pm).

Behind the Old Museum over Bodestraße lies the *Neue (New) Museum* and the *National Gallery.* Only the ruins of the New Museum are left. However, its reconstruction is planned and then it will house the Egyptian department, which was held here before the war. The National Gallery exhibits paintings and sculptures from the 19th and 20th centuries. Its weighty architecture reveals its historical origins: Wilhelmine classicism. It's remarkable, incidentally, that you cannot enter the building up its stately front steps, but only through a relatively small door at street level (Wed-Sun 10am-6pm).

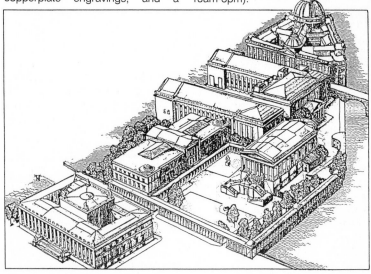

North of the New Museum lies the heart of the island: the **Pergamon Museum,** built between 1912 and 1930. The entrance hall was only completed in 1976. Here you will find the *Antiquity Collection* with its *Pergamon Altar* and the *Processional Road of Babylon*, the *Near Eastern Museum*, the *Islamic Museum* and the *East Asian Collection*. In addition it houses the Ethnological Museum, badly depleted during the war. Naturally the exhibits of the Pergamon Museum are symptomatic of an archaeology closely linked with colonialism. But it is still worth spending some time in the museum (open daily 10am-5:30pm, Mon and Tue the museum is only partially open).

At the North-Western end of the island is the **Bode Museum** (until 1958 the Kaiser-Friedrich Museum) It houses a remarkable Papyrus Collection, the Early Christian-Byzantine collection, the Sculpture Collection, the Painting Gallery, the Coin Collection as well as the Egyptian Museum and the Museum of Pre-and Early History. As you can see from this assembly, the Bode Museum is completely full. Even so, parts of the museum have lain in West Berlin since the end of the war. The East German government was tireless in demanding, for example, the *Head of Nefertiti* from the West Berlin Senate. The remarkable exhibits include the life-sized X-ray of a female mummy and the Apsis mosaic of an Italian church (Wed-Sun 10am-6pm).

S-Bahn trains thunder between the Pergamon and Bode museums over the swampy Spree island. If you're lucky, you can see from the moving train into the antique collection of the Pergamon museum.

The building boom of the foundation years also benefited Berlin's museums. In 1871 there was plenty of money in the capital, and the director of the museums, *Wilhelm von Bode*, only had to ask the many potential donors. This was how Berlin gained an art collection which could compete with the Louvre. The collection experienced its first losses in 1937, when the Nazis destroyed virtually the entire modern art section. But this loss was minor compared to the damage wrought

by the Second World War. The whole collection was shipped out of the museums and put in bunkers throughout Germany. Whole sections, such as *Priamo's Gold Treasure*, have remained missing since the end of the war.

In 1947 the state of Prussia, the owner of the collection, was dissolved by the Allied Control Council. There was no dispute about its legal successors, but certainly about their property. The *Prussian Cultural Heritage Foundation*, founded by the Federal Republic (West Germany) in 1957, was not recognised by the East German government. This was to be expected. More surprising was the fact that a number of West German provinces mounted legal challenges to the removal of parts of the collection found on their territory after the war.

A cultural agreement with East Berlin could not be secured for a long time. The SED (Socialist Unity Party) considered that exhibits such as the *Head of Nefertiti* and *Rembrandt's Man with the Golden Helmet* belonged by right in East Berlin. In the meantime the West Berlin museums and galleries were established in Dahlem, Charlottenburg Palace, and in Tiergarten. Perhaps the collection will now also be "reunited", but then that will cost money.

Regardless of whether the New Museum will be reconstructed or built anew, the work will cost 400 million marks. The renovation of the Bode Museum, the National Gallery and the Old Museum, as well as the completion of the Pergamon Museum adds another 530 million marks. If you consider that under the museums the whole Spree island is still swampland, then the renovation of the island will cost around 1.5 billion marks. And today it is not as easy as in 1871 to find art sponsors...

Back Under the Lime Trees

Back on Unter den Linden the old **Zeughaus** (armory) stands on the bank of the Kupfgraben. Built between 1695 and 1706, it is one of the most beautiful German baroque buildings. Today it houses the *Museum für Deutsche Geschichte* (Museum of German History), but until now this has meant only the history of Socialist East Germany. So visitors should hurry if they want to cast their eyes over the other German state's historical-materialist view of history (April-September Mon-Thu 9am-7pm, Sat/Sun 10am-5pm; October-March 9am-6pm, Sat/Sun 10am-5pm, closed Fridays). The four women at the building's entrance symbolise the art of fire, arithmetic, geometry and mechanics, and were designed by the French artist *Guillaume Hulot*. The rest of the facade's frieze and the inner courtyard are the work of *Andreas Schlüter*.

The Armory, the oldest monument building on the Unter den Linden, has had a turbulent history. During the March Revolution of 1843, then still in use as an arsenal, it was stormed by the citizens of Berlin. In 1877 it was transformed into a weapons museum. Heavily damaged during the Second World War, it was rebuilt in a simpler form.

Directly beside the Armory stands the **Neue Wache** (New Watch), built by *Schinkel* and modelled on a Roman fort. Originally used as a detention center, it was rebuilt after the First World War as a "Memorial to the Fallen". Misused by the Nazis as a parade square for "Heroes Memorial Day" and damaged in the war, it was rebuilt in 1957 as a "Memorial to the Victims of Fascism and Militarism". Inside an eternal flame burns in a crystal cube. In the vault underneath lie urns with the ashes of the Unknown Soldier and the Unknown Resistance Fighter (whoever that may be). There are also urns with earth from concentration camps and battlefields of the Second World War. However, reunification has deprived the New Watch of much of its attraction. Before reunification the changing of the guard was accompanied by some very smart goose-stepping, lifting the heart of every militarist.

On the other side of the street you will find another building with an exciting history: the **Kronprinzen-palais** (Crown Prince's Palace). It has only had this name since *Friedrich II*, before which it was the

residence of the Berlin Governor. In 1732, during *Old Fritz's* early years, the house was bought by the prince's father, partly as compensation for the "Katte affair" and rebuilt as a residence for his son. As king, *Friedrich Wilhelm III* lived in the palace, the 30 rooms here were after all more habitable than the huge City Palace. Until 1920, when the National Gallery's modern art section moved here, the building was architecturally tidied up and extended. After that a walkway to the adjoining Princesses' Palace was added. The Crown Prince's Palace and what is today the Opera Cafe were completely burnt out in the last weeks of the war. They collapsed in the 1950s, but were rebuilt, and are thus really new buildings. Finally the SED ended up using the palace as a guesthouse.

Behind the palace in a pavilion you will find the *Schinkelklause* restaurant (Oberwallstraße, Wed-Sun 11am-12pm, Tel. 9-207 12 09), a reminder of the *Schinkelian* Building Academy. All that is left of the academy is a portal, through which you enter the restaurant on Oberwallstraße.

West of the *Operncafé* (Unter den Linden 5, open daily 11am-12pm, Tel. 9-208 21 92), opposite Humboldt University, lies **Bebelplatz**. The square contains some of the city's most beautiful architecture. Before the war it was called Opernplatz (Opera Square) and it was here that the Nazis burnt the first books in

May 1933. It was mainly the works of leftish and Jewish authors like *Kurt Tucholsky, Alfred Döblin, Lion Feuchtwanger, Egon Erwin Kisch, Carl von Ossietzky, Henri Barbusse, Sigmund Freud, Karl Marx* and *Heinrich Mann* which were brought to the flames. But "apolitical" authors like *Thomas Mann, Erich Kästner, Erich Maria Remarque* and *Ernest Hemingway* were also gathered from the nearby University Library.

On the left Bebelplatz is bordered by the **Deutschen Staatsoper** (German State Opera), for once not the work of Schinkel, but that of *Georg Wenzelhaus von Knobelsdorff* in 1741-43. The opera house, on the "Forum Fridericianum", was the first theater to be built independently of the palace. Free-standing on all sides, it resembles a Corinthian temple. Damaged by a bomb in April 1941, it was rebuilt amid much propaganda during the war, only to be bombed again in 1945. The inscription over the entrance *"Fridericus Rex Apolini et Musis"* was only returned to its place in 1986, the year communist East Germany reconciled itself with its Prussian past.

At the rear of Bebelplatz stands the domed **St. Hedwig's Cathedral,** built in 1747 and modelled on the Pantheon in Rome. *Friedrich the Great's* goal with this construction, the first Catholic church after the Reformation, was to integrate the Silesian Catholics who streamed into the capital after the Prussian conquest.

In 1930 the St. Hedwig Bishop's Cathedral - the bishopric of Berlin then encompassed the whole of the Mark of Brandenburg - was put under the authority of the Archbishop of Breslau. It is not worth going inside the church, as the interior has been renovated by an East German architect in a 1950s style.

The whole **Forum Fridericianum** is closed off on the right by the **Königlichen Bibliothek** (Royal Library). It is still popularly known as the *Kommode (commode)*, because legend has it that *Friedrich II* had it modelled on a commode. The same legend also has it that the model for St. Hedwig's Cathedral was an upturned teacup. The building was constructed in Austrian high Baroque style following a design by the architect *Fischer von Erlach*. Curiously, the Viennese original, Hofburg's Michaeltrakt, was only completed in 1893. *Friedrich II* moved his library with 150,000 volumes here. After the construction of the State Library the Friedrich-Wilhelms University took over the building. Today the "commode" is part of Humboldt University.

The **Equestrian Statue of Friedrich the Great** has stood in the middle of Unter den Linden since 1980. It was removed in 1950 and lay spread out in pieces in the Sanssouci Palace park. 150 figures are immortalised in the monument's pedestal, although Prussian scientists and artists are under the horse's rear end. *Old Fritz* is not represented here as a good king, but as a soldier who turned an insignificant Protestant Prussia into a leading central European military power. German political consciousness and nationalism first arose around this man.

Humboldt University, on the other side of the street, can look back on almost 200 years of history as an educational institution. The initiator of its 1809 reconstruction was the humanist and philologist *Wilhelm von Humboldt*, whose name it has borne since 1946. Some important scientists and philosophers studied here: *Hegel,* the *Brothers Grimm, Max Planck, Albert Einstein, Otto Hahn, Rudolf Virchow, Ferdinand Sauerbruch* and *Robert Koch*. The statues of the Humboldt brothers can only be admired in summer. In winter they are packed away in wooden boxes, because of the damage done by smog.

Directly alongside Humboldt University stands the 170 meter long and 105 meter broad **Staatsbibliothek** (State Library) (tours every first Sunday of the month at 10:30am). The current state library was first opened in 1905. Before that the spot was occupied by the *Academy of Science* and the *Academy of Art*. The first rector of Berlin University, *Johann Gottlieb Fichte*, delivered his famous "Speeches to the German nation" here in 1807. *Fichte*, an advocate of the ideas of the French Revolution, attacked the Napoleonic war of conquest. A deed which was all the more courageous because Berlin lay under French occupation.

As early as 1661 the Berlin Palace housed the "Elector's Library of Cölln on the Spree". *Friedrich II* then stored the books in the commode. Today's state library has a collection of over five million books, of which 130,000 are on the shelves.

If you follow Charlottenstraße south, you will come to one of the most beautiful squares in Berlin: **Platz der Akademie** (Academy Square), formerly known as the Gendarme Market. The main market place got its name from the regiment "Gens d'armes" which had its guardhouse and stables here. The rechristening took place in 1950 in conjunction with the 250th anniversary of the *Academy of Science*.

The two churches which frame the square were built in 1701-08. However, the two identically decorated domes and the three-sided columned front halls were first added between 1780 and 1785. This was when *Friedrich II* decided to turn the market into the most beautiful square in Berlin, following the example of the Piazza del Popolo in Rome. The regimental stables were torn down and prestigious buildings took their place.

Theodor Fontane's expression "Deep down Berlin bears the mark of Schinkel" is impressively brought to life here. The middle of the square is occupied by the **Schauspielhaus** (Theater), which *Schinkel* designed in 1817 on the site of *Langhans the Elder's* burnt-down National Theater. The foundations and the Ionic columns of the portico were retained, but overall *Schinkel* reinforced the impression of Greek architecture.

The **Schiller Memorial** by *Reinhold Begas* stood in front of the Schauspielhaus between 1871 and 1936. Until 1986 it could be seen in West Berlin's Lietzensee Park. Since 1989 it has stood on its old spot. After its reconstruction the Schauspielhaus will only be used as a concert hall.

On the southern side of the square, running up to Leipziger Straße, stands the **Deutsche Dom** (German Cathedral), whose reconstruction is still incomplete.

The north side borders on the **Französischer Dom** (French Cathe-

dral) (Viewings: Tue-Sat 10am-5pm, Sun 1pm-5pm). The name says it all. This church was built for the congregation of French *Huguenot families* who settled in Berlin after 1685 to avoid persecution in France. *Elector Friedrich Wilhelm I's Potsdamer Edict* offered the 20,000 "refugees" not only freedom of religion, but also freedom of trade, making every third Berliner a foreigner. In this way the *Great Elector* brought the Berlin textile industry to life. In the tower of the French Cathedral there is a small **Huguenot Museum** (Mon-Sat 10am-5pm, Sun 11:30am-5pm) which displays the history of the "refugees" until 1898. There is also a wine bar in the tower with a very good view (Platz der Akademie 5, open daily 10am-12pm, Tel. 9-229 93 13).

So much culture makes you thirsty, and you should now enter the very beautiful *Café Arcade* (Französische Str. 25, open daily 10am-12pm, Tel. 9-208 02 73). The entrance is not easy to find: you have to go through a driveway and enter the restaurant from the rear. The restaurant offers a good view over the Gendarmenmarkt, and the service is always good. On cold days the cappuccino with egg and mocca liqueur (first try it, then turn your nose up) is a hot tip in the real sense of the word. If the Café Arcade is too common then *Café Bauer* in the Grand Hotel (Unter den Linden, open daily 8am-1am, Tel. 9-209 20) may be more to your taste. The entrance is in Friedrichstraße. Apart from the name, *Café Bauer* has nothing in common with the cafe of the same name which used to stand opposite in Friedrichstraße.

Friedrichstraße really deserves a chapter of its own, but it would be a chapter which could only be reconstructed from old books. Here was where Berlin's heart beat strongest. Friedrichstraße was no glittering boulevard, but a lively thoroughfare. Here were the famous variety shows and dance cafes in which Berliners amused themselves. Friedrichstraße was destroyed by the war-time bombing, and through the building of the Wall in 1961 it lost its function as a North-South artery. What was rebuilt in the 1950s has all the charm of an old boot. Only one new building, the Grand Hotel, resonates architecturally with the arcades of the old buildings.

From here on Unter den Linden also loses its historical charm. On the northern side the **French Cultural Center** is worth seeing. It often holds good exhibitions, films and concerts. On the other side lie the Embassies of the Allied victors.

Until the war the most beautiful, but also the most expensive residences lay on the eastern side of **the Brandenburg Gate,** on **Pariser Platz.** The painter *Max Liebermann* lived here and until his death in 1935 had to experience a number of fascist processions. His comment on the Nazis: "I can't eat the amount I'd like to throw up."

The history of the Brandenburg Gate is described in the chapter "From Checkpoint Charlie to the Reichstag: all along the wall". Directly behind it, already in the Western part of the city, stands the **Soviet Monument.** It is not to be confused with the memorial in Treptow, built from the stones of Hitler's Reichs Chancellery, which lies only a few minutes south from here on foot. The monument is extra-territorial, no-one except the Soviets is allowed near it. There is a justification for the Berlin police keeping pedestrians off the sidewalk. Often the Red Army guards have been attacked by Berlin citizens, once they were even shot at. The result was that Straße des 17. Juni was blocked at this spot for a number of years.

The battle for Berlin raged particularly fiercely in this part of the city during the last days of the Second World War. More than 7,000 Red Army soldiers died in the fight for the former government quarter.

The Platz der Republik (formerly Königsplatz) in front of the Reichstag is now a spare time football park. Tiergarten, Berlin's largest green area in the inner city, begins here. In 1945 the park looked more like the Gobi Desert; in the cold winters Berliners went to "wood auctions" and took the valuable fuel from Tiergarten.

Crossing the by-pass westwards, you will soon get to the **Kongresshalle** (Congress Hall), popularly known as the "pregnant oyster". It

was constructed in 1956-57 as the USA's contribution to the Berlin International Building Exhibition. A terrace standing on 1000 concrete pillars supports a round building topped off, tent-like, by a shell-shaped roof. In 1980 the roof's partial collapse gave Berlin's most innovative rock group its name: *Einstürzende Neubauten* (Collapsing New Buildings). After lengthy discussions the building was recon-structed in 1984-87 and took up in 1989 its new function as *Haus der Kulturen der Welt* (World Cultural Center).

This part of Tiergarten was known as "In den Zelten" ("In the tents") in the 18th century when travelling traders were housed here in tents in the summer months. Excited discussions took place here in 1848,

preceding the March revolution. Today there are again two tents. Directly beside the Congress Hall is the ***Tempodrom,*** with a large and a small circus tent. It offers space for all sorts of entertainment. But even if nothing is on in the Tempodrom, you can happily sit in the beer-garden.

If the agenda in this chapter was too much for you, bear in mind Alfred Polgar's comment that Berlin is a city "in which a little leisure can't be had in a leisurely way." (See also the chapter on "From Checkpoint Charlie to the Reichstag").

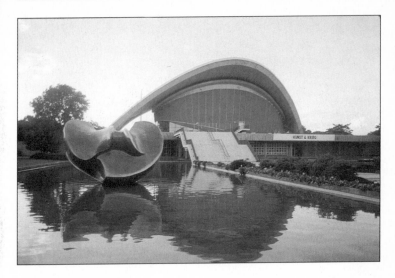

Friedrichshain *(R.Schuler)*

The little ones always cause the most trouble, and it is no different with Friedrichshain. The smallest eastern district, 9.8 square kilometers, doesn't fit into any pattern. It is difficult to walk through, the sights lie too far apart, industrial and residential areas are too haphazardly mixed together, and it doesn't have any particular character. Friedrichshain has always been a workers' district, which is not surprising, as the little late-comer borders on Prenzlauer Berg. Nonetheless, today it is one of the better places to live. The alternative scene here doesn't have the sometimes doubtful reputation of its famous neighboring district.

Everyone who moves around in Berlin has to pass through Friedrichshain. The largest traffic arteries divide even this small district into different pieces.

Despite being the dwarf in East Berlin, Friedrichshain is almost as densely populated as Prenzlauer Berg, with 126,000 inhabitants. Where there are now industrial sites and residential quarters grouped around the **Volkspark Friedrichshain,** there used to be picturesque meadows and fields.

In the past there was only dense settlement along the major trading roads. For example, Landsberger Straße (today Leninallee), Große Frankfurter Allee (today Karl-Marx-Allee), and the Mühlen- or Holzmarktstraße. After the city's growth in population led to the removal of

Friedrichshain

U-Bhf.
1 Strausberger Platz
2 Marchlewskistraße
3 Frankfurter Tor

S-Bhf.
4 Leninallee
5 Ostbahnhof (Hauptbahnhof)
6 Warschauer Str.

1 Cinema International
2 Fairy Tale Fountain
3 Lenin Memorial
4 Cemetery
5 Karl Friedrich Friesen Swimming Stadium
6 SEZ (Sport and Leisure Center)
7 Hühner Gustl
8 Studio Otto Nagel
9 Photo Gallery
10 To Oberbaum bridge

the old toll and excise wall in 1732, the Prussian state was forced in 1737 to erect another construction. This was erected mainly to prevent customs fraud and, above all, desertion. Many recruits appear to have had little interest in hard drill. Some fled the short distance over the city border to the Mark of Brandenburg, where one could disappear easily. The new wall ran roughly as high as the **Oberbaumbrücke** along Warschauer Straße, cutting diagonally through what is today Friedrichshain.

The street maps of the area between the Spree and Prenzlauer Berg are based almost entirely on building plans from 1826. (Luckily this area was spared the destruction of the Second World War, so you can still use these maps today.) At that time the residential capacity of Berlin's inner city was no longer capable of keeping up with the rapidly expanding industries. Along the Spree and where today the **Ostkreuz S-Bahn Intersection** lies, there were many factories and workshops. As a result of this overcrowding *James Friedrich Rudolf Hobrecht* (1825-1902) put forward a building plan which was later to have disastrous consequences for Berlin. The engineer and building assessor's design, approved by *Wilhelm I* despite considerable criticism, sealed Berlin's development into the largest apartment-block city in the world. Disregarding the experiences of other cities, and against the wishes of *Friedrich Wilhelm IV.*,

Hobrecht orientated himself faithfully to a Parisian example. He ultimately produced only a poor copy, which is certainly partly responsible for the social misery and the wretched living conditions of Berlin's workers.

The well-intentioned star-shaped street plans with the occasional prestigious building are smoke screens for the *slum quarter*. These smoke screens hide concrete jungles of courtyards and mini-apartments.

The worker's housing associations which were founded later, and *Alfred Messel's* reformist building in Weisbach- and Proskauer Straße, could only partially help. Between them they produced a few buildings suitable for human habitation.

The fact that the people living under these conditions tended to be dissatisfied and disloyal servants of the state is hardly surprising. Just as Berlin's East End was generally notorious for being "red", the history of Friedrichshain is also a history of the labor movement. Critical plays were performed in the *Freie Volksbühne* East-end theater, workers' educational associations were founded and many large demonstrations took place. The Brown Shirts, who first achieved success in Berlin, only ventured carefully into this district, and wild street battles were the result. Even in March 1933 the Nazis could not achieve a majority here.

The Second World War left behind a pile of rubble. After the last major American air raid in April 1945, the area around what was then Große Frankfurter Allee lay in rubble and ash. The smart new buildings which were supposed to hide the broken city's face did the opposite.

The constructions and monuments built here in the spirit of Stalinist gigantism and vulgar architectural egalitarianism have in turn become memorials. The former Stalin Allee, today Karl-Marx-Allee, and the standard concrete pre-fabricated buildings (popularly known as "workers' lockers") on Lenin-Allee stand as remnants of what was hopefully a mistake overcome in the search for a better city.

If you would like to go directly from West Berlin for a brief walk through Friedrichshain, the ideal starting point is the former border crossing at **Oberbaumbrücke.** For Berliners the bridge is a painful reminder: in winter 1984-85 two men swam through the icy waters of the Spree to get to West Berlin. One made it, the other was arrested by the border guards after he had already reached the other side. Even in GDR law it was illegitimate to arrest someone on West Berlin soil.

The bridge itself, which used to carry U-Bahn Line 1 to its terminal station Warschauer Brücke, was torn down after the building of the Wall. A symbolic act for the way they envisioned the future: nothing would connect Berliners arbitrarily divided by the Wall.

When you leave the bridge a large building comes into view on the

right, covered in white-beige plastic sheets. In what was unfortunately a familiar case of foolishness, lack of building materials made the former town planners cover this very imposing *Bauhaus Project* in this unattractive material. Instead of keeping the dark red facade in good repair, they decided instead on this disfigured exterior. The protocol tour for state VIPs runs past here...

The Bauhaus school of architecture led by *Walter Gropius* developed a number of buildings for this harbour complex in the 1920s. They were intended to be a synthesis of functional building and constructive beauty.

On the left *Mühlenstraße* doesn't offer any exceptional views, but is an example of East Berlin life. The monotonous Wall ran along the street for more than a kilometer, making the people living here particularly aware of the years of separation. Behind the smooth stone wall there was a strip guarded by watchtowers and dogs, and then an electric fence. Water police patrolled the Spree, and the watchtowers kept a lookout over the whole area. Today a few Berlin artists have painted this stretch of the Wall, unfortunately only to be spoiled by more radical scribblers.

The interesting route leads along *Warschauer Straße* and then over *Warschauer Brücke.* The red wall is all that remains of the former U-Bahn station. The station served as an important junction in the Berlin transport network, therefore the wall as a monument is worth preserving. The East Berlin transport authority, which owns the land, has rented it out for years to the Berlin electric light company *"Rosa Luxemburg"*.

The company buildings them-selves are under protection, like the old signal box on the bridge. Presu-mably the company will have to be renewed, as the whole complex, despite a fairly modern assembly line is completely obsolete. Under a thick layer of dirt you can still see the well-thought-out building plans for the factory halls.

If you'd like to go to Friedrichshain directly from the East Berlin city center, it is best to get off the S-Bahn (from Friedrichstraße or Alexanderplatz) at Warschauer Straße. In front of the exit in the middle of the bridge you can get a good view of the whole area. To the south lies the Spree and the former border. To the west the huge symbols of the Old East Berlin center rise against the sky: the Television Tower, *Hotel Stadt Berlin* and closer, the Central Station, formerly Ostbahnhof (Eastern Station). A short distance to the left of the Central Station lies the former Wriezener Bahnhof. It is now only recognizable from a few insignificant remains as it was almost completely demolished after the damage of the war. Its name still stays fixed in the language though. Young people are often helpless when older colleagues direct them to Wriezener Bahnhof, when they really mean the streets around it. To the east from

Warschauer Bridge you can see the next station on the S-Bahn, the largest station in East Berlin: ***Ostkreuz***.

To the north Warschauer Straße leads to the residential area between Revaler and Boxhagener Straße.

Coming off the bridge, Warschau-er Straße leads around the tram station (Lines 3 & 4) and turns into Helsingforser Platz. No matter what the exhibition currently is, the bright studio of the ***Photo Gallery*** (Hel-singforser Platz 1, Tue-Fri 11am-7pm, Sat 10am-1pm), although not so inviting from the outside, is almost always worth a visit. Local and foreign photographers display their photographs either thematically or in exhibitions devoted to the work of one artist.

It is briefly worth leaving War-schauer Straße and going a few meters up the Revaler to **Libauer Straße**. Here you can see some of *building assessor Hobrecht's* famous apartment blocks.

Friedrichshain was also recon-structed, and for the sake of increased efficiency the communists removed all "superfluous" decora-tion, such as ledges and trimmings. Some raw plaster was then slapped over the top and like magic the workers had comfortable houses. Libauer Straße is a good example of this kind of thinking. The road surface keeps cars jumping and drivers' heads bouncing off the roof. Trees line the streets and occasion-ally you'll see large garbage con-tainers with cars parked - more or less competently - around them. The local culture produces few exotic blossoms. There are some graphic artists, actors and other free-lancers, but the majority are workers and students. With the general housing shortage they have managed to find a roof over their heads around Boxhagener-, Grünberger-, Koperni-kus- and Wühlischstraße. Naturally these places are not in the best of condition, but they are still roomier than new flats. Because there is only row upon row of apartment blocks, a more nature-oriented lifestyle is confined to the weekend, when you can go to some park or beyond the city.

Libauer Straße meets **Simon-Dach-Straße,** which is just as quiet as everywhere else. The geraniums grow silently in window-boxes, the occasional tenant looks wearily out of the window at life passing slowly by. The taverns are also less com-mon here than in Prenzlauer Berg.

Leaving noisy Kopernikusstraße behind you, there is the opportunity to study traditional buildings without noisy renovations being carried out. Usually the courtyards are unorigi-nal, damp and dark. In some buildings, however, the costly embellished entrances have been maintained or consequently re-stored. The ornamental mouldings and rosettes contrast with the crumbling plaster and the flaking oil paint which seems too tired to stay on the walls.

If you turn into **Krossener Straße** or walk along Grünbergerstraße a little to the right, you find **Boxhage-ner Platz**. The square is used as a leisure spot. Locals sit on the benches, exchange general com-plaints about life, and watch over the little ones. The *Quelle* corner tavern (Seumsstraße 25, Wed/Thu closed) is mainly for the locals, outsiders should merely look over the interior.

On the way from Boxhagener Platz back to Warschauer Straße, on the left you will come across a *small "people's" art gallery* in **Studio Otto Nagel** (Grünberger Str. 60, Mon-Fri 2pm-6pm). This place used to represent the old cultural concept of a "healthy people's art" made by creative workers. Today it is more artistically-inclined intellectuals wanting to gather experience or those with an artistic occupation who come here. The exhibitions occasionally offer a glimpse of the work of non-professionals.

Walking along Simon-Dach-Straße to Boxhagener Straße, you will reach the *Gullasch Hütte* restaurant (Simon-Dach-Straße 1, Mon-Fri 8am-12pm, Tel. 9-430 08 14; ext. 461). Diagonally opposite is the *Intimes* **cinema** (Niederbarnimstr. 15, Tel. 9-59 32 87); with less than 100 seats it is the smallest cinema in East Berlin.

If you cross Warschauer Straße into **Grünberger Straße** you will encounter the reality of ordinary East Berlin life. Streets with little color to relieve the sad indifference.

In **Warschauer Straße** there are shops in which one can find everything from records and textiles to groceries - but always the same selections. Only recently have the odd entrepeneurs and shop-owners tried to make something of the unused shop-spaces in the hitherto deserted side streets. It will take some time before people get to know about the area's growing attractiveness.

On the corner of Grünberger and Lasdehner Straße stand the *Kurt Schlosser* and *John-Sieg High Schools*. The schools are housed in a massive building, designed by *Ludwig Hoffman* and built in 1909, during the Wilhelmine era. A little further, on the other side of the street, we find a well-known **Grünberger Straße** address: the *Hühner Gustl* (No. 6, Mon-Fri 10am-12pm, Tel. 9-589 20 77). This family-owned tavern has existed for more than 50 years. It serves high quality traditional Berlin food ("Eisbein" - pickled pork knuckles, bratwurst, broiled chicken and pea soup) and cool beer. The *Hühner Gustl* takes pride in the quality of its chicken as opposed to some of the chicken served elsewhere. The food is served in a typical old Berlin tavern interior. *Gustl* himself, for the master oversees the business, ensures a cosy atmosphere in the common room behind the restaurant. There you can ask for the old tunes, and a chat about vintage cars is compulsory. Occasionally a gleaming jewel from the tavern-owner's own collection is started up. The *DEFA film studio* is always keen to borrow the noble chariots from Grünberger Straße. *Gustl's* team provides an open house.

Further along on the other side of the street there is yet another spot awaiting the gourmet. The *Jägerklause* (Grünberger Str. 1, Tue-Sat 11am-12pm, Tel. 9-589 22 50) serves dishes of the highest quality. "Jägerspieß" (hunters spear), roast venison, special flambeed dishes with the "Fruit of the South", and wonderful game soups. All this in the fitting surrounding of antlers and other forest decorations.

Over Gubener Straße, which runs to the right from just beyond the Jägerklause, is East Berlin's first high-rise building erected after the war. Not very pleasing to the eye, but nevertheless a sight of historical significance.

Nearby, the *Weberwiese* (weaver's meadow), a narrow field with a small pond in the middle, is the site of the annual district fair. The fair offers secondhand stalls, fast food, portraits in five minutes, and various artistic endeavors on the small stage. The Weberwiese got its name from the weavers who laid out their cloth for bleaching around the Frankfurter Gate area.

Still, back to East Berlin's first high-rise. It was meant to be a sign of the peaceful, hopeful reconstruction of the first year. Designed by the former, chief city architect *Henselmann*, the builders erected this 40 meter building, laughably tiny by today's standards, in 121 days. The enthusiasm of the year 1951, deliberately promoted to be sure, is barely imaginable today. Just as the opening of *Thälmann Park* in Prenzlauer Berg in 1986 was meant to be an encouraging example for everyone, so too was the inauguration of this first high-rise building. It motivated many people to believe in the future of this new social order. But the optimism did not last long; the strike which unleashed the uprising of 17 June 1953 took place only a year later and only a few meters away.

It was built from the rubble of this badly damaged district. The 33 families who moved in each got a telephone connection (still a rarity today), central heating, and electric hot water systems. Also some comfortable extras like garbage disposal units, lifts and glassed-in

roof terraces. Since then the rent of 90 Marks a month has sufficed for what is no longer such a luxurious apartment.

Crossing over Hildegard-Jadamowitz-Straße you come to **Straße der Pariser Kommune.** Between the recently built 10-storey blocks of flats and the *Henselmann apartment blocks*, stand some examples of the original housing. They stand alone on the edge of the city, punished by the neglect of a communist building industry . The more they decline, the less their chances of being rebuilt and maintained as heritage buildings.

From Hildegard-Jadamowitz-Straße you cannot avoid **Karl-Marx-Allee** running off to the right. *Henselmann* intended this road to be a tribute to the "great" Stalin, whose name it bore until 1961. It was also meant to convey the irresistable dynamism of socialist reconstruction

("We don't need any Marshall Plan ..."). Not coincidentally, the tiled facades are reminiscent of Moscow Prospect.

On 21 December 1952 some "Heroes of Labour" moved into the first 148 apartments in **Stalinallee.** What was seen on one side of the Wall as a great symbol of the new socialist Germany, was referred to in the West as the "Russians' Via Triumphalis", or the "gigantic Bolshevist-Stalinist confectionery store". You can see that there were once other plans for the avenue. The *Ludmilla Herzenstein Collective* buildings, built in 1949, are a testimony to this. They stand inconspicuously between other buildings lining the avenue. However, in April 1950, a delegation of the "Ministry

for the Reconstruction of the GDR" went on a study tour of the Soviet Union. The Ludmilla Herzenstein Collective remained lonely relics. After the later proclamation of the "Sixteen Principles of Town Planning", a plan originated in the USSR, they were meant to have been demolished.

Stalinallee acquired tragic fame in 1953, when the building workers on Strausberger Platz called a strike against impossible productivity requirements. On 17 June 1953 they joined up with other workers and proceeded to the city center to demonstrate their dissatisfaction. Western gloating over the riot in the other half of the city led to the Soviet occupation forces being asked to put a halt to the incident with tanks. While the productivity increases were retracted, this first and only test of democracy remained a painful upheaval in the history of Communist East Germany.

It took until 1989 for protests to re-emerge, the last in East Germany.

If you'd like to avoid the extensive walk through Friedrichshain and instead just look at this historic avenue, you should take the U-Bahn from Alexanderplatz. It travels along Karl-Marx-Allee in convenient stages, so that you can emerge here and there to see whatever takes your fancy. And you can also get quickly back to the center. From Alexanderplatz the U-Bahn goes via Tierpark all the way to Hönow.

Where Straße der Pariser Kommune crosses the Allee, it may be

worth making a detour to **Straus-berger Platz**. This takes you past the Karl Marx bookshop and on towards the center. Behind Straus-berger Platz is the largest **first-run cinema** in East Berlin, the *International* (Karl-Marx- Allee 33, Tel 9-212 58 26).

In the other directions along the Allee there are some **specialty restaurants** of other ex-socialist nations: the *Budapest*, *Bukarest* and *Warschau* restaurants. Unfortunately they don't always live up to their reputations for high quality.

Shopping can be done on either side of the street, and between U-Bahn stations if you're short of time.

A few meters past Karl-Marx-Allee, Straße der Pariser Kommune changes its name to **Friedens-straße.** The gates in the red brick wall which begins here lead to the **cemetery** of the parish of *St. George*. In the cemetery you can turn your back on the ever-present traffic and get a little peace and quiet. A little neglected in some corners, over-grown with ivy and weeds, and at other spots tended with extreme care, the cemetery runs to Lenin-allee, which is where its main entrance is.

The **Church of the Resurrection** (Auferstehungskirche), Friedenstra-ße 84, lost its spire during the war. It has never been replaced. The church was once surrounded by four cemeteries and on the spot where the church now stands there used to be a pauper's cemetery.

The wall along the Friedens-and Auerstraße surrounds the ceme-teries of the *Parochial*, Evangelical *St. Petri-Georgen*, and *Georgen parishes.*

Leninallee without busy traffic is a very rare sight. In the Middle Ages it was a trading route and after 1818 it became the main postal route. Turning left out of Friedenstraße onto Leninallee you will see Lenin-platz and the Lenin Memorial. The memorial created by the Moscow artist *Nikolai Tomski* was unveiled on 19 April 1970. The city fathers thought it fitted in well with the ensemble of concrete blocks behind it. Apart from devoted Leninists and those who would like to try the Russian specialties prepared by

211

German cooks in the *Baikal* restaurant (Leninplatz 1, open daily 10am-12pm, Tel. 9-436 61 55), this side-trip isn't especially worthwhile.

Instead you could go for an extended walk through the **Volkspark Friedrichshain** (Friedrichshain Public Park). At 52 hectares this is the largest park in the eastern half of the city. The park was originally created for the less well-to-do inhabitants of Berlin. The Tiergarten was reserved for the wealthy. *Peter Joseph Lenné* had developed a design for the park, which was in fact reworked and extended by his student *Johann Gustav Heinrich Meyer* in 1848. In 1874/75 the area's extension was designed by *Meyer*.

The city hospital lies directly opposite the cemetery entrance. It was built under the supervision of *Virchow* by *Martin Gropius* and *Heino Schnieden* in 1868-75 and is in a way part of the park.

The park with its large open spaces, rhododendrums and small woods, is a perfect place for people of all ages. In the summer countless sunbathers enjoy this cheap solarium. In the park there are two small ponds, some fast-food stalls and open-air restaurants.

The war, which destroyed the park's hundred-year-old trees, left behind an unmanageable pile of rubble which had to be removed somehow. Two blown-up and unsightly anti-aircraft bunkers, reminders of the 12-year dictatorship, became the recipients of 2 million cubic meters of rubble. On maps they are still shown as the small (48m) and the large (78m)

212

bunker hills. Berliners call them *Mount Klamott*. From these two hills you get a good view over the neighboring city landscape.

Directly in front on Leninallee lies the **Friedhof der Märzgefallen** (Cemetery of the March Fallen). Those who fought and died in the 1848 Revolution are buried here, alongside the victims of the 1918 November Revolution. Beside the bunker hills is the *Karl Friedrich Friesen Swimming Stadium*. In 1951 they wanted to put on a good show for the World Youth Games, and built this complex in the park. It was subsequently named after the great mathematician and teacher *Friesen* (1785-1814).

The **Fairy Tale Fountain**, (Märchenbrunnen) a neo-baroque fountain installed at the instigation of the Social Democratic faction of the city government, bubbles in the western corner of the park. It is a favorite playground, particularly in the summer, for children. *Ludwig Hoffman* must have had this in mind with his design based on Grimm's fairytales. The figures around the edge of the large water basin were carved by *Georg Weber*, those on the colonnades by *Joseph Rauch*, and the animal sculptures were created by *Ignatius Taschner*. For lovers of detail, between the water-spouting frogs and witches, one gnome unmistakably bears the features of the Berlin painter *Adolph Menzel*.

The remaining monuments in the park are memorials to the anti-fascist struggles of the *International Brigades* as well as the joint struggle of German and Polish resistance fighters in the Second World War. No-one takes such monuments particularly seriously. There are simply too many of them; no one wanted to be left behind in unveiling monuments. If you end your city walk at the Märchenbrunnen you should continue to nearby Straße Am Friedrichshain. Here you will have no problems in getting back to the center with Bus 57. It stops at Alexanderplatz and then travels down Unter den Linden to Fried-richstraße station. If you want to go to Invalidenstraße, you can stay seated at Friedrichstraße and get out when the bus stops at the former border crossing.

As was said at the beginning of this chapter, Friedrichshain is a difficult district to understand. So we should not be surprised if this intractability also works against city tourist-guides. Not all the sights or inter-esting spots can be discovered in one round trip.

The **Sport und Erholungszen-trum** (*SEZ*) (Sport and Leisure Center) is the easiest to include, as it lies on the corner of Leninallee and Dimitroffstraße, not far from the public park. If you wish to use the indoor sporting facilities, you need only walk along Leninallee as far as Bersarinstraße to catch sight of this unmistakable steel and glass building. The SEZ (Leninallee 77, Tel. 9-588 62 15) offers a range of activities. Whether it's swimming in the wave-pool or the outdoor pool, splashing in the cascades or diving

in the diving pool, you are guar-anteed pleasure in the water. Super-fluous flesh can be removed with body-building, the sauna, volleyball, handball or football. The center also offers various eating establishments which specialize in "energy-rich" food and drink. There are also out-door lawns, a billiards room and a solarium.

In the summer rollerskaters circle around the skating rink, which is too slippery in the winter. Information about the center's countless events, from aerobics to cabaret, can be found on the noticeboards. The hostesses in the foyer will also be pleased to help you. The SEZ is open Mon-Fr 10am-9pm, Sat/Sun 10am-6pm. Every first Monday in the month the doors stay closed, except for the bowling alley.

Simply watching other people exercising is also enjoyable and less strenuous. In *Café Kaskade* (open daily 12am-9pm) you get the best view of the swimming pool. In the *Kristall* (Mon-Fri 10am-12pm, Sat/Sun 9am-12pm) the view of roller or ice skaters is enriched by the excellent offerings of a good restaurant. In addition there is *Foyer Treff* (Mon-Fri 10am-6pm, Sat/Sun 9am-6pm). *Zur Molle* is a pub (Mon-Fri 10am-12pm, Sat 9am-12pm, Sun 9am-10pm) which one can also get to through a side entrance. The *Hallenbar* and *Wellen-treff* are only open to swimmers.

All sorts of gastronomic variations are also on offer in the Central Station, even though it is not strictly

on the route. There are no problems in getting there by any S-Bahn line from Friedrichstraße or Alexanderplatz, and you can't miss it. The ***Hauptbahnhof*** (Central Station) - many Berliners still have difficulty getting these words past their lips - has a chapter all to itself in Berlin's history.

It has had a number of names, but none were so ill-suited as the current one. It is the last of a generation of great Berlin railway stations, and the third to come into operation, on 23 October 1842. Then it was called "Frankfurter" station, because the 81 kilometer stretch to Frankfurt an der Oder had just been opened. Apart from this station only the "Potsdamer" and "Anhalter" stations (direction Sachsen-Anhalt) existed.

In 1843 the "Stettiner" station was ready for the trains to the Ostsee, "Hamburger" followed in 1846 and "Görlitzer" in 1868. Because the Frankfurt stretch was extended to Schlesien (Silesia), it soon became known as "Niederschlesisch-Märkische" station. After 1882, when the metropolitan railway (S-Bahn) was to connect all the city stations with each other, both the platforms and the rails had to be raised by six meters. The former terminus station, which was now called "Schlesische" station, became a through station.

"Schlesische" station was a starting point for excursions east of Berlin. The demand was enormous and between 1884 and 1894 the number of departing trains increased from 46 to 102. Around 50 long-distance trains departed from the station, steaming to Breslau, Danzig, Königsberg and even Russia.

In 1941, the papers showed the laughing faces of soldiers boarding trains at "Schlesische" station on their way to the Eastern front. But only four years later trains overflowing with refugees from the eastern territories began to arrive. The glass covering over the platforms and the foyer building was badly damaged during the war.

In 1950 "Schlesische" station was renamed "Ostbahnhof". This was to indicate that with the recognition of the Oder-Neiße border, Silesia was no longer part of Germany. The other Berlin stations were all demolished and cleared away because of the heavy damage. With today's thinking it was a crime, as many could easily have been saved.

Ostbahnhof stumbled on, declined and rusted. The kiosks had little to offer, service was slovenly, and the roof let little light into the dimly-lit hall. But because a socialist capital also had to have a central station, (this would indicate that the Eastern half was Berlin's main part), the SED decided during the 750th anniversary to erect a new Central Station on Stralauer Platz. Naturally the anniversary's timetable had to be kept to, so the foyer, as the first stage of the station, was handed over punctually in May 1987. However, it has still not become the metropolitan railway station it was supposed to be.

Light natural stone behind the glass facade of the Ostbahnhof does now give the large hall a brighter feel. Escalators also make it easier to get to the platforms. But the station has never shaken free of the atmosphere of a construction site. The steel frame of the hall is constantly being restored. In the foyer hairdressing salons, travel agencies, flowers shops and a number of cafes wait for customers. Perhaps the old hall and its entrance decorated with polished steel sculptures will one day become a real metropolitan railway station, but one cannot be sure...

And if you've looked at your map to discover that the *Halbinsel Stralau* (Stralau Island) is also part of Friedrichshain, you can climb aboard Bus 34 at Helsingforser Platz and go there. There is certainly not that much to see. Apart from the old village church and the glass-works, the old tram tunnel under the Spree is the little island's main attraction. It is said to have been flooded after the war, but you can still find the entrance.

Prenzlauer Berg
(R. Schuler)

Prenzlauer Berg is a legend. The peculiarity of naming a small district (10.8 square km.) after a similarly insignificant little hill is matched by the wonder of a suburb whose daily life runs counter to all normality. It is a suburb often idealised just a little too much and enveloped in a melancholy romanticism. In reality it is little more than a piece of dreary new-building-monotony.

The real legend appears to have begun in the 1970s. The "initial" phase of "socialism" was clearly over, and it could no longer sustain the illusion that it was the "better side". Every little attempt at independent thought, pitiful by today's standards, immediately brought not just temporary injury, but permanent scars. Little was left of the dream of a community of well-intentioned people working for the good of the whole society. Now slogans and a rigid power apparatus tried to shape reality to its will. For every enlightened individual not yet inclined to run into the arms of the West there was only one way out: they had to find a niche, a place they could live out their ideas undisturbed. Although their convictions gave them no right to a comfortable new apartment, they could certainly lay claim to the run-down shanties in Prenzlauer Berg.

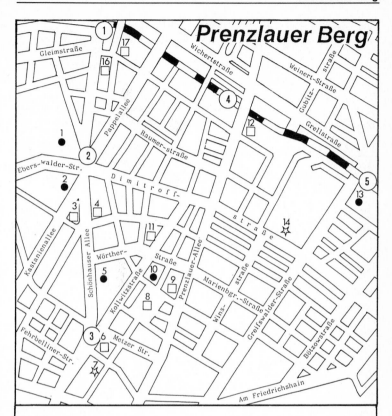

U-Bhf.
1. Schönhauser Allee
2. Dimitroffstraße
3. Senefelderplatz

S-Bhf.
4. Prenzlauer Allee
5. Ernst-Thälmann-Platz

1. Friedrich Ludwig Jahn Sportpark
2. Prater
3. Pratergalerie
4. Franz-Klub
5. Jewish Cemetery

6. Metzer Eck
7. Alibi Night Bar
8. Water Tower
9. Synagogue
10. Kollwitzplatz
11. Museum Berliner Arbeiterleben um 1900 (Museum of Berlin Working Life around 1900)
12. Zeiss Planetarium
13. Ernst Thälmann Park
14. Culture Centre /Wabe Disco
16. Exhibition Hall
17. Gethsemane Church

Increasing numbers of young people began to embark on some form of *"internal emmigration"*. They stopped participating, but still wanted to stay close to the action, to the capital, its information and its culture. Prenzlauer Berg was perfect. Even the authorities felt that if people were willing to live in these barely habitable apartments, they'd be left in peace. These people could have their desired place on the fringe.

After that a whole army of young alternatives and the like, otherwise unable to find an apartment, streamed here to fix up the smallest of apartments. There are more important things in life than luxury, said everyone who lived here.

Always a worker's district, Prenzlauer Berg was nothing special at the beginning of the 1970s. When Berlin slowly began to expand around 1866, there was little happening here: a few windmills, breweries and a few hundred inhabitants. Within 40 years, however, the suburb had become the most densely populated in Berlin. Expanding industry helped, as the labour one needed every day had to be housed quickly. An apartment block quarter sprang up, at some points with more than 2,000 inhabitants per hectare (100 x 100 meters!).

By the 1930s there were around 350,000 people living under what were at times catastrophic conditions. The SPD and the Communists had a strong electoral advantage here, at least until the National Socialists put their brown stamp of terror on the district.

It has remained the most densely populated district to this day: there are now only 190,000 inhabitants, but they are still tightly packed.

There are essentially three main roads, which run through Prenzlauer Berg: Greifswalder Straße, Prenzlauer Allee and Schönhauser Allee. The latter is to some extent the heart of "Prenzelberg". Life is condensed along this route, gathered together and pulsating. Around the "Schönhauser" you can obtain everything.

Coming from Alexanderplatz the U-Bahn is recommended. The line winds through the whole of **Schönhauser Allee,** at times underground and at others high over the heads of pedestrians. From Friedrichstraße station you can also get Tram 70 or 46, which take you to the railway embankment behind the unmistakeable International Trade Center. It runs a little way along Friedrichstraße, over Invalidenstraße and after a short stretch along Kastanienallee it reaches the junction of Schönhauserallee and Dimitroffstraße.

However, the U-Bahn has the advantage of allowing you to step out into Schönhauser Allee wherever you like.

If you leave the U-Bahn at **Senefelderplatz,** which lies a few steps from the U-Bahn, you'll find yourself on a large green square. This is the southernmost tip of Prenzlauer Berg.

On the left, looking from the city center, there are a number of streets. These maybe considered the last traces of the former Jewish quarter **Scheunenviertel.** The closely-packed rows of facades date from the end of the last century. Like the rest of the district, the graceful cornices disappeared long ago, leaving only the scars from the war's bullet holes. People have never made the effort to smooth over the craters created in the plaster by machine-gun and pistol fire. Originally there must have been some well-to-do people living around Christinenstraße and Teutoburger Platz, in the *Herz-Jesu-Church* area. Some of the apartments are very spacious, when they haven't been divided up into smaller partitions. Often there was even a second servant's entrance.

On **Senefelder Platz** there is a memorial to the inventor of lithography, *Alois Senefelder*. In 1892 a certain *Pohle* erected this sculpture beside the U-Bahn exit.

If you're on Senefelder Platz late in the day, you can walk a few meters back towards the city to Saarbrücker Straße and the night bar *Alibi* (No. 14, Wed-Sun 7pm-2am, Tel. 9-281 18 07). Right on Senefelder Platz is the *Metzer Eck* (Metzerstr. 33, Mon-Thu 2pm-1am, Fri-Sun 2pm-3am, Tel. 9-448 25 55) which opens its doors to everyone not just artists and the like.

Walking further along this early part of Schönhauser Allee, not yet a shopping mile, you'll see the main

police station on the right. This attractive building was built in 1883-87 as the Jewish community's home for the elderly, later to be occupied by the Nazis. The **Jewish Cemetery** lies right beside it.

The East German Jewish community had all of its original property returned to it after the war. If buildings are to be put to any other use, it has to be with the permission of the community, buildings are only rented to other institutions. This does not mean, however, that the state has bothered to help maintain these historical buildings. In the past this was left to the Jewish community itself, which with its meagre financial resources was frequently pushed to the limit. Only in recent years has the state supported the care of Jewish cultural heritage, financially as well as in words.

In the context of an organised campaign, as always, *FDJ (Free German Youth) groups* took to the cemetery to repair the damage inflicted by the war and the elements. In the process there were often conflicts between the *FDJ* blue-shirts and the Jewish community. They were outraged at the FDJ's disrespectful treatment of the cemetery, paying no regard to Jewish traditions. Where could young people have learnt any respect for a religion in the middle of "atheistic socialism"?

The ivy-covered gravestones in the Jewish cemetery on Schönhauser Allee are tightly packed together. Splendid resting-places were created by prominent artists and you will find the graves of some famous names: the composer *Giacomo Meyerbeer*, the publisher *Leopold*

Ullstein or the painter *Max Lieber-mann*, who was President of the Prussian Academy of Art until 1933. Unfortunately in recent years the cemetery has not been spared by the vandals. Right-wing skinheads tear up gravestones and destroy the greenery.

A little further up Schönhauser Allee on the corner of Sredskistraße you will see a particularly beautiful yellow brick building. This used to belong to the **Schultheiss brewery.** The former production and storage area is classic late nineteenth-century style industrial architecture. Besides a furniture store-room, the renowned *Franz-Klub* (Schönhauser Allee 36-39, Tel. 9-448 55 67) is now housed here. It is the local in crowd who come and go here, for the casual visitor it is difficult to make contact: people know each other in the "Franz". Opening times and programs are best obtained from the current notices on advertisement pillars or in the city magazines.

Of course Prenzlauer Berg also has a number of good taverns. In fact there are so many, that only a truly dedicated beer drinker could have tried them all. They are well-represented on Schönhauser Allee, but the best are in the side-streets. If on your way from Senefelderplatz you've passed by *Eistüte* in Wörther-straße (No. 35, Tue-Sun 11am-6pm, Tel. 9-448 04 95, cakes and drinks, ice-cream Russian style) and don't want to know about *Wörther Eck* (Schönhauser Str. 27, Wed-Fri 3pm-11pm, Sat/Sun 10am-8pm, Tel.

9-448 49 93), there's always *Würz-stübchen* in Sredzkistraße (No. 43, Mon-Fri from 6am, Tel. 9-449 94 70). Good and inexpensive are the right words for this small selection of taverns. The quiet Sredzkistraße crosses Knaakstraße (*Kneipe Zum Wasserturm*, open daily 3pm-10pm) to Husemannstraße.

For many years the authorities had given up on reconstructing the Prenzlauer quarter, regarding it as a lost cause. But a few years ago sociologists discovered the progressive tradition of worker's taverns and apartment blocks. They also discovered that the nucleus of the "revolutionary fighters" must have been located here. As a result the authorities, to show how conscious and proud they were of their working-class roots, decided to reconstruct one street. At great expense **Husemannstraße** was renovated.

A picture-book scene with general stores and original taverns was meant to appear. Stucco was produced and iron cast for the balcony rails (roughly 20,000 balconies in the district were in danger of collapse). Guild emblems were placed above the small shops and cooperative stores, and the **Museum Berliner Arbeiterleben um 1900** (Museum of Berlin Working Life around 1900) (No. 12, Tue-Sat 11am-6pm, Tel. 9-448 56 75) was established. In the 750th anniversary celebrations Huse-mannstraße could boast of its cosy working class background. Sadly this benefited only those with the good fortune to have moved into one of the renovated apartments, for such comfort exists nowhwere else in Prenzelberg.

If you wander through Husemann-straße today you will see the street is crumbling already. Cracks are appearing in the fresh plaster and the dirt is gathering on the light-colored facades and ornamen-tal borders. It won't be long before the slovenliness of local building workers returns the show-case to its former state.

Have a look at the art nouveau surroundings in the *Kaffeestube* (No. 6, open daily 11am-10pm, Tel. 9-449 52 80). *Budike* (No. 15, Mon-Sun 10am-10pm, Tel. 9-449 18 20) or *1900* (No. 1, Mon-Sat 4pm 12pm, Tel. 9-449 40 52) have become popular taverns, visitors from West Berlin included, where good food and a comfortable atmosphere make up their charm.

Turning right from Sredzkistraße into Husemannstraße you will get to **Kollwitzplatz.** The Square and street are named after *Käthe Kollwitz* and her husband, the pauper's doctor *Dr. Karl Kollwitz*, who used to live at the former Weißenburger Straße 35. A sculpture in memory of the famous couple, "The Mother" (by *Fritz Diedrich*) now stands where the home of the artist and her husband stood until a bombing raid in 1943. On Kollwitzplatz itself *Gustav Seitz* designed a **monument** in honor of the artist. She would certainly have enjoyed the swarms of children in the square in the afternoons.

In Kollwitzstraße, *Café WC*, also known as *Westphal* (No. 64, Mon-Fri 6pm-8am, Sat/Sun continuous) has recently set itself up in a former liquor factory. Word has spread quickly about this establishment, and not just because of its unusual opening hours. In a small room toast and beer are served at no more than 5 tables, and fast music is played.

If you turn left from Kollwitzstraße into Knaackstraße you approach a local landmark: the **water tower** on Belforter Straße, first put into service in 1877. During the Nazi period there was a notorious and feared torture chamber in the cellar. The tower was relieved of its function in 1952. Playgrounds and trees surround this peculiar construction, today containing apartments, presumably shaped like cake-slices.

Running left off Knaackstraße at the water tower, Rykestraße also leads through an interesting area. The buildings along **Rykestraße**

(*Ryke* or *Reiche* was the name of an influential patrician family which produced a number of mayors between 1290 and 1540) are more or less at that final stage which separates a building from demolition. Due to the condition of these buildings, there are finally plans to begin a special assistance program here. The alternatives being discussed are demolition versus costly reconstruction. The inhabitants want to maintain the well-situated three-sided facades and masonry. For tourists, who don't have or want to live here, it's all very interesting. A side-trip into the courtyards is worthwhile.

As the area used to be occupied primarily by Jews, a **Synagogue** (Friedenstempel) was erected towards the end of the previous century on Rykestraße. In 1938 the synagogue was desecrated by Nazi troops during the infamous "Kristallnacht", and to degrade the Jewish

inhabitants it was used as a horse stable. It was not until 1953 that the building was reconstructed with state support and returned to service after reconsecration.

Just a short distance away is Prenzlauer Allee which runs parallel to Rykestraße. From here trams will take you quickly and easily back to the center.

The **Dimitroffstraße** U-Bahn station lies more or less at the heart of Prenzlauer Berg. This is where Schönhauser Allee and Dimitroff-straße meet, joined by Pappelallee, Kastianienallee and Eberswalder Straße. The clatter of the trams, the roaring motor cars and then on top of that the rythmically rattling yellow trains over your head, can only be borne on a full stomach. Luckily the *Konnopkes Würstchenbude* (open daily from 6:30am) is conveniently

close by. In time with the hurrying clients the currywurst and bockwurst is handed out of the little window, and then it's the next customer's turn. *Konnopke* has turned this into an institution, and despite all the new fast-food chains it still prospers. For the man and woman with little time and little money Konnopke is perfect. A sausage stall like the old days. Some now ask what kind of face the market economy will give this congenial enterprise, pehaps a yellow "M" on a red background?

Looking from the city **Kastanien-allee** runs to the left off Schönhau-ser Allee. Just a few steps away from the intersection is another local attraction: the **Prater** (No. 7-9, Tel. 9-448 14 56) offers music in its large garden in the afternoon as well as on weekends. The Prater was built early this century as the Berlin twin

to its namesake in Vienna. Today the most diverse groups gather in the garden, weather permitting. With a beer or a wine glass in your hand this place is an enjoyable little oasis in the middle of the noisy big city.

To get tickets for evening performances, which usually take place in the open in summer, you should go early. Acts like the pantomine artist Eberhard Kube, attract more than just the Prenzlauer Berg community. The program is well filled with fun, action and good cheer, like the monthly "Prater Ball". The ball is a favorite with men and women of a more advanced age. And since new, wild, independent artists have increasingly been encouraged, many fresh avant-garde people are also climbing onto the stage.

The *Pratergalerie* opposite the Prater's entrance is worth a look.

Artists of various types and origins are invited to exhibit here.

If you want to see a bit of local life, have a look into one or two of the courtyards down *Kastanienallee*. No. 12 is a particularly good example. After a number of driveways and courtyards you suddenly look into a square of painted walls and flourishing ivy. With a little luck there'll be a courtyard party underway, to which strangers will no doubt also be welcome.

A few steps further and *Oderberger Straße* crosses Kastanienallee. If you turn left into Oderberger Straße, at No. 57/59 you'll find the splendid entrance to the *City Baths*. The baths were constructed in 1899-1902 and designed by *Ludwig Hoffmann*. The sculptures on the sandstone-covered building were the work of *Otto Lessing*. Unfortunately this German Renaissance-style building is in poor condition. Sponsors have to be sought for reconstruction and renovation. Its own cash boxes - you only have to look around you - are incapable of generating as much as needs to be invested in the building.

The stretch of Oderberger Straße from Kastanienallee to the former border is crumbling. In certain parts ledges and mouldings, once put on as decoration, have fallen off long ago, leaving only scars. Balconies are mostly closed off - for fear of collapse. In the courtyards sculptors or children work with their "toys" - often the two groups are only distinguished by their age. A colorful alternative kindergarten named *SpielUNKE* has been set up in a ground floor apartment.

Zum Oderkahn (No. 11, Tue-Sat 4pm-1am, Tel. 9-449 44 62) is where the locals go in the evening, when the walls of their one or two room apartments start to close in, or the summer's evening air is too sticky and dry, and only draught beer can come to the rescue.

Right at the end of Oderberger Straße, behind the fire station, East and West Berlin meet. There were few other spots where the naked concrete of the Wall was so obvious and intrusive. The *"anti-imperialist protective wall"* was built between the houses, diagonally across the street. Overnight neighbors were turned into foreigners.

Just around the corner begins ***Eberswalder Straße,*** which will take you back to the intersection of Dimitroff Straße and Schönhauser

Allee. On the left side of Eberswalder Straße lies the **Friedrich Ludwig Jahn Sportpark**. This is the home ground of one of Berlin's football clubs, *1. FC Berlin* (formerly BFC Dynamo). Swarms of fans pile into the stadium on the appropriate Saturdays. But the club has its problems. It used to be well cared-for financially by the Ministry of the Interior and State Security, but now without that help public support and cash reserves have declined.

Older people refer to the stadium just as "Exer", short for "exercise square". Until the Second World War it was one of Berlins' most feared drill and training grounds.

The **St. Elisabeth Foundation** on the right side of Eberswalder Straße is one of the many church institutions which took in the often helpless older people. This in spite of the existence of arrogantly announced state care. Compared to what were occasionally dreadful conditions in the state-run homes, the Foundation's workers managed to offer a pleasant life to pensioners.

About 40,000 people in Prenzlauer Berg are above retirement age, and they are the most affected by the miserable housing situation. For young people it is just a relic of past times that the bathroom is half a flight of stairs up, but for the elderly it becomes a real problem. It is no different with hauling coal for heating. The situation is particularly cruel when you think that it is those who are 60 and 70 years old today who rebuilt Berlin. They sat in the air raid shelters and then cleared away the rubble.

Back again to Schönhauser Allee. Now continuing towards Schönhauser Allee U-Bahn station you get a sense of the considerable achievements of the original U-Bahn builders. The 35 kilometer U-Bahn stretch from Alexanderplatz was handed over to the public on 25 July 1913. In 1930 the overground railway was extended to Pankow. Many regard the Berlin U-Bahn as something special due to its practical and yet graceful construction. The Dimitroffstraße and Schönhauser Allee stations were built following the designs of the renowned architects *Alfred Grenander* and *Johannes Bousset*, and they clearly determined the image of the road. Cunning details facilitate the operation of trains: the stations lie a little above the level of the railway track, so that brake power is spared entering the station, and departures are slightly accelerated.

After this little Schönhauser tour it is worthwhile turning off to the right into **Stargarder Straße,** shortly before the Schönauser Allee S- and U-Bahn station.

Just around the corner at No. 3 the *Krusta Stube* attracts the attention of strangers to the district. Whether or not the combination of pizza and onion tart is to your taste, you can give the place a try.

The **so-called Messel buildings** at Stargarder Straße 3-5 exemplify the attempt to turn progressive architectural concepts into reality. The architect *Alfred Messel* (1853-1909) designed this group of residential buildings for the *Berlin Savings and Building Society*, which runs into Greifenhagener Straße 56/57. Above all he wanted to replace the dark narrow courtyards with lighter ones, and the facades were to be relieved with imaginative shapes, balconies, gables and colors.

A side-trip into Greifenhagener Straße is also worthwhile for hunger's sake. Hot food can be found in *Anker* (open Wed-Sun 8pm-3am) until 2:30am. This private restaurant, maintained in the style of a coastal harbour tavern, can be classed as a rarity in East Berlin. In the *Papillon* at Greifenhagener Straße 16, you can have a drink outside in the courtyard.

Café Flair at Stargarder Str. 72 (Mon-Fri 10am-6pm, Tel. 9-448 34 88) is all done up in purple. High society enjoys its wide range of offerings.

The **Gethsemane Church** in Stargarder Straße stands on the highest point in the district. When the landowner's widow *Griebenow* wanted to donate this land to the church, she was at first refused: the area was too sparsely populated. Finally the church decided not to look a gift-horse in the mouth, and in 1891-93 had *August Orth* erect the red building. When it was completed it was opened with a great deal of pomp by the Kaiser himself. The church is surprisingly spacious and offers a haven of quietness amid all the surrounding crowds.

In more recent times the church has captured a lot of headlines. It was here, during a prayer service, that police brutally intervened against a peaceful demonstration. The demonstrators, outside the church, were doing no more than quietly lighting candles. This brutality was a decisive contribution towards

a large part of the Berlin - and GDR-population in October 1989 being unwilling to bear the chains of the stagnant regime any longer.

This church was the catalyst which roused the people's protests, repressed for so many years, and ultimately encouraged the peaceful rebellion which made it possible to embark on a new beginning. Never had the militant authorities ever been so provoked as by this gathering of mourners. And never had the repressed emotions on both sides been released so brutally. Even the current Rector of Humboldt University found himself among those arrested. Months later, after the fall of the regime, commissions of inquiry were still trying to discover who was responsible and to punish them. It was only partially success-ful, for the old hierarchy covered its tracks, and the cornered former rulers in uniform closed ranks.

On the way through Stargarder Straße to Prenzlauer Allee the occasional digression into the side streets can do no harm. Here you will experience Prenzlauer Berg in the raw.

Where housing is cramped and uncomfortable, the tavern serves as a meeting place. Certainly the days are long gone when members of a political party would stick strictly to their local tavern. Today you will seldom see brawls like those between the "Reds" (communists) and the "Browns" (Nazis) that occurred in the 20's and 30's. But here the times of general unity

against the old regime are slowly coming to an end. The papers report more and more incidents where right-wing radicals have broken in somewhere and damaged person and property. The aggression against foreigners and fringe groups is growing in this district too, and both sides are polarising.

Where Stargarder Straße meets Prenzlauer Allee, you'll see the new *Zeiss Großplanetarium* (Zeiss Planetarium) (Prenzlauer Allee 80, Tue-Sun, 1pm-8pm, Tel. 9-43 28 40). If you are interested in an explanation of the night sky, tickets can obtained from the cashier.

To the right is the *District Council Complex.* The attractive red and yellow brick buildings are surrounded by a wall, and only citizens with business to do with the council are allowed inside.

Returning a little way down Prenzlauer Allee towards the city center, behind the city hospital there lies a housing complex. The complex is worth taking a look at, not because of its good craftsmanship, but more as an example of town planning under the previous "socialist" regime.

Until 28 July 1984 the spot now occupied by the "*Ernst Thälmann Park*" was where the old gasometer of the former "City Gasworks in Danziger Straße" was situated. It was a circular brick building reminiscent of the Roman Colosseum, where the city's gas used to be stored. After Berlin founded its own gasworks in 1872, a number of gasometers were erected between 1889 and 1900, primarily to serve the street lighting. They were destroyed during the Second World War, leaving only the walls standing. Reconstruction was not considered worthwhile. Only students of the Weißensee Art School produced imaginative ideas for their use in their assignments.

As an example of how little the views of the people were taken seriously, ambitious party functionaries decided to erect a housing estate for "our workers". The ensuing flood of protest letters, civil action campaigns, and an attempt to occupy the gasometer were all to no avail. All were repressed by every conceivable security measure, to the point of imprisonment by the *state security* forces during the demolition. Because Berlin demolition experts refused to do the job, colleagues from Magdeburg had to be called in.

In 1986, in honor of the former chairman of the German Communist Party, *Ernst Thälmann*, who was murdered in Buchenwald concentration camp, the whole area and the Greifswalder Straße S-Bahn station was named after him.

It is beyond question that the apartments - comfortable and cheap, with a swimming pool, shops and cultural center close by - were and remain to the liking of the Berliners who moved in. But the project was far more an attempt to obscure the generally miserable housing situation with one, highly publicized spectacle. The fact that the far more attractive gasometer had to give way to a huge and monstrous **sculpture** is particularly lamentable. The monument, with its clenched fist, bold look and waving flags, is by the Moscow sculptor *Lew Kerbel*.

The **Cultural Center** in Ernst Thälmann Park offers a rich and varied program. Behind the obscure title there lies a whole complex including the *Theater unterm Dach* (Tel. 9-430 06 10) as well as the *Wabe* disco. The disco meets all expectations and brings a diverse range of people together. The center in Dimitroffstraße 101 offers amusements ranging from rock to art. If you are interested you should check the noticeboard or just ring up. Eating places are naturally also included.

Another small excursion, between Grellstraße and Naugarder Straße, takes you into the housing estate designed by *Bruno Taut* in 1927.

Depending on how tired you are, you could close your pilgrimage through Prenzlauer Berg either at the Ernst Thälmann Park S-Bahn station or the Prenzlauer Allee S-Bahn station. The S-Bahn is not, however, a particularly advantageous way of getting back to the city, as you have to change trains at least once. Instead a tram ride down Prenzlauer Allee to the intersection of Wilhelm Pieck/Mollstraße and Karl Liebknecht Straße can be recommended. Lines 71 and 72 take you directly back to the city. In this way you will travel right through the apartment blocks which were in the forefront of the city extensions at the end of the last century. They were largely based on plans by *James Friedrich Ludolf Hobrecht*. A look at the map will make it easy to see that this was part of the concept (*George Eugene Hausmann's*) of streets radiating from a center, to be connected with each other by ring roads. The whole street network still follows the old farm boundaries.

Where the tram turns right into Wilhelm Pieck Straße you should step out and walk the final stretch back to Alexanderplatz.

Köpenick (Ralf Schuler)

Köpenick, like almost all of Berlin's districts, bears a number of historical reminders. After the Second World War "only" 7% of Köpenick lay in rubble and ash. Sadly the following years saw much of what remained of this typical suburb neglected and allowed to decay. Köpenick is Berlin's largest district and covers 32% of East Berlin's total area. Unfortunately the 7,600 hectare forest within the district has fared as badly as Köpenick's buildings and streets.

Köpenick has always been inhabited by fishermen. The districts coat of arms portrays the key of St. Peter and two fish. At the end of the last century, the city center had become too cramped. Industry began to exploit the favorable conditions on the banks of the **Spree** and **Dahme** rivers in the southern fringe of the city. Since this time things have steadily declined for fish and fishermen. Although people argued over the type of fish that ought to be represented in the coat of arms, pike or perch, it is only very rarely that an angler will find a fish at the end of his line. The water is getting filthier by the day.

Elsengrund and Wolfsgarten

There are two ways of approaching *Berlin's Green Lung*, as Köpenick is known due to its wealth of forests and lakes: by S-Bahn or by car. The journey from Alexanderplatz to Köpenick station takes 25 minutes. On arrival you can choose between a walk northwards (turning right from the station) through a residential area and on into the countryside, or directly towards the district's center (left from the station).

Directly opposite the station's north exit you will come across a statue of the district's world-famous original: the **Hauptmann (Captain) of Köpenick.** In 1906 the poor wretch was caught dressed up in a self-assembled copy of the mayor's uniform, and with his hand in the town treasury. The bungler, named *Wilhelm Voigt*, had only just been released from jail, and apart from the mayor himself, no one would have held his prank and its wonderful portrayal of the petty Prussian infatuation with uniforms against him. He was released soon after his arrest and thanks to international sympathy he quickly became a wealthy man who got a good price for his memoirs. Because of his addiction to extravagance, however, he was still buried a pauper in a Luxemburg graveyard. Beside the statue the similarly named *restaurant* (Mahlsdorfer Str. 1, open daily 11am-2 am, Tel. 0372-657 20 76) is recommended for lovers of quality German food and good beer.

Stellingdamm, which begins here at the station's north exit, leads to the garden suburb **Elsengrund.** It runs peacefully between the well looked after detached houses. The birch and fir trees, but above all the pine trees manage quite well on the poor soil which is really best suited for Prussian exercise yards. They produce a pleasant atmosphere and the greenery is easy on the eye. The houses were built between 1921 and 1929 by *Otto Rudolf Salvisberg*. The housing layout follows the garden suburb concept favored during the Weimar period.

You can watch life pass by in Elsengrund. Within these enclosed garden plots it was easier to bear the "socialist" times. From a garden swing one can also approach the troubles of the as-yet unknown, but clearly fascinating, market economy calmly: when the price of vegetables goes up, there's always your own beetroot.

Köpenick

S-Bhf.

1 Köpenick
2 Hirschgarten

1 Mecklenburger Dorf
2 Luisenhain/Weiße Flotte (White Fleet)
3 Kunstgewerbemuseum (Arts and Craft Museum)
4 Schloßinsel (Palace Island)
5 Elcknerplatz/Heimatkundliches Kabinett Köpenick (Köpenick Local History Collection)
6 St. Laurentius Church
7 Köpenick Town Hall
8 Flußbad Gartenstraße (swimming pool)
9 Mandrellaplatz
10 Bellevuepark

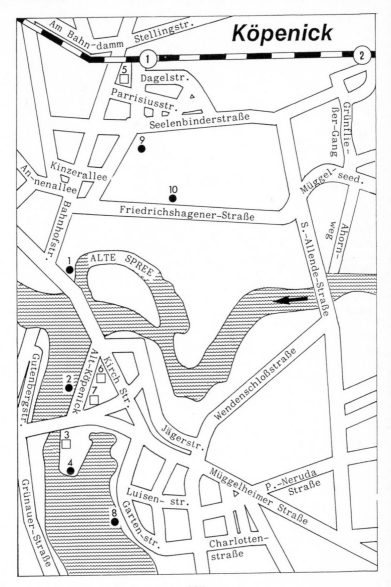

Elsengrund is a very pleasant area to walk through. The tiny Neuenhagener Mühlenfluß river flows through here. To the east lies the **Mittelheide** countryside reserve, and to the north, **Wolfsgarten**, the next garden suburb. The winding Mittelheide forms the border to a small area called the "Märchenviertel" (Fairy Tale Quarter). So dubbed because of its magical street names. A variety of prominent characters have settled here, including pop singers and actors. The makes of the cars standing in front of some houses reveal the high status of the people living here.

If you would like to acquaint yourself with a piece of secluded, isolated Berlin life, you should take the time for a walk through either Elsengrund or Wolfsgarten. Only a few steps into Mittelheide or the Uhlenhorster forest in the north, and the walker is surrounded by inviting greenery. Behind the forest lies the district boundary with Hellersdorf.

Some of the street names in Elsengrund are reminders of a darker chapter in German history.

Only a few weeks after Hitler's seizure of power in June 1933, SA troops began a frightful offensive against the Köpenickers. For some reason they were regarded as progressive, especially the intelligentsia. What went into the district's history as *Köpenicker Blutwoche* (Köpenick Blood Week) is one of the most sensitive wounds to have been inflicted on this tranquil little district. The streets are named after men such as *Stellig, Schmaus* or *Janitzky*, who were among the 19 citizens who met their death under dreadful torture in the local court. No matter how heavy-handed "socialist" propaganda has been in the past, the Köpenickers have never forgotten that these were simple, good people. The various bronze plaques which refer to the events of "Blood Week" are thus futile attempts to embody doctrinaire state anti-fascism, which could never reflect the people's real sorrow.

Also north of the station, but on the left side of Mahlsdorfer Straße (served by tram lines 82, 83 & 86), Dammfeld stretches as far as **Kaulsdorf.** Close to the station you will find 5-storey buildings; later the streets around Gehsener and Kaulsdorfer Straße change to 3-storey buildings, built in the 1950s. Finally the terrain changes to

gardens and detached houses. Out of the Uhlenhorster Forest rises the transmission tower of the East Berlin radio stations, an unmistakable sign of Köpenick's boundary.

If you are tired of the not very productive walk through this part, you can take a bus. They leave from the exit of the station and offer a comfortable ride through the area, over the Köpenick border to Kaulsdorf station or the Elstwerdaer Platz U-Bahn station. From there you can get quickly and easily back to the city; the *Faltin* beer tavern (Kaulsdorfer Str. Tel. 0372-657 22 83) is on the way.

The Center

If you would like to track down the real heart of Köpenick, the former fishing village, you should take the southern exit from the S-Bahn station. You will have to decide for yourself whether it is worth walking down Bahnhofstraße. The buildings are not very attractive and a few facades are crumbling. The former "Bali" cinema diagonally opposite the station exit is hardly recognizable; older Köpenickers still remember the expansive building behind the uninteresting facade.

Next to the station lies **Elcknerplatz,** where the **Heimatkundliche Kabinett Köpenick** (Köpenick Local History Collection) has its home. If you would like to immerse yourself in the district's history, as far back as the Slavic tribes who settled here, you will only be able to do so on Tuesdays (9am-6pm).

Although a wander along **Bahnhofstraße** doesn't offer much, you can always turn it into a little tavern tour. *Buffet am Elcknerplatz*, at the S-Bahn, offers food and drink for customers in a hurry from 7am. Continuing past some apartment buildings, built shortly before the turn of the century, you quickly come to the intersection with Seelenbinderstraße. Here *Café Espresso* serves freshly brewed coffee and snacks (Mon-Fri 10am-10pm, Sat/Sun 2pm-7pm, Tel. 0372-656 03 23).

A side-trip into **Seelenbinderstraße** to the left is well worthwhile because of the lighter traffic. The tram runs about 200 meters from Bahnhofstraße to **Mandrellaplatz**. This square is dominated by the District Court, formerly the Lower Court and built in German Renaissance style. It was built by *Paul Thoerner* between 1899 and 1901. In the building's courtyard, where the remand prison still stands, more than 500 of those arrested during "*Blood Week*" in 1933 were "ques-

tioned". This really meant tortured and beaten into submission. A plaque commemorates *Rudolf Mandrella*, after whom the square was named. He was a judge here, executed in 1943 for his refusal to cooperate with the Nazis.

Tired visitors can rest a little in *Mandrellaeck* tavern directly opposite the court, before they decide where to go next. Of course you could also stay in Mandrellaplatz and move to the *Gerichtsklause* (Mon-Fri 11am-10pm, Sun 4pm-10pm, Tel. 9-657 14 78).

Along Parrsiusstraße, leading off from Mandrellaplatz, you will find quiet, cobblestone streets and old original buildings. Nearby the *Fröhlicher Weinberg* tavern (No. 39, Tel. 9-657 14 53) is open Wed-Fri 4pm-10pm and Sat/Sun 5pm-10pm.

Seelenbinderstraße then leads directly past some horrible barracks. On towards Friedrichshagen, to the *Artur Becker Clubhouse*, which is reserved for the local youth's weekend disco.

The route continues along noisy Bahnhofstraße towards Lindenstraße passing the *Köpenicker Weinstuben* (No. 7, open daily 12am-12pm, Tel. 9-657 29 93). This wine bar always serves good food, but it does cut corners with the wine. A little further along you'll see the letters *AKLA* (a locally-known ice-cream) above the building now housing *Eiscafé Eggert* (No. 2b, Mon-Fri 11am-7pm, Tel. 9-656 21 90). Here the visitor is offered cool refreshment in a cone or a bowl, with fruit or liqueur. From this ice-cream parlor it is only 5 minutes to the *Mecklenburger Dorf* on **Platz des 23. April.** It is open October-March 11am-6pm, Mon/Tue closed; April/May/Sept 11am-7pm, Tue closed; June-August 11am-8pm.

If you are not afraid of a longer detour, just before you reach the Mecklenburger Dorf, you can turn into **Friedrichshagener Straße**. After about 15 minutes walking you will reach Bellevuepark. It begins on the left side of the street shortly before an unattractive industrial complex. This quiet little spot, covered with trees and formerly named "Weinberg", belonged for a long time to the court chaplain *de Saint-Aubin*. He received it as a gift for his efforts from Princess *Henriette-Marie*.

Unfortunately nothing is left of the little castle erected by the chaplain; such relics fitted poorly into the "Socialist" regime's image of a progressive heritage. The poet/-writer *Bernhard von Lepel* bought the park and castle in 1836, and soon the writer's circle "Tunnel over the Spree" was meeting here.

If you don't want to continue beyond Bellevuepark, you will have to walk back to Bahnhofstraße.

How long the monumental **stone fist** will stand on Platz des 23. April as a symbol of revolutionary struggle, no one knows. Incidentally, 23 April marks the day in 1945 that victorious Soviet troops entered Köpenick.

The turn of the century building which dominates Platz des 23. April between Dammbrücke and Bahn-

hofstraße, the Post Office, also lends its name to a tavern. It should only be entered in cases of emergency, and then only for a quick beer (*Zur Post*, Mon-Fri, Tel. 9-657 29 03). On the other corner of the junction with Bahnhofstraße, the former Körner High School stands crumbling. Today it educates junior high school teachers. It is an attractive building with battlements and high windows, which deserves more attention than renovators have given it in the past.

After a few hundred meters Lindenstraße turns into Straße An der Wuhlheide, which you should only traverse by car, the footpaths are that unfriendly. The street comes alive every two weeks when the local football club, *1. FC Union*, plays. The team often loses, but it has loyal, if sometimes unsophisticated fans.

Going left from Bahnhofstraße you will quickly be on the **Dammbrücke** (bridge). From here you get the best view of the two rivers, the Spree and the Dahme, meeting in the middle of Köpenick's old town. Underneath the Dammbrücke rattle the various trams and buses heading towards the outskirts (Müggelheim). From here you can go directly to old Köpenick, the heart of the settlement.

Walking along **Straße Alt Köpenick** towards Luisenhain you will encounter the remains of the original town, which has always been very proud of its seclusion. Although the odd gaps have appeared in the town's facades, from too long a period of neglect, the buildings

opposite the **St. Laurentius Church** still date back to the 17th centuries. But in general the buildings date from the 18th and 19th centuries. Alt-Köpenick 15, for example, belonged to the previously-mentioned court chaplain *de Saint-Aubin*: the *Anderson Palace*. On the ground floor the recently established *Alte Laterne* can be recommended for a quick snack and a friendly beer. Unfortunately the tavern opposite is less attractive.

The **Köpenick Town Hall** next door is unmistakable because of its 54 meter high tower. The neo-Gothic red brick building was erected between 1901 and 1904. As mentioned before, the town hall was the scene of the prank by the self-appointed captain, *Wilhelm Voigt*. Because it generated so much amusement, a parade with a uniformed captain weaves through Old Köpenick every year in the last week of June. It opens with the symbolic handing over of the town treasury to the "Köpenick Summer", a week-long festival with much fun and entertainment.

The *Ratskeller* is open Sun-Thu 10am-11pm and Fri/Sat 10am-1am. Good food is served in the rustic vaults.

Directly opposite the Köpenick Town Hall, where the Dahme runs its last few meters before joining the Spree, **Luisenhain,** a bright promenade, runs along the riverbank. In summer ice-cream is sold here and on the *pier of the Weiße Flotte* (White Fleet). The pleasure boats of the

fleet will take you around Köpenick and the Müggelberge (-hills) (information on Tel. 9-27 12 0). The major dock for all the boats is in Treptow, not far from the Treptower Park S-Bahn station .

Straße Alt-Köpenick leads directly from Dammbrücke to *Schloßinsel* (Palace Island). Before reaching the island it crosses Schloßplatz. This formerly built-up square is now empty and only good for changing over between bus and tram lines. From Schloßplatz you can take a short walk through Grünstraße. This street is becoming more and more attractive by the day, gaining new shops and slowly returning to its old town atmosphere.

A wooden bridge, formerly a drawbridge, is the only way of reaching Schloßinsel. If you look closely at the archway, you will see the remains of the bridge machinery. To the right, in *Köpenicker Schloß* (Köpenick Palace), there is the well-known *Kunstgewerbemuseum* (Arts and Crafts Museum). It exhibits a truly remarkable collection of furniture, porcelain, glass, gold and silverwork spanning the last 1,000 years. Open Wed-Sat 9am-5pm and Sun 10am-6pm. The showpiece, displayed a number of times a day, is a desk with more than 100 drawers, some of them secret drawers....

The palace, built in 1677 by *Rutger von Langerfeld*, acquired its large baroque entrance in 1682 from *Johann Arnold Nehring*. The palace chapel opposite (which serves the Evangelical-Reformed congregation

and offers a varied concert program) is also in baroque style. Again it is the work of *Nehring*, who had it built between 1682 and 1685.

When you have seen enough of the splendid halls in the palace and the chapel, you can walk through the small palace garden. This has something to offer at all times of the year. Beginning with the colorful rhododendron blossoms to the squirrels chasing each other over the bare trees in winter. From the bank beside the palace one can see as far as Cölln, once referred to as "red". The tavern brawls between the communist party members from beyond Langen Brücke and the Social Democrats from Köpenick seen almost romantic now.

At the island's cape one looks over the Dahme flowing from Langen Lake. Virtually all year round tugboats work their way laboriously through the water and sound their melancholy horns. The friendly boats of the *White Fleet* carry waving passengers through the waves. While boats from the Grünau regatta race each other, either using musclepower or with the help of outboard motors.

Beside the palace chapel is the *Schloßcafé*, good for a brief rest (Mon-Thu 2pm-8pm, Wed-Sun 11am-8pm). The din from the nearby swimming pool, **Flußbad Gartenstraße** (open daily 8am-7pm) does not seem to bother the grannies who drink their coffee here. From

244

the cafe's terrace there is a fine view of the traditional fishing settlement, the "Frauentog", which one should inspect at one's leisure.

The "Frauentog" owes its name to a legend in which local fishermen repeatedly returned home with empty nets. The women decided to take matters into their own hands and of course returned with full nets, so giving the stretch of water its name.

If you don't immediately want to return to town, you can cross Lange Bridge and take a detour to *"Cölln"*. This part of Köpenick is dominated by the various industries which have settled here. Going from Lange Bridge and following the tracks of tram line 84, the route leads to Spindlersfeld. On the way you'll pass a striking building on the **corner of Oberspree and Menzelstraße**. This building was built following *Bauhaus* plans and used to house a school for domestic science. A number of years ago, however, the facade of *Majolika-Fliesen* was covered with rough plaster by incompetent architects.

Spindlersfeld owes its name to what was once Berlin's largest laundry. Spindler, who moved his expanding business here late last century, introduced revolutionary work methods. He also built associated worker's quarters, which give the square its character. Spindlersfeld S-Bahn station is the terminal

station of the connecting line to Blankenburg, which offers innumerable connections with other lines. The district border with Treptow runs along here.

A culinary pearl in East Berlin's poorly served and not exactly colorful restaurant scene is *Fioretto* in Oberspreestraße 176 (Tue-Sat 6pm-1am, Sun 2pm-9pm, Tel. 9-657 26 05). It has a fine Italian kitchen, which makes its own pasta. The owner has been given a number of awards by international gourmet guides.

Grünau

Tram Line 86 is suited to those who would like to push on to the furthest and southernmost tip of Köpenick, to *Grünau* or *Schmöckwitz*. The long trip on the rattling tram proceeds down Grünauer Straße, which runs to the left immediately after the Lange Bridge, and later down Regattastraße. At first houses and the *Rewatex* laundry line the road. These are followed by boathouses and gardens on the left and a concrete works and shop fronts on the right. On the way you'll pass the *Weißer Mohr* restaurant (Regattastr. 126, Mon-Fri 11am-9pm, Sat/Sun 10am-6pm, Tel. 9-681 67 41) which offers good simple fare.

Where the tram turns right from Regattastraße into **Wassersportallee** you should get out. Here things become more interesting not only in culinary terms, but also environmentally. *Café Liebig* (No. 158) offers selected snacks, coffee and cakes from 3pm-11pm. Special orders are also taken from groups for foreign dishes.

You'll find a nightspot named the *Riviera* in the Grünau Community Center (Regattastr. 161, Tue-Sun 8pm-4am).

On lazy days a walk is recommended along the banks of the Dahme to the Langer See lake. The Regattastrecke (Regatta Course) puts on a regular calendar of motorboat and rowing races. The adjoining residential area was established in the 1950s especially for artists and intellectuals. It is the home of some famous representatives of German culture, such as *Stefan Heym*.

Long bathing beaches stretch as far as Karolinenhof and Schmockwitz. Tourist cafes like *Hanff's Ruh* (Rabindranath-Tagore-Straße; Thu-Mon 11am-9pm, Tel. 9-681 33 68) or *Richtershorn* (Sportpromenade, open daily 11am-6pm, with the *Schiffahrtsklause* Tue-Sat 5pm-11pm and a nightbar Wed-Sat 9pm-5am) invite you to relax and have a good time. The tram will take you back to Köpenick.

Another possible trip is from Grünau (Wassersportallee) to Wendenschloß. This takes the visitor from one favorite excursion spot to another.

Leaving from Schloßplatz walk along Müggelheimer Straße and swing right into a lane named **Kietz.**

Here the *Kietzer Krug* (No. 18, Mon-Fri 3pm-10pm, Sun 9am-1pm, Tel. 9-657 28 60) serves good solid food with the beer. The pavements along Kietz are buckled and bumpy. Squat houses which were once fisherman's cottages lie beneath rows of trees on either side of the street. But there is really little of the old romance left, the fishermen have been brought together into a collective and the streets lined with "civilized" houses. The further one goes, the more the first impression fades. Kietz becomes first Garten- and then Charlottenstraße. Finally you reach Wendenschloßstraße and the good-looking tram station where Line 83 stops. You can also get to Wendenschloßstraße by simply walking down Müggelheimer Straße from Schloßplatz.

At the intersection of Müggelheimer Straße and Wendenschloßstraße you will have to decide between two equally attractive outings. Wendenschloß on the River Dahme or the area around Müggelsee. If you've got a whole afternoon and good legs, you can do both.

Müggelsee

Bus No. 169 stops right after the intersection, and it will take you quickly and easily to the large open air restaurant, *Rübezahl* (Am Großen Müggelsee, Mon-Fri 10:30am-6:30pm, Sat/Sun 10:30am-7:30pm, Tel. 9-657 25 34). This trip makes it necessary to forget the smaller restaurants like *Clubgaststätte Freundschaft* (Pablo-Neruda-Str. 3, restaurant open Sun-Thu 11am-

10pm, Fri/Sat open 11am-5pm, 6:30pm-1am, beer parlour Mon-Fri 2pm-11pm, Sat/Sun 10am-11pm) or *Café Kränzchen* (Alfred-Randt-Str. 11, open daily 2pm-12pm, Tel. 9-662 01 05) which are on the way.

Apart from the open air *Müggelsee-perle* restaurant (Am Großen Müggelsee, open daily 10:30am-11pm, Tel. 9-657 14 86), the *Rübezahl* is the largest excursion amenity in East Berlin. There is music on the large terraces on weekends. The boats of the *White Fleet* also stop here, either for disembarking passengers or for the start of the trip to Friedrichshagen and around the Müggelberge hills.

You can walk from the *Rübezahl* either to the Spree tunnel or past the *Müggelseeperle* to the **Kleiner Müggelsee** lake, where further refreshment awaits you. *Neu Helgoland* (Odernheimer Straße, Sun-Tue10am-6pm, Fri/Sat 10am-8pm, Tel. 9-656 82 47) and the smaller *Café L B* (Am Kleinen Müggelsee, Wed-Sun, 11am-7pm, Tel. 9-656 82 24).

If you'd like neither "Eis" (ice-cream) nor "Eisbein" (pig's trotter's) in *Rübezahl* then you can enjoy the path towards the **Müggelberge** hills. Halfway along Teufelssee awaits with a remarkable nature trail. The little *Gaststätte Teufelssee* restaurant is close by (Wed-Sun 10am-6pm, Tel. 9-657 28 32).

Legend has it that the devil imprisoned a snooty princess in a glass bell at the bottom of the Teufelsee lake. She could only be released by someone who would carry the emerging princess on their back to Köpenick at midnight on midsummer's night. They then had to circle three times around the church tower. All this without ever looking back at the princess. One person is supposed to have managed it twice, but then looked around...

Leaving the rich natural environment of Teufelssee, with its interesting variety of animals and plants, you climb the **Müggelturm** (Müggel Tower), which probably offers the best view over Köpenick. The current Müggel Tower (126 steps, 30 meters) was preceded by a wooden tower, built in 1890. It was more attractive, but burnt down in 1958. Naturally the *Müggelturm* restaurant on top of the 115 meter high hill, offers a hearty meal for the hungry traveller (Mon-Fri 10am-7pm, Sat/Sun 10am-8pm, Tel. 9-656 97 97).

From the tower the return trip towards Müggelheim takes you via the Müggelbaude, where the bus ensures a swift return. Really keen excursionists head towards Langer Lake and walk down the steps from the hill to the *Marienlust* restaurant (Mon-Fri 11am-7pm, Sat/Sun 10am-8pm, Tel. 9-656 98 00). It can also be reached by car, and the boats of the *White Fleet* also dock here.

A further short walk and you stand at the next open air establishment, the *Schmetterlingshorst* (Am Langen See, Thu-Tue 10am-7pm, Tel. 9-681 39 95). This pub, once a good location, has declined somewhat after a number of changes in ownership, but it still has a good beer garden.

The paths along the Dahme and Langer See are not well-established, but still easily walked, except when they become very muddy during heavy rain.

Continuing from the pub the path leads past **Seebad Wendenschloß** (Wendenschloß Swimming Pool) (open daily 8am-6pm, in July / August until 8pm) to the terminus of tram lines 83 and 85. With either line you can easily return to Köpenick and the S-Bahn station.

The Wends are supposed to have had a castle in this part of Köpenick, which gave the tribe widespread fame.

Friedrichshagen

You haven't seen Köpenick if you overlook *Friedrichshagen.* The S-Bahn line terminating at Erkner stops at Friedrichshagen, two stops after Köpenick. If you'd like to go further into the suburb, to Schöneiche or Fredersdorf, you can change over to the Schöneiche tram, left of the station exit. To the right Bölschestraße leads away from the station.

Friedrichshagen, incorporated into Berlin shortly before the end of the First World War, is special in every sense. It has more culture to offer than other parts of the city and you can comfortably wander about. Friedrichshagen is older, looks a little more run down in parts but is still very attractive. People who live here rarely move away. The foundation years left their ornate traces in the richly-decorated facades. You come across unexpected pomp not only in **Bölschestraße,** a wide artery running right through the area, but also in the side-streets. It must have once been pleasantly quiet, and not just because writers and the well-to-do moved here. Until the beginning of this century Bölschestraße is said to have still been a sandy waste.

After victory in the Franco-German War of 1870/71, favorable financial rains fell on the capital, and expanding industries began to look for open spaces. Where once, thanks to the *Niedersächsisch-Märkischen railway* and its station (built in 1842), one could only see a flood of holiday-makers, modern properties soon began to dominate the skyline. Gas lanterns, a racecourse, two schools, a town hall and Berlin's hitherto largest water works appeared, along with a steamboat ferry over the Müggelspree. The railway was electrified after 1906.

If you come from the station, past the *Union* cinema, you walk down an avenue which today has few trees. At one time it must have been lined with mulberry trees - a well-known restaurant's name still refers to them. But they have long since disappeared, you can count the remaining trees on one hand. What was called "Friedrichsgnade" in the first written references has become a favorite shopping and residential area.

Although there are few sights to report in the conventional sense, you should take the opportunity to walk the streets and enjoy the isolation from the big city crush. Here there are still corner butchers, the private chemist with friendly service, and the baker who gives you the tip to wait another five minutes for oven-fresh bread.

An unusually large amount of cafes and restaurants makes carefree sauntering that much easier. On Bölschestraße alone there is the *Eiscafé Schmock* (No. 25, Mon-Fri 11am-7pm, Sun 1pm-7pm, Tel. 9-645 37 57), the *Ladencafé* (No. 101, Tue-Fri, 10am-6pm) and the *Friedrichshagen* (No. 77, Mon-Fri & Sun 9am-10pm, Sat 2pm-10pm, Tel. 9-645 51 01). As everything in Friedrichshagen is a little more chic and elegant, so too are the culinary establishments. The *Spindel* (No. 51, Wed-Mon 12am-10pm, Tel. 9-645 29 37) is one of East Berlin's finest offerings. The *Friedrichshof* (No. 56, Wed-Sun 6pm-2am) has for a long while been a leader in Friedrichshagen for its quality as well as its prices. The *Monas Bierbar* (No. 64, Mon-Fri 10am-10m) falls more under the heading of "tavern". The *Maul-*

beerbaum (No. 121, Tue-Sat 11am-10pm, Tel. 9-645 81 30) provides an earthy atmosphere of boozing and chatting. Besides the good Berlin cuisine there is also a five-country-menu.

The writer *Johannes Bobrowski*, one of the greats of post-war literature, lived at Ahornallee 26 until his death in 1965. The writer *Erich Mühsam* lived a few houses further on, but a stranger will find no trace of them. There are no plaques or memorial rooms.

Coming from the station everything in Friedrichshagen focuses on one thing: beer. The **Linden Brewery,** established in 1869, and since 1901 the location of the *Berliner Bürger Bräu brewery* (only producing quality and expensive export beer), stands at the end of Bölschestraße. If you go through the 160 meter long **Spree tunnel** from the bank of Müggelsee, you can observe the brewery's imposing building from across the water. Perhaps, though, you should wait until you have tried the house beer in the brewery's *Biergarten* (open daily 10am-12pm).

A favorite among connoisseurs of the area is the *Müggelseeklause* tavern (Tue-Thu 4pm-11pm, Fri 4pm-12pm, Sat/Sun 10am-12pm, Tel. 9-645 54 22). It's about a hundred meters from the BBB brewery, at Müggelseedamm 233 and was formerly known as the "Friedrichshagener Bilderkneipe" (Picture Tavern). After the forced departure of its original owners to the West, the traces of their pre-

sence had to be removed. The name was changed, but what has remained are the cosy, old tavern style atmosphere and the numerous pictures; artists fall over each other to exhibit here. Every first Monday in the month there's jazz.

On the way from the brewery you'll also come across the *Riff* (Tue-Thu, Sun 10pm-4am, Fri/Sat 10pm-6am), an inconspicuous night bar right beside the fire station. It's interesting not only for its elegant interior, but also for its good food and hot music.

If you've found the way to the Spree tunnel - you only have to turn towards Müggelsee at the brewery - you'll see the pier where boats from all directions dock. The view here over the Müggel countryside is very enjoyable. Through the tunnel you can get to either the *Rübezahl* restaurant or back to Köpenick. Buses 168 or 169 will take you back to Köpenick station.

Schöneweide

The last remaining part of Köpenick is *Schönweide*. City tours normally avoid or ignore this industrial area. Usually only the boat trip which begins at Treptower Park is recommended. Schöneweide indeed has very little to offer. Neither the new, but still uncompetitive color television factory, nor the *Karl Liebknecht electrical engineering works* are aesthetic sights. A few brick buildings along Wilhelminenhofstraße might arouse the interest of devotees of industrial architecture. The

251

remaining residential buildings are badly neglected and have for some time awaited various fates, ranging from total demolition to complete renovation.

Schöneweide can be reached from Karlshorst S-Bahn station with trams 16 and 17 towards Johannisthal or Köpenick hospital (four or five stops). The area is dominated above all by factories. The houses are unattractive, but have character, say the locals. A *cinema* named *UT* (Wilhelminenhofstr., Tel. 9-635 09 83) and a few taverns appear to suffice in providing the young, house-hunting and community-building generation with the required atmosphere.

Straße An der Wuhlheide, with its large leisure and relaxation center, borders the Schöneweide housing estate. The other side of Wilhelminenhofstraße does offer some cafes, but sadly the cream of the catering trade hasn't ended up here. Naturally there's a tavern on every corner.

By car to Köpenick

Visitors who travel by car from the city center reach the western edge of the district at the large broadcasting center, shortly after the Klingenberg power station. All the former-GDR's national radio stations were produced here and transmitted from the two transmission towers in Uhlenhorst.

Rummelsburger Landstraße leads past the Wilhelmstrand garden settlement, named in honor of the last emperor. Over the bridge, you cross Edison-/Hermann-Duncker-Straße and then a relatively good road takes you to Old Köpenick. Where Weißkopftraße meets *An der Wuhlheide* on the left, is the entrance to the former Pioneer Park. The park was quickly renamed the *Leisure and Relaxation Center* after the fall of the Wall and it has its own restaurant (*Clubgaststätte Pionierpalast*, open daily 10am-10pm).

A few hundred meters further along An der Wuhlheide stands the *Erich-Weinert-clubhouse* which clumsily tried to supervise the working class's cultural politics. Another 200 meters along, at the old forester's house, the road meets the Spree.

The Spree is probably Berlin's dirtiest river, as it carries all of East Berlin's sewage. It is processed in two stages, but the pollution is still severe enough to produce eczema. From this point on bathing in the Spree is forbidden. A number of years ago the "Flußbad Oberspree" swimming pool had to be closed for swimming, and today serves only for sunbathing.

Finally you reach the intersection of *Lindenstraße and Bahnhofstraße* and continue over the Dammbrücke bridge to Straße Alt-Köpenick. As long as you are not heading straight for Müggelheim, you should park your car here and follow the suggested walking routes. The true Köpenick can only be discovered on foot!

Potsdam - the German Versailles

(*Peter Höh*)

Southwest of Berlin, surrounded by the innumerable lakes, forests and hills of the Lower Havel area, lies the city of Potsdam. It appears as if on an island.

The Prussian military spirit, which Germany brought forth in two World Wars, was originally shaped in this city under the *Soldier King Friedrich Wilhelm I.* To defeat this spirit once and for all, the Allies signed the Potsdam Agreement in 1945, in *Schloß Cecilienhof.*

Historical Background

The Slavic settlement of *Potztupium* was first referred to in **993.** For centuries it remained an unimportant fishing and farming village. This first changed in 1660, when the Hohenzollern family, who had reigned over Brandenburg since 1415, made Potsdam its residence and began building the residental palace in **1664.** From this point onwards the town experienced an unrestrained political, economic and cultural boom. It developed into the center and symbol of Prussia's splendor and glory.

In **1685** *Elector Friedrich*'s "Potsdam Edict" formed the basis of the development of the whole Berlin region from an insignifcant settlement to a world metropolis. The edict ensured freedom of religion for the Huguenots, persecuted in France, and supported their settlement in Brandenburg with limited tax exemptions and favorable land acquisitions. This also explains the many French-sounding names in the Berlin telephone book. These Huguenots and other immigrants - especially the Dutch - made a substantial contribution to the town's subsequent rise.

In *1713* *Friedrich Wilhelm I*, the Soldier King, assumed the monarchy and systematically developed Potsdam into a garrison city. He allowed the city to expand and made room for the many soldiers and immigrants. The Dutch quarter and the new town arose, and the Old Town was extended. In *1769* the city already had 17,000 inhabitants. The fact that more than 8,000 of them were soldiers made the significance of the military to Potsdam abundantly clear.

The Soldier King died in *1740* and his son, *Friedrich II*, *Old Fritz*, took over the regiment. He extended the military machine, but also began to

reshape Potsdam into the seat of representative government. With the construction of *Schloss Sanssouci* (Sans Souci Palace) and its extensive grounds, Potsdam became the German Versailles. Almost all of the old town and parts of the new town were torn down and rebuilt.

By *1786,* the year of *Old Fritz's* death, the reconstruction of the city was more or less complete, and the population almost 50,000. Due to the construction of numerous magnificent buildings, the cream of artisans and architects had concentrated in Potsdam. Also the intellectual and cultural life at Court had attracted many representatives of the fine arts.

At the **end of the 18th century** Potsdam fell increasingly under the shadow of its rapidly growing neighbor Berlin. It became Brandenburg's economic center, while Potsdam remained the seat of government and the royal residence.

It was no coincidence that after his seizure of power in *1933,* *Hitler* had the newly elected Reichstag opened in the Potsdam Garrison Church. With this selection, this symbol of the "Spirit of Potsdam", he wanted to demonstrate the connection between the old might of Prussia and its "virtues" of order, obedience and discipline with the young power of Fascism.

In *1945* this spirit, together with a number of valuable buildings, was covered in a mound of rubble. The city palace, the garrison church and Barberini Palace were all destroyed.

The goal of the Allies when they met in *Schloß Cecilienhof* to sign the Potsdam Agreement and determine the future of post-war Germany was to finally defeat the "Spirit of Potsdam" and ensure that it never rose again. The zones of occupation laid down in the agreement established the division of Germany. These zones made it impossible to visit this historical city for more than 40 years. Despite the deep wounds inflicted by the war on Potsdam's features, its many historic buildings make it one of the great tourist attractions close to Berlin. In particular *Schloß Cecilienhof* and *Schloß Sanssouci* with their lovely park gardens attract visitors from all over the world.

A Roundtrip

Coming from the station over Lange Brücke (bridge), the first thing you see is Potsdam's center, dominated by large socialist-style buildings. Potsdam's main traffic artery, **Friedrich-Ebert-Straße,** runs right through the city to the parks of Cecilienhof and Belvedere. At the start of Friedrich-Ebert-Straße stands the **Film Museum** (open daily except Mon, Tel. 03733). It owes its position to the legendary *UFA*, later *DEFA*, which had its production facilities in the suburb of Babelsberg. It is housed in the baroque-style Royal Stables (1675), which belonged to the former City Palace's Lustgarten.

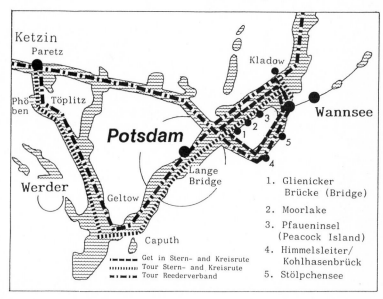

Ketzin
Paretz
Kladow
Phö-ben Töplitz
Wannsee

Potsdam

3
2
1
5
4

Werder
Geltow
Lange Bridge

Caputh

▪▪▪▪ Get in Stern- and Kreisrute
▪▪▪▪▪ Tour Stern- and Kreisrute
▪▪▪▪ Tour Reederverband

1. Glienicker
   Brücke (Bridge)
2. Moorlake
3. Pfaueninsel
   (Peacock Island)
4. Himmelsleiter/
   Kohlhasenbrück
5. Stölpchensee

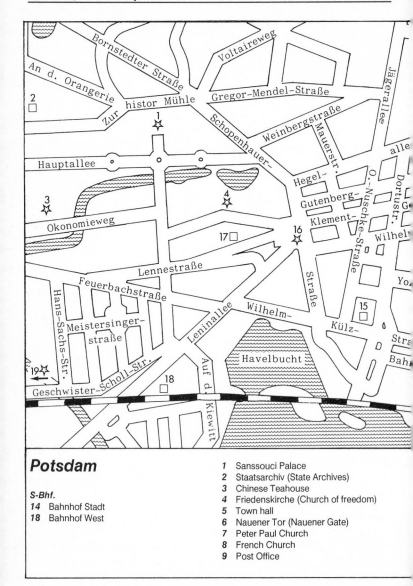

Potsdam

S-Bhf.
14 Bahnhof Stadt
18 Bahnhof West

1 Sanssouci Palace
2 Staatsarchiv (State Archives)
3 Chinese Teahouse
4 Friedenskirche (Church of freedom)
5 Town hall
6 Nauener Tor (Nauener Gate)
7 Peter Paul Church
8 French Church
9 Post Office

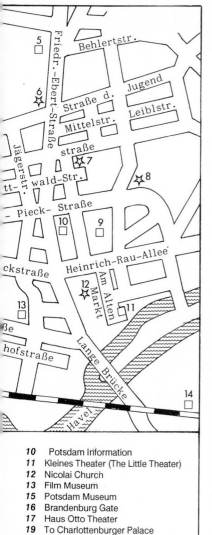

The **Stadtschloß** (City Palace), burnt out by an air raid on 12 January 1945 and finally torn down in 1960, was located near the old market place. The old market, along with the palace, Nicolai's Church and the city hall was the artistic center of the city. The city hall and Nicolai's Church were rebuilt.

The **City Hall,** a baroque building from 1753, today houses the *Kulturhaus Hans Marchwitza*. The stepped dome of the old city hall is crowned by a gold-plated statue of *Atlas* carrying the world on his shoulders. It is in fact the second Atlas. The first, made in 1754 entirely of lead, was too heavy weighing well over 5 tons, and fell to the ground in 1776. The second, which has stood on the dome since 1777, was made of copper.

The **Nicolai Church,** a masterly *K. F. Schinkel* construction, is regarded as one of the most significant examples of classicism in Germany. With its dome it dominates the market place and Potsdam's skyline.

On the **obelisks** which stand in the market place you will find portraits of Potsdam's great builders. Until 1969 pictures of the Hohenzollern family could be seen here. Unfortunately they did not fit with the SED's political concepts, and were exchanged for less significant architectural characters.

The **Knobelsdorffhaus,** a baroque building from 1750, is connected with the old city hall by a modern building.

On the spot where the Hohenzollern's lovely City Palace once stood, the *Interhotel* now rises 16 storeys into the sky. Remnants and parts of the palace can be seen in the hotel's garden, once the Lustgarten.

Immediately next to the *Interhotel* there is a pier for the *White Fleet*, with which you can make a number of outings into the Havel lake area. If you want to take a break, it is worth going the few steps back to Langen Brücke. There, in the Havel, lies **Freundschaftsinsel** (Friendship Island), where you can pause for a while in the *Inselcafé*. On the island you can rent boats, look at the exhibition in the pavilion, or walk around the garden. On a memorial erected in the garden by its founder, *Karl Förster*, the alert visitor can read the words: "To turn dreams into reality, you have to be awake and dream deeper than others".

After the coffee-break you can work your way up Friedrich Ebert Straße.

First you will come to **Bassinplatz** and the **Peter Paul Church,** a late-classical building from 1751/52, with Byzantine elements reminiscent of the *Hagia Sofia*. The church's bell tower was modelled on the *San Zeno Campanile* in Verona, Italy. Behind the church, at the end of **Wilhelm-Pieck-Straße,** stands the **French Church,** another baroque building from 1752/53 designed by *Knobelsdorff*. Here at Bassinplatz you will have to choose which direction you wish to go, Cecilienhof/New Garden or Sanssouci.

Cecilienhof

If you chose the Cecilienhof direction, just continue along Friedrich-Ebert-Straße. On the corner with Gutenberg-Straße lies Potsdam's next jewel - the **Dutch Quarter:** 134 houses in Dutch style, arranged around 4 courtyards. *Friedrich I* had it erected in 1734 to house the Dutch building workers who were to move to Potsdam as a result of His Majesty's trip to Amsterdam. However, the whole idea was a flop. Far fewer Dutchman came than expected, and many of the houses had to be given to soldiers and local artisans. Today the quarter is in a state of very poor repair. With the energetic assistance, financial support and technical know-how of former West Berlin squatters, the inhabitants have tried to halt the houses' decline and carefully restore them.

Further along Ebert-Straße you look through the **Nauener Tor** (Gate) to a neo-Gothic building, erected in 1755 following an English example. If you look down Hegel-allee, you'll see the **Jägertor,** the only remaining gate from the city wall erected around the new town in 1735.

At the end of Ebert-Straße, where it turns into Puschkinallee, lies *Alexandrowka*, the **Russian colony.** Its 12 richly trimmed log houses, designed in Russia, were erected by *Friedrich Wilhelm III*, to keep 12 singers of a Russian soldier's choir at court. To ensure that they felt at home, a Russian Orthodox church was also built for them. The 12 singers belonged to a choir - originally of 62 soldiers - taken prisoner during the Napoleonic campaign. Later they were allowed to stay with the Prussian army as part of the military pact between Russia and Prussia.

The **Russian Orthodox Church** tops the Kapellenberg (Chapel Hill). Behind the Kapellenberg, on the **Pfingstberg**, stands the **Belvedere** (1849/62). This building, constructed in Italian Renaissance style, is a fragment of a large set of terraces. They were supposed to reach back to the Neuen Garten park. On the slope of the Pfingstberg you can get a lovely view over the Havel area. The city's **Jewish Cemetery** also lies on the slope. In 1743 it was set out here, on ground "which was otherwise unsuited to any purpose".

Schinkel's first building in Potsdam, an unfortunately badly damaged tea pavilion also stands on the Pfingstberg.

Going from the Pfinstberg down **Weinmeisterstraße,** you will reach the **New Park.** The 74 hectare landscaped park created by the landscape architects *Lenné* and *Eyserbeck*, was modelled on Wörlitzer Park.

At its northern end, where it borders on to Jungfernsee, stands **Schloß Cecilienhof** (open daily, Tel. 03733-225 79). The palace was erected in 1913/17 in the style of an English country manor. The *Potsdam Conference* met here between 17 July and 2 August 1945, with *Stalin, Truman, Churchill and Attlee* hammering out the *Potsdam Agreement.* The conference rooms are today a museum, the rest a hotel.

The extensive grounds of the park run parallel to the banks of Heiligen See lake. If you pass the Green and Red Houses, two old garden houses from before the park was established, you come to the **Marmor Palace** (1787/92). The palace lies on the river bank and is one of the best examples of the Berlin school of architecture's early Classicism. Its rooms have housed the Army Museum since 1961. South of the palace lies the kitchen, disguised as an antique temple to Mars, and connected to the palace by an underground tunnel. The pyramids lying north of the palace are not a

graveyard, but once served as the Marmor palace's ice-box. The small temple at the southern end of the park was *Wilhelm II's* library.

Between the palace and the cavalier's houses lies the Orangerie. Its eastern facade has a large Egyptian gateway including a sphinx. The former cavalier's houses, the ladies house and the gate house together with the coach house and stables, are now the **Planetarium,** the **Bruno H. Bürgel Memorial** and the **Educational Center** .

Sanssouci

If you decided to go to Sanssouci from Bassinplatz, then turn down **Klement-Gottwald-Straße.** This is Potsdam's main shopping street, a pedestrian precinct with lovely renovated buildings. At the far end lies the **Platz der Nationen,** with its own **Brandenburg Gate,** which is actually older than its namesake in Berlin. It was erected in 1770 as a Roman triumphal arch.

From the Platz der Nationen the avenue leads to Sanssouci.

Naturally it is impossible to describe the 290 hectare **Sanssouci Park** and all its buildings in detail here. That would be a book in itself. If you are interested in delving more deeply into the palace's history, you should gather some information from the Visitor's Information Center at Grünen Gitter 2 (Tel. 03733-238 19).

The Sanssouci grounds are the work of generations. It began in 1744 when *Friedrich II* had terraces constructed on the deserted hill to turn it into a vineyard. Between 1745 and 1747 Sanssouci palace was erected by *Knobelsdorff* according to *Friedrich II's* sketches. Friedrich wanted an intimate spot, where he could pursue his private life "without care" (French: *sans souci*).

You enter the park through the **Main Portal,** erected in 1747 and modelled on the garden portal in *Schloß Rheinsberg.* Here Hauptallee , the main path through the grounds, begins. It winds through the park and ends at the New Palace 2.5 kilometers away.

At the beginning of the path stands a copy of an **Egyptian obelisk** (1748). Continuing past 12 marble

busts the **Dutch Garden** lies to the right. *Neptune* perches here in his grotto, flanked by two mermaids with water pitchers. Behind the grotto lies the **Picture Gallery** (1755/63). Most of its treasures (including Italian and Flemish Renaissance and baroque masters) disappeared in the confusion of the Second World War. The pictures here have been gathered together from other palaces.

To the north of the gallery is the **Kastellenhaus** (1790) with its grotto-like base.

The **Schloß Sanssouci Palace** is reached from the picture gallery up a small staircase decorated with a wonderful 18th-century cast-iron banister. In the palace's alcoves stands *Friedrich II's* death chair. The *Voltaire room* in the palace is named after the famous French writer who visited Berlin and Potsdam in 1750-53 at the invitation of the King.

From the uppermost palace terrace one goes up a staircase to the **New Chambers.** The building, erected in 1747 by *Knobelsdorff*, was later reconstructed as a guest house. The New Chambers used to be fronted by the Cherry Garden, and in 1956 a rose garden was laid out here. The heart of the park is the vineyard, on which the palace stands. In 1773 the terraces were enclosed in greenhouses. This meant that the most foreign of grapes could be grown to produce a passable drop of wine even in Northern Europe's harsh climate.

From the Musenrondell - with its statues of the Muses - you can see the **Felsentor.** Originally (1749) only represented in a painting on a wooden partition, it was later properly built of stone.

Southwest of the Musenrondell lies the **Chinese Teahouse** (May-October open daily). Life-sized statues of Chinese eating fruit or drinking coffee decorate the entrance hall and the small rooms. Today you will find an exhibition of Chinese and European porcelain in the pavilion.

Further along Hauptallee you come to the entrance of the **Reb Gardens**. Continuing on towards the New Palace, you'll reach the **Sicilian Garden.** In summer there are various types of palm trees here, intended to create a more southern atmosphere. In winter they are housed in the **Orangerie,** which lies on Maulbeerallee, running parallel to

Hauptallee. The Orangerie was erected in 1851/60, and was to be the only building along the triumphal road planned by *Friedrich Wilhelm IV*. The road was to lead over the Klausberg as far as the Belvedere. Today the building, erected in Italian Renaissance style, houses the Potsdam State Archives. Opposite the Sicilian garden lies the Northern garden, with pines and firs instead of palm trees.

The **Dragon House,** like the Orangerie on Maulbeerallee, was built in 1770 as a residence for the wine growers. Its roofs are decorated with gold-plated dragons. At the top of the hill diagonally behind the Dragon House stands the **Belvedere** (1770/72). From here you can look over the whole park grounds.

Round Table of Friedrich the Great in Sanssouci.
From an original drawing by Ad. v. Menzel

The circular building with its two rooms never had any real purpose, and was therefore left unused.

At the end of Hauptallee, flanked by the Friendship Temple and the Antique Temple, stands the **New Palace,** the most magnificent building in the park. It was built in 1763/69 as the Royal Family's summer residence. One of the building's curiosities is the Grotto-Hall. Originally the Hall was decorated with glass shavings, mussels and coral. These were replaced by precious stones, minerals and fossils in the 19th century. In the southern wing is the palace theater, a beautiful roccoco-style auditorium with 300 seats.

Behind the New Palace lies the **Gommuns** (1766/69). In the past they served as kitchen, service rooms, servants' quarters, and so on. Today they belong to the Potsdam College of Education.

South of the Palace a new district was constructed in 1825: **Park Charlottenhof.** Schloß Charlottenhof lies embedded in *Lenné's* landscape, a small palace with a modest exterior (May-October open daily, Tel. 03733-927 74). *Alexander von Humboldt* lived for a time in the "tent room", a room with a tent-shaped ceiling. The scientist did not create the design, it was already there. He is said to have felt very much at home in this tented environment and to have dreamed of his research trips under the canopy.

The **Hippodrom** (1886) was planned as part of an exclusive housing estate, to be modelled on an antique model, but the estate was never built. West of the Hippodrom, *Lenné* established a pheasant reserve in 1841/44, and in 1844 *Persius* added a pheasantry in an Italian villa-style. Close to the little lake are the **Roman Baths**. The baths are assembled around a group of houses which in turn are arranged around a garden (1829/35). Exhibitions are held in one of the houses, **Hofgärtnerhaus,** in the summer months.

Past the Chinese Teahouse, through Marlygarten (formerly Küchengarten), and shortly before the obelisks at the exit from **Frie-denskirche,** you will reach a late-Classical, columned basilica. Built in 1845/54 it was modelled on *Basilika San Clemente* in Rome.

The park's fountains and water-works were supposed to have been driven by the water basin laid out for that purpose within the hill. However only once, in 1754, did they pump enough water from the Havel into the basin to drive the little fountain - for a whole hour. In 1841 a steam-driven pump was installed, which would finally drive the fountains in the park continuosly. *Persius* built a **Mosque** around the pump, in a Moorish style, with the chimney disguised as a minaret. If you'd like to take a look at this curious technical and cultural monument, it stands at the corner of Leninallee and Wilhelm-Külz-Straße.

Babelsberg

After Sanssouci and the New Garden, Babelsberg Park is the third largest garden in Potsdam. The 130 hectare park was started by *Lenné*, and later extended and completed by *Elector Pückler-Muskau* (1843-49). It was preceded by a wildlife park, which *Friedrich I* had established together with the Glienecke Hunting Palace.

The park contains **Schloß Babelsberg** (1843/49), which today houses the Museum for Prehistory and Early History. The palace grounds include the **Small Palace,** built in 1841/42 as a ladies house, the **Marstall** (Royal Stables) (1838), and the **Matrosenhaus** (Sailor's Home) (1842). The Matrosenhaus housed the sailors who worked the gondolas and sailing vessels.

The park's trademark is the **Flatow tower,** which can be seen from far away. Also a water fort, it stands in a pool which serves the park's irrigation. It can be reached by crossing a draw-bridge. North of the tower stands the **Gerichtslaube** (courthouse). It originally stood in Berlin by the old city hall. When the new *Red City Hall* was constructed, the building was carried off in 1871/72 and reconstructed in Babelsberger Park.

If you like walking through lovely, peaceful landscapes, you should go to Babelsberger Park. Lying somewhat off the beaten track, it is the least well-known and least spectacular of Potsdam's three garden parks. It is impossible to walk so undisturbed in New Park, or Sanssouci especially on weekends. In Sanssouci the tourist buses pull up before the grounds are even open.

If you'd like to stay longer in Potsdam you should obtain the *Tourist Stadtführer Atlas Potsdam* (Potsdam Tourist Atlas). It contains a comprehensive and very detailed description of the city. The book's somewhat heroic socialist undertone can be understood as part of a historical document. Available in bookshops.

Potsdam Information is in Friedrich-Ebert-Str. 5 (Mon-Fri 9am-6pm, Sat 9am-4pm, Sun 12am-4pm, Tel. 03733-32 92 17). Here you can obtain information about accommodation, restaurants and the many ways of enjoying yourself in Potsdam.

Potsdam is best reached by train from Wannsee.

Practical Hints, A-Z

Contents

AN1483059K1

Note: Addresses are all prefaced with the postcode for that district, marked on most maps. 1-61, for example, refers to Kreuzberg.

1. Banks

Outside normal banking hours you can **change money** and do other bank business at the following branches:

●*Bank für Handel und Industrie* in KaDeWe, 1-15, Tauentzienstr. 21, 1st floor, open during the department stores opening hours.
●*Berliner Bank*, city service, 1-15, Ku'damm 24, Mon-Fri 9am-6:00pm, Sat 9:30am-1:00pm or at Tegel Airport, open daily 8am-10pm.
●*Berliner Sparkasse* at the Gedächtniskirche, 1-15, Ku'damm 11, Mon-Fri 9am-6pm, Sat 10am-1pm.
●*Berliner Commerzbank*, 1-15, Ku'damm 211, Mon-Fri 9am-6pm, Sat 10am-1pm.

Money Exchange

You can exchange money at the Zoo station; in Joachimstaler Straße; in the Europa Center; at the airport; and in Georgenstraße at Friedrichstraße S-Bahn station (open day and night).

2. Cinemas

●*Recorded message for West Berlin first-run cinemas*, A-K on Tel. 115 11 & L-Z on Tel. 115 12
●*Recorded message for local cinemas* in Kreuzberg, Neukölln, Schöneberg, Steglitz, Wilmersdorf & Zehlendorf on Tel. 115 14; for Charlottenburg, Reinickendorf, Wedding & Spandau on Tel. 115 15
●*Hotline to the city magazine Prinz*: Tel. 88 42 01 45

3. Climate

If the climate in the city sometimes seems a little harsh, it lies less in the weather and more in the various social contradictions and conflicts. The temperatures seldom reach extremes. Winters are usually mild, Summers rarely unbearably hot. The months May-October are ideal for a visit.

The so called "inversion situation" which often results in a first-level smog alarm in winter, arises from cold air fronts pushing hot air and all it contains to the ground. The burning of brown coal by industry and private households in particular, burdens the air with sulphur dioxide.

4. Disabled

Berlin is certainly not a disability-friendly city. Although some initial attempts are being made to change the city's landscape so that disabled people can also take part in life unaided, the results so far are limited.

●The *Interessengemeinschaft von Geburt an Behinderter e.V.* (1-10, Otto-Suhr-Allee 131, Tel. 341 17 97) offers advice and rents wheelchairs.
●The *Telebus-Zentrale* (1-15, Joachimstaler Str. 17, Tel. 880 03-113) gives advice on problems with transportation.
●The *Ambulanten Dienst* (1-61, Gneisenaustr. 2, Tel. 693 70 31) offers a variety of services Mon-Fri 10am-5pm.

5. Eating and Drinking

In culinary terms Berlin ranks highly as a city with a truly cosmopolitan choice of food and drink. There are innumerable restaurants, taverns, bars and fast-food stalls spread all over the city. The praiseworthy task of covering the whole culinary scene has been taken on by the city magazine "Zitty". The Zitty special issues on eating, drinking and dancing in West and East Berlin (Spring 1990 with "all 999 taverns") are the best guides to the gastronomic jungle. The tourist bureau also puts out a comprehensive survey of good eating establishments. But as trends and quality changes rapidly, you should rely as much as you can on tips from the locals.

The oft-repeated cliché about Berlin, that it is open round the clock, is primarily true for the Western half. The restaurants in Mitte or Prenzlauer Berg tend to close around midnight.

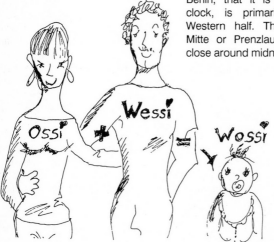

6. Excursions

Bundesgartenschau and Berliner Gartenschau (The Federal Garden Show and The Berlin Garden Show)

A number of institutions and organizations exist in duplicate at the moment. So there are still two garden shows on the Spree: the *Britzer Garten*, the former Federal Garden Show, as well as the *Berliner Gartenschau* in Marzahn (East Berlin).

Attractive amusement areas have been created in both parks. Each offers a wealth of interesting impressions for visitors to the city as well as locals. **Britzer Park** first appeared as the Federal Garden Show beween 1979 and 1985 in the South-East of Berlin. Today the area encompasses around 100 hectares of dog-free relaxing countryside with lakes, hills and meadows. Britzer Garden also contains Berlin's only functioning Dutch windmill, built in 1896.

●The Berlin Garden Show is open in the summer months daily 10am-7pm. The entrances are in Eisenacher Straße and in Otto-Buchwitz-Straße, admission 1 DM.

Lübars

Before 9 November 1990, any West Berliner who wanted to see the countryside and its animals could only follow the road to Lübars. The village, north of Berlin, with its broad fields and meadows has in the past become the target of many, perhaps too many, weekend excursions. The heart of the village, first mentioned in 1247, has been maintained with a number of historic buildings and their facades.

●Britzer Park is open daily from 9am to dusk, admission 1 DM.

The other attractive park, the **Berliner Gartenschau** was established during the 750th anniversary in 1987. It is situated on an area of more than 20 hectares between the districts of Marzahn and Hellersdorf. Large open stretches, woods and theme gardens as well as a varied display of plants and flower beds characterize the park. Bicycles can be rented during a visit to the park.

You can walk from Lübars along the Nordgraben, which flows into Tegel Lake, along the old border as far as Tegel (U-Bahn Line U6, roughly 10 km).

●Bus Line 222 travels to and from Lübars.

Treptower Park

Even Kreuzbergers and Neuköll-ners haven't yet recognised what a beautiful park sits on their doorstep since the opening of the Wall. Treptower Park was built in 1896 precisely for the relaxation of the populations of these two districts.

●The park alongside the Spree in the East Berlin district of Treptow can be reached with the S-Bahn (Treptower Park or Plänterwald) or by foot from Schlesisches Tor U-Bahn station (U1).

Surroundings: Signs from the S-Bahn direct you to the harbour of the *Weißen Flotte* (White Fleet). Here lie the excursion boats for the Müggelsee roundtrip or trips to Schmöckwitz, Woltersdorf and Charlottenburg.

If you walk or cycle along Pusch-kinallee, you will soon reach the so-called *Insel der Jugend* (Island of Youth), with its suspension bridge over the Spree. On Sundays the sounds of jazz music can be heard from *Jugendclub "Pablo Neruda"* (Tel. 9-272 55 23). In summer open-air concerts are also held on the island. You can watch everything happen-ing on the island and the Spree from the beergarden in *Zenner* (Sun-Thu 12am-8pm, Fri/Sat 12am-12pm). But *Zenner* is to be recommended not just for lazy summer nights. The restaurant, in a room large enough to be a ballroom (Tel. 9-272 72 11, Mon-Thu 11am-8pm, Fri/Sat 11am-1am, Sun 11am-10pm), serves generous helpings of excellent traditional food.

Fortified by this refreshment, you will now be able to head for the *Soviet Memorial* (see memorials) or the *Plänterwald Culture Park*. The culture park is an amusement park open between April and October. Rust eats away at the carousels and stalls, but the ride on the ferris wheel is to be recommended for its wonderful view of the inner city.

7. Fairs and Festivals

The cultural offerings in both halves of the city easily measure up to comparable metropolises. In addition to the huge variety of events in Berlin's daily calendar, there are also Berlin's fairs and festivals.

International Filmfestspiele
(International Film Festival)

This film festival is not just for the professional film crowd, but a February "happening" for "normal" film people. The festival has been

Wintergarten.

Direction: **Dorn & Baron.**

Neues Programm. 12 Debuts. Neues Programm.

Mlle. Gabriele Juniori
vom Empire-Theater in London.

The Eugens, **Mr. Tompson** **Die Wüstensöhne,** **Brüder Marko,**
die berühmten Hochturner.   mit seinen drei Elephanten.   8 Araber.   die sonderbaren „Zwillinge".

Griffin u. Dubois, **Rheingold-Trio,** **Egger-Rieser, Pettenati,**
Excentriques.   Komisches Gesangs-Terzett.   Tyroler National-Sänger u, Tänzer. Italienisches Quartett.

Neu! **Das Bioskop.** Neu!
Die interessanteste Erfindung der Neuzeit.

Maisanos,
musikalische Excentriques.

Ferner: **Familie Sylvester Sch**
in ihren unerreichten ikarischen Spielen

Lona Barrison, Sie
singende Schulreiterin.
Anfang 7½ — Sonntags 7 Uhr. — Vorve

Emil Skladanowsky
Erfinder der lebenden Photographien
(Bioskop)
in Firma Gebrüder Max & Emil Skladanowsky
1890 — 1897
Erste öffentliche Vorführung am 1. November 1895 im Wintergarten zu Berlin

Berlin O. 34,   Warschauer Str. 27

going for 40 years. The gloss and glamour of earlier days is over, but the significance of this the third-largest film festival in the world is undisputed. Since 1990 the film screenings have taken place in both halves of Berlin.

●Information: *Berliner Festspiele*, 1-30, Budapester Str. 48.

Freie Berliner Kunstausstellung
(Independent Berlin Art Exhibition)

Berlin artists exhibit their work here at the Exhibition Grounds every year (April/May).

Theatertreffen Berlin (Berlin Theater Gathering)

The cream of the German-speaking theater meets every year in May in both halves of Berlin.

●Information: *Berliner Festspiele*, 1-30, Budapester Str. 48.

Jazz in the Garden

A summer jazz festival with open-air concerts in the National Gallery's Sculpture Garden or, in bad weather, the College of Art.

Kino in der Waldbühne (Cinema in the Forest stadium)

A large-screen cinema experience in Berlin's best open-air location. Tightly-packed, over 20,000 cinema fans sit and enjoy cult films like *The Blues Brothers*, *The Rocky Horror Picture Show* or *Charlie's Aunt*.

Berliner Festwochen

A **series of classical music concerts** with international participants, which takes place every year in Autumn. Because the events are always well-attended, it is worth booking tickets early. Information and tickets: *Berliner Festspiele*, 1-30, Budapester Str. 48.

8. Getting there, getting back

By air

Air traffic to and from Berlin is in a state of flux because of the opening of the border. The three air corridors assigned to the Allies in 1945 still exist, and airlines still have to stay within them. Originally this was to ensure that no air traffic to or from West Berlin could pass unnoticed.

There are four airports in the city: *Tegel*, *Gatow*, *Schönefeld* and *Tempelhof*. Virtually all of West Berlin's civil air traffic passed through Tegel airport, opened in 1975. It still remains almost exclusively the destination of the various Allied airlines. But this too is certain to change in the future. An improved connection between Tegel and Schönefeld is anticipated. A bus service for the route was introduced in July 1990.

Information
- Tegel Airport, Tel. 410 1-2306
- Tempelhof Airport, Tel. 6909-1
- Schönefeld Airport, Tel. 9-672-4031

Reservations Tegel

Aeroflot	41 01 26 88
Aero Lloyd	41 01 26 08
Air France	41 01 27 15
Alitalia	41 01 26 50
Austrian Airlines	41 01 26 15/16
British Airways	41 01 26 47
Dan Air	41 01 27 16
Delta Air Lines	41 01 34 90
Finnair	41 01 26 15/16
Iberia	41 01 26 98
Istanbul Airlines	41 01 28 72
KLM	41 01 34 22
Lufthansa	88 10 11
Olympic Airways	41 01 26 45
Pan Am	01 30 55 66
SAS	41 01 26 80
Swissair	41 01 26 15/16
TAP Air Portugal	2 61 16 87
Tempelhof Airways (Tempelhof)	69 09 431-34
Trans World Airlines	41 01 27 34
Turkish Airlines	41 01 34 16
United Airlines	41 01 34 35

Reservations Schönefeld

Aeroflot	9-6 72 20 39 / 6 78 82 43
Air Algerie	9-5 89 26 53
Air China	9-6 72 23 06
Austrian Airlines	9-6 72 33 81
Balkan	9-6 72 31 74 / 6 78 83 44
Chosonminhang	9-6 72 20 70
CSA	9-6 72 38 42 / 6 78 80 66
Cubana	9-6 78 81 18
El Al Israel Airlines	9-8 81 10 58
Japan Airlines	9-2 61 13 74
JAT	9-6 72 23 04 / 6 78 80 64
LAM	9-6 72 23 08 / 6 78 80 62
LOT	9-6 78 82 50

Lufthansa	9-6 72 35 15
Malev	9-6 72 38 54 / 6 78 80 61
Singapore Airlines	9-6 72 26 67
Syrien Arab	9-6 72 23 44 / 6 78 82 58
TAAG	9-6 78 80 65

Lufthansa has plans to enter into the Berlin air traffic to and from both large airports. The first step in this direction was the opening of an office in East Berlin:

• *Deutsche Lufthansa AG*, Hotel Metropol, Friedrichst. 150-153, 1086 Berlin, Tel. 9-220 40. The West Berlin office is also centrally located:
• *Deutsche Lufthansa AG*, 1-15 Kurfürstendamm 220, Tel. 88 75 0

Getting to the Airport

Tegel airport is connected to the city center by a **shuttle bus** on Line 109. This bus runs every 15 minutes (travel time, 20 minutes, normal fare). Bus Line 128 departs from the airport towards the northern districts and terminates at Osloer Straße U-Bahn station (Line U8/U9).

A **taxi** to the city costs around 20 DM.

By Train

Trains travelling to Berlin usually stop at Wannsee or Spandau, and stop whatever at Zoo Station (West) and Friedrichstraße Station (East). A lot will change in the near future with respect to rail comfort and the number of rail connections. Until now the *Deutsche Reichsbahn* (GDR) has been responsible for the railways in West Berlin. The antici-

pated cooperation with the *Deutschen Bundesbahn* (FRG) will hopefully make train travel, which suffers from a lack of comfort and long travelling time, more attractive.

Information

●Bahnhof Zoo (Bundesbahn), Tel. 194 19
●Bahnhof Zoo (Reichsbahn), Tel. 31 10 21 11
●Bahnhof Friedrichstraße, Tel. 9-495 31 or 495 41

By Bus

A number of bus companies connect Berlin with West Germany and the GDR. The bus station in West Berlin is the "ZOB" on the Messegelände, in East Berlin it is at the Hauptbahnhof (Central Station).

Timetable Information

At the ZOB, up to 6pm on Tel. 302 52 94, after 6pm on Tel. 301 80 28.

Lift Services

Throughout West Germany there are some unique enterprises called "Mitfahrzentralen". These operations make hitch-hiking in Germany a remarkably civilized affair, taking much of the pain out of the whole process. People offering lifts approach the lift service saying when and where they are travelling, and those seeking lifts do the same. The service brings them together,

charges a small fee, and the hitch-hiker pays the driver for petrol. Occasionally you may also be asked to share in the driving, but that will be made clear at the Lift Service. If you would like to leave Berlin this way you should simply ring one of more than 15 Mitfahrzentralen to be found in West Berlin. Just say where you would like to go and when. They will understand English! It's a cheap way of getting about.

●*Frauen-Mitfahr-Zentrale* (Women's Lift Service), women take women!, 1-30, Potsdamer Str. 139, Mon-Fri 10am-2pm and 4pm-8pm, Sat/Sun 12am-3pm, Tel. 215 31 65.
●*Mitfahrzentrale im Ku-Damm-Eck*, 1-15, Ku'damm 227, Mon-Sat 8am-9pm, Sun 10am-6pm, Tel. 882 76 04 (for seeking lifts), 881 22 83 (for offering lifts).
●*Mitfahrzentrale im U-Bahnhof Zoo*, on the platform on Line 1 in the direction of Schlesisches Tor, Mon-Sat 8am-9pm, Sun 10am-6pm, Tel. 31 03 31.

Hitch Hiking

If you want to save the Lift Service's fee, you can use your own outstretched thumb and a sign with your destination. It is best to start at the Dreilinden (entry Potsdamer Chausee) or Staaken border crossing. The dangers associated with women hitch-hiking alone cannot be over emphasized. Sad as it may be, women are better advised to turn to the women's lift service.

Border Crossings

There is no longer any passport control at the internal border crossings. For a born and bred Berliner this sentence is still sensational. All the streets (more than 140) which were divided by the concrete wall can now be passed through freely. No long queues at the control stations, no anxious bag inspections and of course no troublesome compulsory money exchange.

9. Information

(mostly English-spoken)

●*Auskunftstelle im Bahnhof Zoo*, open daily 8am-11pm, Tel. 313 90 63/64

●*Auskunftstelle Dreilinden*, open daily 8am-11pm, Tel. 803 90 57

●*Auskunftsstelle Flughafen Tegel*, open daily 8am-11pm, Tel. 41 01 31 45

●*Auskunftstelle Staaken*, open daily 8am-11pm, Tel. 363 40 21

●*Berlin Tourist Information* 1-30, Europa Center (entrance Budapester Str.). open daily 7:30am-10:30pm, Tel. 262 60 31-33, Fax 21 23 25 20

●*Informationszentrum der Berlin Information* at the East Berlin Television Tower, Mon 1pm-6pm, Tue-Fri 8am-6pm, Sat/Sun 10am-6pm, Tel. 9-212 46 75

●*Zentraler Touristen-Service*, East Berlin, Alexanderplatz 5, Mon-Fri 9am-7pm, Sat/Sun 9am-12am & 12:30am-6pm, Tel. 9-215 41 61 & 212 33 75

10. Language

You will encounter a number of German words fairly often. Here is a list of the more common words, particularly the ones of relevance to a visitor. Use the list when you need to or, better still, try to remember it.

Amt	office	*Markt*	market
Autobahn	freeway, highway	*Mensa*	cafeteria,
Autonome	anarchist		usually student
	streetfighter	*Messe*	fair, show,
Bad	bath, pool		exhibition
Bahnhof	railway station	*Naturschutzgebiet*	protected park,
Bezirk	district		national park,
Bibliothek	library		nature reserve,
Brauerei	brewery		sanctuary
Brücke	bridge	*neu/e*	new
Bühne	stage, theater	*Ost*	east
Buchhandlung	bookshop	*Passage*	arcade
Büro	office	*Platz*	square
Café	coffee-shop	*Polizei*	police
Currywurst	curried sausage	*Rat*	council
Ecke	corner	*Rathaus*	town hall
Eis	ice-cream	*S-Bahn*	metropolitan
Etage	floor		railway
Fahrt	trip, journey	*Schuh*	shoe
Feld	field	*Schiff*	ship, boat
Flughafen	airport	*See*	lake
Freilicht	open-air	*Silvester*	New Year's Eve
Garten	garden	*Stadion*	stadium
Gasthaus	guest-house,	*Stehcafe*	standing cafe
	restaurant	*Strand*	beach
Gericht	court	*Straße*	street
Gesellschaft	society,	*Süd*	south
	association	*Tor*	gate
Groschen	dime, ten pfennig	*Turm*	tower
Gründerzeit	foundation period	*U-Bahn*	underground
Haus	house, building		railway, metro,
haupt	main, central		subway
Imbiß	fast-food stall	*Viertel*	quarter, district
Insel	island	*Wald*	forest
Keller	cellar	*Weihnachen*	Christmas
Kino	cinema,	*Werkstatt*	workshop
	movie theater	*Weg*	way, path
Kirche	church	*Wurst*	sausage
Kneipe	tavern	*Zentrum*	center
Kunst	art		

11. Living in Berlin (Accommodation)

Hotels

●The *Berlin Tourist Information* office in the Europa Center issues an annotated listing of Hotels and Pensions in Greater Berlin. This list can also be requested by mail (address see Information).

●Rooms for rent in *East Berlin's Hauptbahnhof* (Postfach 33, 1017 Berlin, Mon 10am-7pm. Tue-Sun 9am-7pm, Tel. 9-436 24 68)

●*Wohnwitz* offers rooms for rent in East and West Berlin; 1-31, Holsteinische Str. 55, Mon-Fri 11am-8pm, Sat/Sun 11am-2pm, Tel. 861 82 22, 861 82 42, 861 91 92 or 861 63 38; East Berlin, Immanualkirchstr. 11, same opening times, Tel. 9-439 24 94

Camping Spots

The *Deutsche Camping Club*, 1-30, Geisbergstr. 11, Tel. 24 60 71/72 provides information about the possibilites for setting up a tent in West Berlin.

●*Campingplatz Haselhorst*, 1-20, Pulvermühlenweg, Tel 334 59 55

●*Zeltplatz in Kohlhasenbrück*, am Griebnitzsee 39, Tel. 805 17 37 (also caravans)

●*Zeltplatz in Kladow*, 1-22, Krampnitzer Weg 11, Tel. 365 27 97 (also caravans)

●*Campingplatz Dreilinden*, 1-39, Albrechts Teerofen, Tel. 805 12 01

For the **East Berlin campsites** which lie in the Köpenicker Forest, you will have to obtain a "Zeltschein" (tent permit) from: *Rat des Stadtbezirks Berlin-Köpenick, Zeltplatzvermietung*, Am Katzengraben 20, 1170 Berlin, Tel. 9-657 14 13

●*Zeltplatz Große Kampe I*, Tel. 9-656 22 37 & *Große Kampe II*, Tel. 9-656 34 65

●*Zeltplatz Kleiner Müggelsee*, Tel 9-656 18 60

●*Zeltplatz Seddinsee*, Tel. 9-656 23 36

●*Zeltplatz Krossinsee*, Tel. 9-685 86 96 (also caravans)

● *Zeltplätze Zeuthen I*, 9-685 82 49 (also caravans) and *Zeuthen II*, Tel. 9-685 94 45

●*Intercamping Krossinsee*, Tel. 9-685 86 87

●*Jugendcampingplatz "Kuhle Wampe"*, Tel. 9-660 86 21

Youth Accommodation

The Berlin Information Center's brochure *Berlin für junge Leute* lists a range of affordable accommodation, and it can be requested free of charge.

The German Youth Hostels Association (*Deutsches Jugendherbergswerk*, 1-61, Tempelhofer Ufer 32 has information about its hostels in Berlin.

●*Jugendherberge Ernst Reuter*, 1-28, Hermsdorfer Damm 48-50, Tel. 404 16 10

●*Jugendherberge Bayernallee*, 1-19, Bayernallee 36, Tel. 305 30 55

●*Jugendgästehaus am Wannsee*, 1-38, Badeweg 1, Tel. 803 20 34

●*Jugendgästehaus Berlin*, 1-30, Kluckstr. 3, Tel. 261 10 97/98

●*Jugendgästehaus Feurigstraße*, 1-62, Feurigstr. 63, Tel. 781 52 12

●*Jugendgästehaus am Zoo*, 1-12, Hardenbergstr. 9a, Tel. 312 94 10

Information about accommodation in East Berlin is provided by the *Jugendtourist Service*, 1080 Berlin, Friedrichstr. 79a, Tel. 9-226 63 22/23

●*Jugendtouristenhotel "Egon Schultz"*, 1136 Berlin, Franz Mett Str. 7, Tel. 9-510 01 14

Mitwohnzentralen (Housing Associations)

Literally "co-living agencies". Mitwohnzentralen bring together people wanting to rent their apartment or house for any length of time, and those looking for somewhere to live, for a small service charge. You can rent **private quarters** for weeks or for months.

●*Mitwohnzentrale für Berlin-Besucher*, 1-61, Mehringdamm 72, Mon-Fri 10am-7pm, Sat 11am-4pm, Tel. 786 60 02, 786 60 03, 786 22 70

●*Mitwohnzentrale Ku-Dam-Eck*, special offers for women from women, 1-15, Ku'damm 227/228, Mon-Fri 10am-7pm, Sat/Sun 11am-3pm, Tel. 882 66 94, 882 62 84

●*Mitwohnzentrale Berlin*, 1-36, Wiener Starße 14, Mon-Fri 12am-8pm, Sat 12am-4pm, Tel. 618 20 08/09

●*Mitschlafzentrale*, 1-36, Reichenbergerstr. 54, Mon-Fri & Sat 2pm-8pm, Tel. 611 80 01

12. Lost Property

●*BVG-Fundbüro* (U-Bahn & S-Bahn), 1-30, Potsdamer Str. 184, Mon, Tue, Thu 9am-3pm, Fri 9am-2pm, Wed 9am-6pm, Tel. 216 14 13

●*Fundbüro der Polizei* (Police), 1-42, Tempelhofer Damm 3, Mon & Tue 7:30am-2pm, Wed 12:30am-6:30pm, Fri 7:30am-12am, Tel. 69 9-0

●*Zentrales Fundbüro*, East Berlin, Wilhelm-Pieck-Str. 164, Tue/Thu 10am-1pm & 2pm-6pm, Fri 10am-1pm, Tel. 9-280 62 35/280 62 57

13. Markets

There are a number of **fleamarkets** in Berlin, where individuals offer the most improbable things for sale. Even if you can't shell out any money, you should still take the opportunity to rummage about and absorb the atmosphere.

●*Krempelmarkt am Reichspitschufer*, a huge flea market in a dusty area, Sat/Sun 8am-3pm, reached with Bus 24, 29, 75 or Gleisdreieck U-Bahn station

●*Flohmarkt am Kolk*, flea market for private vendors in the north of the city, Sat 1pm-10pm, Sun 7am-5pm, reached with Bus 13, 34, 54, 55, 56, 63, 97, 99

●*Trödelmarket am Fehrbelliner Platz*, an interesting mixture of kitsch and everyday items, mostly private vendors, Sat 8am-4pm, Fehrbelliner Platz U-Bahn station

●*Trödelmarkt und Kunstmarkt an 17. Juni*, Berlin's largest and most interesting flea market, Sat/Sun 8am-3:30pm, Ernst Reuter Platz or Hansaplatz U-Bahn stations, Tiergarten S-Bahn station.

In addition there are always **special markets** like record or film exchanges, which are announced in the city magazines.

14. Media

Newspapers

●*Berliner Morgenpost*, a conservative newspaper from Axel Springer, Sunday edition has the largest classifieds section, daily except Mon, 1-61, Kochstr. 50, Tel. 25 91-0

●*Berliner Zeitung*, East Berlin, Karl Liebknecht Str. 29, Tel. 9-244 36 08

●*BILD and BZ*, local, patriotic tabloid, daily except Sun, 1-61, Kochstr. 50m Tel. 25 91-0

●*Neues Deutschland*, East Berlin, Franz Mehring Platz 1, Tel. 9-583 10

●*Neue Zeit*, East Berlin, Mittelstr. 2/4, Tel. 9-200 04 21

●*Tagespiegel*, liberal/conservative, daily except Mon, Wed with a "What's On" calendar, 1-30, Potsdamer Str. 87, Tel. 26 00 90

●*Tageszeitung - taz*, only national daily in both halves of the city, left of center, every Fri edition has an extensive "What's On", daily except Sun, 1-61, Kochstr. 18, Tel. 259 02-0

●*Spandauer Volksblatt*, liberal, daily except Mon, 1-20 Neuendorfer Str. 101, Tel. 33 00 06-0

City Magazines

How many "What's On" magazines does a city need? Until recently Berlin managed with two, whether the two new ones will survive, the readers will decide.

●*tip-Magazin*: years on the market and always improving, more extensive and clearly organised "What's On", numerous classifieds, every 2nd Wed, 1-30, Potsdamer Str 96, Tel. 25 49 06-0

●*Zitty*: always been a little less professional and sometimes a little alternative, Zitty is the only magazine to appear exclusively in Berlin, and has held its own in competition with *tip*, every 2nd Wed, alternating with *tip*, 1-12, Sclüterstr. 39, Tel. 88 42 96-0

●*Prinz*: appeared on the market in April 1990 with a strong advertising campaign, at times sloppily researched, with numerous glamour photos, written for a superficial readership, every 2nd Wed, 1-15, Ku'damm 64-65, Tel. 88 42 01-60

●*Oxmox*: offshoot of the Hamburg magazine *Szene*, unusual format, appears monthly, 1-21, Huttenstr. 3, Tel. 391 90 53

Classified Advertisements

●*Zweite Hand* (Second Hand). Three times per week (Tue, Thu & Sat), newspaper exclusively for classified advertisements, placed at no charge. 1-30, Potsdamer Str. 70, Tel. 26 92 61

Radio

•*Sender Freies Berlin*. SFB 1 at 88.8 MHz - Berlin information; SFB 2 at 92.4 MHz - magazine format; SFB 3 at 96.65 MHz - classical music; Radio 4U at 98.2 MHz - young wave, rock, 1-19. Masurenallee 8, Tel. 30 31-0

•*Radio im amerikanischen Sektor*. RIAS 1 at 89.6 MHz - magazine format; RIAS 2 at 94.3 MHz - music around the clock. 1-62, Kufsteiner Str. 69, Tel. 85 03-0

•*Radio 100*. Transmits on 103.4 MHz around the clock, totally unconventional private station. 1-30, Potsdamer Str. 131, Tel. 216 40 81

•*Hundert 6*. Transmits on 100.6 MHz, commercial/funk with popular music and a little information. 1-33, Paulsborner Str. 44,Tel. 896 94-0

•*DT 64*. Transmits on 83.1 MHz and 102.6 MHz, quality youth radio from East Berlin. Nalepastr. 18/50, Tel. 9-636 0

Television

Apart from the transmissions of the East German television, the regional program of SFB, the commerical RIAS-TV and a cable station are all produced in Berlin.

15. Medical Assistance and Advice

•*Medical Service*, Tel. 9-12 59 -
•*Emergency Medical Service*, Tel. 31 00 31
•*Chemists*, Tel 11 41
•*Emergency Drug Service*, 1-30, Ansbacher Str. 11, annonymous advice day and night, Tel. 24 70 39
•*Emergency Dental Care*, Tel 11 41

AIDS

•*Berliner AIDS-Hilfe*, 1-15, Meinekestr. 12, Tel. 883 30 17. Advice around the clock on 194 11

•*Café POSITHIV*, a pilot project supported by Berliner AIDS-Hilfe, supports assertive self-help by AIDS sufferers. Wed-Sat 5pm-10pm, Sun 3pm-10pm, 1-62, Großgörschenstr.7

16. Memorials

Plötzensee

This memorial to the resistance to National Socialism (Nazism) is located on the grounds of the former city prison - today the Plötzensee Youth Detention Center. Over 2,500 people died here during the Hitler dictatorship.

•Hüttigpfad, 1-30, open daily from 8pm, in summer until 6pm, in winter until dusk, Tel. 344 32 26; reached with bus 123 from Hansaplatz U-Bahn station or Tiergarten S-Bahn station.

Memorial to the German Resistance (Gedenkstätte Deutscher Widerstand)

The memorial is located in the courtyard of the former Armed Forces High Command, where the participants in the failed bomb attack on Hitler were executed the same night.

The permanent exhibition, *Resistance against National Socialism*, should not be ignored. A visit to these historic rooms is really a must for every visitor to Berlin.

●Stauffenbergstr. 13, 1-30, Mon-Fri 9am-6pm, Sat/Sun 9am-1pm, Tel. 26 04 22 02; Bus 29/129 from the city.

Memorial to the Victims of Fascism and Militarism

This memorial is located in the former New Watch on Unter den Linden in the Mitte district. An eternal flame burns guarded by soldiers standing strictly to attention.

Soviet Monument

In Treptower Park the larger-than-life bronze figure of a Soviet soldier with a child on his arm, stands amid a strictly symmetrical park landscape. The history of the Second World War is depicted on various marble plaques. As an example of Stalinist architectural art, the monument is thoroughly worth seeing.

●The monument can be reached using the S-Bahn to Plänterwald and then walking through Treptower Park.

17. Men and Gays

If you are inclined towards diving into the largest and most dazzling gay scene in Germany, you can enjoy yourself in the bars and taverns described in the text. Alternatively drop into some of the following meeting points:

●*Beratungs und Kommunikationszentrum homsexueller Frauen und Männer e.V.* (Advice & Communication center for Homosexual Women and Men) 1-62, Kulmer Str. 20a, Mon-Thu 5pm-8pm, Tel. 215 90 00
●*Mann-O-Meter* (Gay switchboard with numerous tips and contact addresses) 1-62, Motzstr. 5, open daily 3pm-11pm, Tel. 216 80 08
●*Prinz Eisenherz bookshop* 1-12, Bleibtreustr. 52, open daily 10am-6:30pm, Sat 10am-2pm, Tel. 313 99 36
●*SchwulenZentrum (SchwuZ)*, 1-61, Hasenheide 54, meetings every 2nd & 4th Wednesday in the month, Fri 9pm-2am cafe. Tel. 694 10 77
●*Vorspiel - Schwuler Sportverein* (Gay Sports Association), Tel. 61 83 88 32
●The independent radio, *Radio 100* (103.4), broadcasts *Eldoradio* Wed 6pm-8pm and Sun 4pm-6pm, a gay program not only for gays.

18. Museums

Apart from the collections already mentioned in the district descriptions, the Berlin Museum landscape still has a lot to offer, and not just on rainy days:

Bauhaus Archive

Exhibitions from the Bauhaus era, industrial products and works by Bauhaus graduates. 1-30, Klingelhöferstr. 13-14, open daily except Tue, 11am-5pm, admission 3 DM, Tel. 261 16 18

Botanical Museum

Museum associated with the Botanical Gardens. Deals with the world's flora. 1-33, Königin Luise Str. 6-8, Tue-Sun 10am-5pm, Wed 10am-7pm, admission free, Tel. 830 06-0

George Kolbe Museum

The artist's more important works collected in his former work rooms. 1-19, Sensburger Allee 25, open daily except Mon, 10am-5pm, admission 2.50 DM, Tel. 304 21 44

Kunstgewerbemuseum (Arts and Crafts Museum)

Arts and Crafts from a number of centuries up to the present, numerous religious treasures. 1-30, Tiergartenstr. 6, Tue-Sun 9am-5pm, admission free, Tel. 266-6

National Gallery

A gallery for contemporary art designed by *Mies van der Rohe*, paintings and sculpture from the late 19th and 20th century (including works by *Menzel, Beckmann, Picasso, Beuys*). 1-30, Potsdamer Str. 50, Tue-Sun 9am-5pm, admission free, Tel. 266-6

Musikinstrumenten Museum (Musical Instruments Museum)

A collection of historical musical instruments spanning four centuries. 1-30, Tiergartenstr. 1, Tue-Sat 9am-5pm, Sun 10am-5pm, admission free, Tel. 254 81-0

Märkisches Museum

Primeval and Early History of the Berlin area, Berlin art from the baroque period to 1945, handicrafts and manufacturing. East Berlin, Am Köllnischen Park 5, at Märkisches Museum U-Bahn station, Wed-Fri 10am-6pm, Sat/Sun 10am-5pm, admission 0.55 DM, Tel. 9-270 04 14

Museum für Deutsche Geschichte (Museum of German History)

The GDR's national history museum. An outline from primeval times to 1949 with well-presented exhibitions of archaeological and everyday life. East Berlin, Unter den Linden 2, Mon-Thu 9am-6pm, Sat/Sun 10am-5pm, admission 0.50 DM, Tel. 9-200 09 41

19. Post Offices

• *Zoo Station*, day and night counter Tel. 313 97 99
• *Tegel Airport*, open daily 6:30am-9pm, Tel. 430 85 23
• *Postamt 17*, East Berlin, Straße der Pariser Kommune 8-10, open day and night
• *Postamt in the Palast der Republik*, open daily 10am-10pm

20. Shopping Hours

As a rule shops are open Mon-Fri between 9am and 6:30pm. Some exceptions are the "service evenings" which allow shop owners to open every Thursday until 9pm. City shops in particular make regular use of this.

On Saturdays you can shop until 1pm, and every 1st Saturday in the month until 4:40pm.

21. Theater

Information about the established Berlin theaters can be found on advertising pillars all around the city and in the U-Bahn stations. The daily newspapers and city magazines also provide information about performances in both halves of the city. Tickets can be bought in

advance (see Tickets) or booked over the phone. In some theaters there are "stand-by tickets" on sale shortly before the performance begins (see also Fairs and Festivals).

●The "What's On" sections in the city magazines list all the performances and programs in East Berlin
●Recorded message for theaters and concerts, Tel 11 56
●Recorded message for cabaret & variety shows, Tel. 115 17

22. Tickets

There are advance sales for tickets to just about everything that happens in Berlin. As you will often be charged horrendous fees for such a service, it pays to ring up the establishment concerned and book.

●*Kant Kasse* 1-12, Kantstr. 54, Tel. 313 45 54
●*Kasse am Quartier Latin* 1-30, Potsdamer Str. 96, Tel. 262 70 70 -
●*Theater & Konzertkasse Zanke* 1-15, Ku'damm 16, Tel. 882 65 63
●*Wildbad Kiosk* 1-30, Rankestr. 1, Tel. 881 45 07
●*Theaterkasse im Palasthotel* East Berlin, Spandauer Str. Tel. 9-212 52 58 & 212 59 02

23. Tours, organised

"Normal" city tours, i.e. 2-4 hour tours (between 20 and 40 DM) to the sights of Berlin and Potsdam are offered by the following firms:

●*Berliner Bären Stadtrundfahrt*, 1-30, Rankestr. 35, opposite the Gedächtniskirche, Tel. 213 40 77
●*Severin + Kühn*, 1-15, Ku'damm 216, Tel. 883 10 15
●*Berlolina Stadtrundfahrten*, 1-15. Ku'damm/Meineckestr., Tel. 883 31 31
●*BVB-Stadtrundfahrten*, 1-15, Ku'damm 225, Tel. 882 68 47

In East Berlin tours can be booked through the travel agent (Reisebüro Service) at Hauptbahnhof (Tel. 372-436 35 509). The tours also start there. The travel agent at Friedrichstraße station is located on Platform B, Mon-Fri 8am-8pm, Sat/Sun 9am-2pm.

Much more interesting than running around the usual tourist attractions are the cultural-historical tours offered by *Kulturkontor* (1-12, Savignyplatz 9-10, Tel. 31 08 88).

Other, irregularly timed tours of the most diverse areas are announced in the city magazines.

Stattreisen (Alternative Tours)

"Stattreisen" (the name plays on the similar sounds of "statt" = "instead" and "stadt" = "city") is a new concept in city tourism. Unlike most tours, the routes taken through the city make it possible to experience something of Berlin's everyday life and history. They also encourage participants to interact with each other.

The object of these inner city tours is to point out everything: normal street signs, disintegrating facades, forgotten war ruins, as well as famous museums and prominent sights. The latter are put in the context of their everyday surroundings; the background information goes beyond cliches.

The city walks are led by competent tour guides. They provide information about the context of what you see, things you would otherwise uncover only with difficulty, and show you "sights" which are rarely regarded as such.

The tours begin at 11am, tickets are sold at the beginning of the tour, no advance sales! Participation is limited to 25 persons. If requested, the tours can also take place in languages other than German, but you will need to book by telephone, in advance. Group tours can also be organised. The details are available at:

●*Stattreisen Berlin e.V.* 1-21, Stephanstr. 24, Tel. 395 30 78

Berliner Geschichtswerkstatt (Berlin History Workshop)

The Berlin History Workshop also organises tours which have nothing in common with the normal tourist

routes. There is, for example, a historical city tour by boat, which provides a wealth of information about Berlin's waterways and the interesting buildings along the shore.

24. Transport

Public Transport - BVG and BVB

Public transport in both parts of the city is well developed. The *S-Bahn* with its deep red/beige painted carriages was once Germany's most modern transport system. After the building of the Wall, it declined in significance, for West Berlin at least. For East Berlin the extensive network of S-Bahn lines remained its most important means of transport.

The **U-Bahn** is the fastest and most environmentally-friendly form of transport in Berlin. It has been well developed in both parts of the city. The times when the U-Bahn travelled under East Berlin through "ghost stations", only stopping at Friedrichstraße, are gone. The S-Bahn and U-Bahn have proceeded without any restrictions since 1 July 1990! Not all stations are accessible yet, but this is only due to the need for renovation.

In eastern Berlin, apart from **buses** there are also **trams**. Trams disappeared from West Berlin in 1967, but there are plans to reopen some of the lines which now stop at the Wall.

Even at night there is never any need to take a taxi in Berlin. There are more than enough buses. At weekends two U-Bahn lines (U1 & U9) run around the clock.

For the visitor to Berlin, it is recommended that you purchase a *Tageskarte* (Day Ticket) at 9 DM. For longer stays, you can get free rides everywhere with a transferable *Wochenkarte* (weekly ticket, Mon-Sat) for 26 DM, or the *Umweltkarte* for 65 DM per month.

Information

●BVG (West Berlin Transit Authority) Customer Service: 1-30, Grunewaldstr. 1 (Kleistpark U-Bahn station), Mon-Fri 8am,-6pm, Sat 7am-2pm, Tel. 256-1
●BVG Information Booth: Hardenbergplatz (Zoo U-Bahn station), open daily 10am-6pm
●BVB (East Berlin Transit Authority) Information Centre: Alexanderplatz S-Bahn station: Mon-Fri 9am-6pm, Sat 9am-1pm, Tel. 9-246 22 55

A worthwhile investment is the current Timetable (Fahrplan), which provides information about all connections and prices.

Taxis

●*Funktaxis (West Berlin)*. Taxis can be ordered around the clock on the following numbers: 26 10 26, 690 22, 24 0202, 24 00 24 or 254 80 88
●*Funktaxis (East Berlin)*. Tel. 9-33 66 for the districts of Marzahn, Hellers-

dorf, Treptow, Köpenick and Schönefeld airport. Tel. 9-36 44 for the districts of Mitte, Friedrichshain, Weißensee, Pankow, Hohenschönhausen
- *Taxi-Stadtrundfahrten* (Taxi Tours), Tel. 9-246 22 55
- Taxis are permitted to travel in both halves of the city, but can only pick fares up in the part they come from.

Boats

A boat trip on one of Berlin's lakes or canals is both pleasurable and practical. While you relax on the Spree or Landwehrkanal, the city with all its facets glides by. Trips along the border-less waterways begin at a number of *piers*:

in the West:

- 1-10, Doverbrücke
- 1-10, Tegeler Weg (also to East Berlin)
- 1-10, Schloßbrücke (also to East Berlin)

- 1-13, Mäckeritzbrücke
- 1-20, Spandau/Lindenufer (also to East Berlin)
- 1-21, Hansabrücke (also to East Berlin)
- 1-21, Gotzkowskybrücke
- 1-27, Tegel/Greenwichpromenade (also to East Berlin)
- 1-30, Kongreßhalle (also to East Berlin)
- 1-30, Potsdamer Brücke
- 1-30, Corneliusbrücke

- 1-38, Wannsee (also to East Berlin)
- 1-39, Stölpchensee
- 1-39, Nikolskoe/Pfaueninsel
- 1-61, Kottbusser Brücke (also to East Berlin)
- 1-61, Hallesches Tor

Boat Companies (West)

- *Stern und Kreisschiffahrt*, 1-37, Sachtlebenstr. 60, Tel. 803 10 55, 803 87 50
- *Reederei Winkler*, 1-21, Levetzowstr. 16, Tel. 392 70 10, 391 70 70
- *Reederei Heinz Riedel*, 1-61, Planufer 78, Tel. 691 37 82, 693 46 46

in the East:

- Treptow/near S-Bahn station (also to West Berlin)
- Köpenick/Luisehahn
- Grünau/regatta course
- Friedrichshagen/Müggelpark

Boat Company (East)

- *Weiße Flotte*, East Berlin, Rosa Luxemburg Str. 2, Tel. 9-271 23 27/28

Bicycles

The streets of Berlin have been overflowing since the opening of the Wall. Public transport, especially during peak hours, is also reaching its limits. The bicycle is thus a good alternative, although the construction of **bicycle paths** in Berlin, especially in the eastern districts, leaves much to be desired. A pleasant novelty is the possibility of taking **bicycles in the S- and U-Bahn**. This allows you to avoid the more nerve-racking stretches.

- **Information** about bicycling in Berlin can be obtained from the *AFDC*, 1-12, Schillersytr. 70, Tue/Thu 4pm-7pm, Sat 12am-2pm, Tel. 313 45 31

Bicycle Hire:

- *FahrradBüro*, 1-62, Hauptstr. 146, Tel. 784 55 62
- *Kreuz Mobil*, 1-36, Oppelner Str 7, Tel. 612 50 85
- *Fahrradladen Mehringhof*, 1-61, Gneisenaustr. 2a, Tel. 691 60 27

Car Rental

All of the major car rental firms have a representative in Berlin's inner city or at Tegel airport. The addresses are best obtained from the telephone book. It is always worth comparing prices and service, there are significant differences.

25. Women and Lesbians

Information and Advice

- *Extra Dry*, advice in a café, 1-12, Mommsenstr. 34, Tue-Fri 12am-11pm, Sat 11am-12pm, Tel. 324 60 38
- *Fraueninfothek Berlin*, free information and advice on discovering the city, 1-12, Leibnizstr. 57, Tue-Sat 9am-7pm, Sun 9am-3pm, Tel. 324 50 78
- *Frauenkrisen-Telefon der Schokofabrik* (Telephone Crisis Line), 1-36,

Naunystr. 72, during office hours Tue, Wed, Fri 9am-7pm, Sat/Sun 5pm-7pm, Thu 10am-12am, Tel. 65 42 43

●*Frauen-Telefon*, Sat 7pm-9pm, Tel. 614 75 64

●*Notruf und Beratung für vergewaltigte Frauen* (Rape Crisis Center), Tel. 251 28 28

Meeting points

●*Begine*, cafe, cultural center, 1-30, Potsdamer Str. 139;Mon-Fri 8pm-1am & Sat/Sun 4pm-1am, Tel. 215 43 25

●*Dinelo*, cafe, 1-62, Vorbergstr. 10; daily except Mon, from 6 pm, Tel. 782 21 85

●*FFBIZ* (Women's Research, Education and Information Center), gallery, art and women's center, 1-19, Danckelmannstr. 47 & 15; Tue 2pm-6pm, Thu 10am-1pm (with breakfast), Fri 3pm-10pm, Tel. 322 10 35

●*Spinnboden*, Archive for the Discovery and Protection of Women's Love, 1-65, Burgdorfstr. 1; Mon-Thu 2pm-6pm, Fri 5pm-9pm, Tel. 465 20 21

Media

●*Blattgold*, magazine for the Berlin women's scene, 1-30, Potsdamer Str. 139, Tel. 215 66 28

●*Dissonanzen*, radio program with abundant information, Mon, Tue, Thu, Fri 7pm-8pm on Radio 100 (100.6 MHz)

Accommodation

●*Frauenhotel "artemesia"*, run by women, only takes female guests, 1-31, Brandenburgische Str. 18, Tel. 87 89 05 & 87 63 73

●See **Mitwohnzentralen** in the "Living in Berlin" section.

Appendix

List of Photographs

The photographs were taken by Uwe Seidel (US), Peter Höh (PH), Carola Köppen (CK), Michael Schulenberg (MS), Heike Schroth (HS), Karin Göllner (KG), Eberhard Homann (EH), Landesbildstelle Berlin (LB), Volker Buslau (VB), Verkehrsverein Berlin (VVB)

General Index

(K) = in Köpenick, (P) = in Potsdam

Sites to See

(K) = in Köpenick, (P) = in Potsdam

Index of Streets, Squares and Districts
(K) = in Köpenick, (P) = in Potsdam

Index of Pubs, Bars, Restaurants and Discotheques
(K) = in Köpenick, (P) = in Potsdam

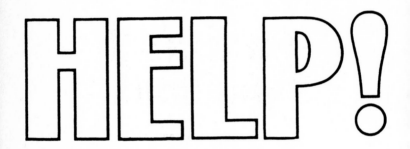

Help us update

This edition of ***Berlin Handbook*** is based on a great deal of first-hand research and last-minute checking. Inevitably, there will be places missed that should be included, others that perhaps get too positive, or negative, and some information will already be outdated.

If you come upon ***details that have changed since publication,*** find things you feel should be featured and aren't, or which are included and shouldn't be, please write and tell us. In putting together updated editions of this handbook readers' information and accounts are invaluable - and a fresh perspective is always very welcome. All contributions will be credited in print, and a copy of the next edition (or any other ***Travel Bug Guide*** if you prefer) is the reward for the best letters.

Please write to:
Peter Rump Publishing Co., Hauptstr. 198, D-4800 Bielefeld 14

TRAVEL BUG

Rainer Krack

Thailand Handbook

The complete guide
for the modern adventurer

This guidebook is packed with nearly 400 pages of practical ideas for the do-it-yourself adventurer. Some information has never been published before in any guidebook in any language.
- From Bangkok and Ko Samui to the Golden Triangle and the steamy jungles along the Malaysian border.
- History, people, religion, festivals, traditions, and forgotten legends.
- Suggestions for trekking, rafting, and diving.
- Remote exotic islands, and the finest beaches.
- Over 1,000 hotels and restaurants.
- Up-to-date prices and schedules for trains, buses, planes, and boats.
- Over 100 maps and 150 photographs, many in color.
- Indispensable for long- and short-time visitors.
- ISBN 3-89416-330-5
  Peter Rump Publishing Co., D-4800 Bielefeld 14

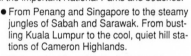
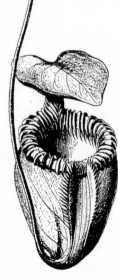

Overcoming the language barrier

The **Kauderwelsch** series of language guides is designed to help travellers actually speak the local language. At long last, here is an approach that dispenses with the old system of memorizingor reading out prepared sentences. After all, the aim of these guides is to help you - as rapidly and with as little drudgery as possible - to speak the language authentically and hold genuine conversation.

German for Travellers will help you overcome the language barrier in German-speaking countries. The book explains enough of the grammar - simply and directly - for you to understand the everyday languages. Superfluous details are omitted.

All the German examples used are translated twice: **word for word** and then into "real" English. This method shows you exactly how the German sentence is constructed, important because this will frequently be very different from the English.

The conversation section of the book then follows up with model phrases and sentences based on the situations you'll encounter when travelling around the country.

The **Kauderwelsch** language guides also deal with rules of behaviour, gestures and body language; after all, getting this type of non-verbal communication right is vital to making proper contact and avoiding misunderstandings.

German for Travellers closes with a vocabulary of about 1,000 essential words.

● The book is available in all good bookshops (in Germany). Ask for the **Kauderwelsch** series. This language guide is geared very much to practical requirements and is richly and humorously illustrated.
It has 144 pages and costs DM 14.80.

Peter Rump Publishing Co., Bielefeld